The Invention of Literary Subjectivity

PARALLAX RE-VISIONS OF CULTURE
AND SOCIETY

Stephen G. Nichols, Gerald Prince, and Wendy Steiner
SERIES EDITORS

The Invention of
Literary Subjectivity

Michel Zink

TRANSLATED BY
David Sices

The Johns Hopkins University Press
Baltimore and London

Originally published as *La Subjectivité littéraire* © Presses
Universitaires de France, 1985

© 1999 The Johns Hopkins University Press
All rights reserved. Published 1999
Printed in the United States of America on acid-free paper
9 8 7 6 5 4 3 2 1

On behalf of the editors of Parallax, the Johns Hopkins
University Press wishes to thank the Florence Gould
Foundation for its support of the translation of this volume.

The Johns Hopkins University Press
2715 North Charles Street
Baltimore, Maryland 21218-4363
www.press.jhu.edu

Library of Congress Cataloging-in-Publication Data will
be found at the end of this book.
A catalog record for this book is available from the
British Library.

ISBN 0-8018-5967-0

Contents

Contents

The Invention of Literary Subjectivity

Introduction

Can we still use the expression "literary subjectivity"? Can we still think that the notion, even supposing it to be definable, has anything to do with the decisive movements that marked the birth of literature? At the present time, examining literary expression of the subject by itself is almost an act of provocation. Doing so to shed light on the origins of medieval French literature seems to ignore the most recent and influential ideas. "Immanent" criticism has for several decades insisted on denying any referent to the text, showing that language functions according to its intrinsic structural laws in a closed circuit and refers to itself alone, casting doubt on the very concept of the author. Meanwhile, the earliest French poetry in the Middle Ages was being defined as "formalist," consisting of variations within a linguistic code and not the expression of subjectivity, affirming that language was all that was at stake in our first romances—Chrétien de Troyes's and, even more, the prose Grail romances. That idea has become so widespread that we may forget how paradoxical it really is.

But despite criticism's general ambitions, medieval literary study has retained a particular point of view. It may not affirm a priori, for speculative reasons, the sole validity of "immanent" criticism, but it does attempt to show that medieval literature obeyed principles com-

I

patible with it and deliberately based itself on the play of language and eliminated all referents: not without guile, since it often seemed to be offering naïve minds a different reading. So one can imagine a special accord, an encounter between the poetics of the Middle Ages and critical choices in the final third of the twentieth century.

Who knows, perhaps such an encounter exists. But the laws of probability make that unlikely. So would it not be better to restate the question: Why does critical thought look for and seem to find affinities in the literature of the Middle Ages rather than some other period? The answer, no doubt, is that the Middle Ages represent our origins and in our view an encounter with our origins seems ample justification. The idea governing any return to the sources—that our choices are justified by such an encounter—explains why the Middle Ages are in fashion even though they are perceived as a somber, almost barbaric period—or, rather, for that very reason, since they are viewed as our Limbo. That is why the Middle Ages have not gone out of fashion for the past two hundred years, through changing and, indeed, contradictory representations serving quite different ideologies, whose only common ground was a preference for them to antiquity as our point of origin. From exalting *The Genius of Christianity*[1] to exalting heresy and marginality; from the romantic notion of literature's roots in national identity and the people's collective soul to regionalist aspirations; from nationalism to a sense of European identity; from Joan of Arc—according to Michelet, Lavisse, or Péguy[2] —to enrolling the women troubadours and Christine de Pizan[3] under the feminist banner; from celebrating mystical asceticism to celebrating mad passion; from Sir Walter Scott to Jeanne Bourin:[4] each sought to base its convictions on a trial by the Middle Ages. Why should literary criticism deny itself that luxury? By emphasizing the formalism, the self-referentiality, the immanence of subject in language of medieval literature, it suggested its own hermeneutics as the one evoked by the function of writing at the dawn of French letters, and felt encouraged by that.

Today, however, we are witnessing an ebb of immanent criticism, which is noticeable in several domains. Everyone generally repeats—

carelessly at times—that structuralism is on the way out. Ethnology and the study of myth are paying more attention to the evolution of history and the weight of historical events.[5] The study of literature once again allows for literary history,[6] even biographical criticism; "genetic"[7] criticism, now increasingly widespread, is in itself a recognition of the writing subject through the modes of writing. As for linguists, troubled by the functioning of linguistic theories *in abstracto*, they are now showing significant interest in the problem of utterance. In this respect, Catherine Kerbrat-Orecchioni's book *L'Enonciation de la subjectivité dans le langage* is exemplary by its very title.[8] The back cover states:

> The essence of [this] study consists of systematic description from concrete examples of the traces of the speaking subject's inscription in the utterance, that is, "subjectivity in language" (Benveniste), subjectivity taken in the strictly linguistic sense, but which continually sidesteps and questions the common use of this term, which is as problematic as it is indispensable.

We applaud this choice and this circumspection, for in the area of literary communication as well recourse to the notion of subjectivity is both delicate and necessary. In her introduction Kerbrat-Orecchioni criticizes the transparency of the communication pattern assumed by Saussurean and Chomskyan linguistics. Quoting Pierre Bourdieu ("Chomsky gives in to the eternal illusion of the grammarian, who forgets that language is made to be spoken, that there is no discourse except to someone in a situation"), she concludes: "It seems, in truth, that a Chomskyan 'immanentist' position is no longer tenable in our day."[9]

The importance of the phenomena of utterance in medieval studies is illustrated by the work of Bernard Cerquiglini.[10] When we examine the first signs of literary subjectivity in early French literature, we are merely following a general trend. Might one add that we are also seeking a justification for our critical choices in the Middle Ages? Not exactly, however, since we will at no time claim any special encounter between medieval thought or sensibility and our own.

But what must we understand by "literary subjectivity"? Quite obviously not spontaneous display or real expression in a text of an author's personality, opinions, or feelings, but rather what marks the text as the point of view of a consciousness. In this sense, literary subjectivity defines literature. The latter truly exists only the moment a text seeks to present itself neither as information about the world, laying claim to general and objective truth, nor as an expression of metaphysical or sacred truth but rather designates itself as the product of a particular consciousness, hesitating between arbitrary individual subjectivity and the constraints of language's forms. For us to indicate the time and conditions of that awakening in the first centuries of French literature—that is, the Middle Ages—means not only to engage in a study about medieval literature but also to shed light on all of French literature and its development.[11]

This perspective—which, like the reception theory to which it is related, is connected to infiltration of the text by consciousness—permits us to account for the evolution of both literature and the idea of literature, which is not always the case with "immanent" criticism.[12] For example, Joël Grisward has shown not only that French chansons de geste reflect in detail the tripartite structure of Indo-European society but that they incorporate in their very details, with surprising fidelity and precision, a host of mythic elements, themes, or narrative sequences, brought to light by Georges Dumézil, throughout Indo-European civilization.[13]

However, no one would think of applying the same investigations and demonstration, so illuminating for the epic cycles of the twelfth century, to Proust's *Remembrance of Things Past* in hopes of discovering in it—if not the three orders of Indo-European society, which we certainly would find—a faithful echo of Ossetian legends. That is because everyone feels that the idea and outlook of literature changed at some point between the twelfth century and the twentieth—much closer to the twelfth than the twentieth, in our opinion, for the problems we are dealing with. Only from the time it became conscious that it was relating the world from a point a view—that is, that it contained not only truth and fiction but also necessity and arbitrariness and a decisive mediation of the subject—did literature exist; but it was saying something other, or was destined soon to be saying something other, than what Grisward revealed.

Any criticism denying a place to referential relationship, enclosing itself within the circle of language and seeing in writing only the desire of language, would cut itself off from an understanding of this transformation. From that perspective it would serve no purpose to study medieval literature in order to understand literature and, paradoxically, the sole justification for examining the texts of the past would be scholarly pleasure. Such a perspective, moreover, would contradict the explicit intent of medieval authors. That argument, of course, is worthless in the framework of thinking that decides the ultimate nature of the text, but neither the historian nor the critic can neglect the idea an era has of its own intellectual life, for by defining its horizon of expectations it influences both the production and reception of works.

In fact, the Middle Ages were a time of subjectivity. Considered in and of itself, this formula seems to come directly from Hegel. But his lesson is worth recalling, though it may seem ridiculous to do so in just a few words. We know that the *Aesthetics* divides the history of art into three periods: symbolic, classical, and romantic. The first was characterized by an arbitrary relationship between the idea and the form in which it was embodied. The idea was seeking both itself and an appropriate form. But the search proceeded by trial and error, and the result was not necessarily clear to the work of art's recipient since the form could refer either to the general idea of the object or to one of its particular meanings, possibly an arbitrary one. Classical art, on the contrary, was characterized by appropriateness of form to content, ensured by the idea's acceptance of its own subjectivity. Finally, in romantic art, which was pure inwardness, content was once again separated from form, no longer by the inability to find an appropriate form but because the idea, produced by absolute subjectivity, was not prisoner to a form imposed in advance.

The French are instinctively tempted to place the Middle Ages in the period of symbolic art. They do so, first of all, because the terms

classicism and *romanticism* designate specific periods of French literature, both of them later than the Middle Ages; and when we think of
classicism and romanticism, we tend to think that what comes before
them consequently falls under the heading of symbolic art. It is still
easier to do so because of the place that symbols held in the thought
and art of the Middle Ages; an important part of that period's literature was allegorical, and Hegel's definitions seem to find convincing
application in them. Going beyond literal interpretation to derive allegorical and tropological meaning from sacred texts, biblical exegesis seems to illustrate the arbitrary relationship between idea and
form. Why was it necessary for the right breast of the wife in the
Song of Solomon to represent compassion, as Saint Bernard would
have it, and for the milk of consolation to flow from it, whereas the
left breast represented encouragement and produced the milk of exhortation?[14] And do we not find proof in secular allegorical fiction—
where we see the signifier reflecting its contingent characteristics on
the signified—that ideas were sought through their incarnation?

However, for Hegel, who considered art's evolution on the scale of
all mankind, the art of the Middle Ages was romantic. In fact, he designated art preceding Graeco-Roman antiquity, or outside its domain, as symbolic; his favorite examples were Indian and Egyptian
art. For him classical art was that of Greek or Roman antiquity, romantic art that of modern times, that is, the art of the West during
the period from the triumph of Christianity to our time. Thus, the
Middle Ages not only belonged to the period of romantic art but occupied an essential place in it, since they constituted the first part of
the period and were particularly representative of it, thanks to the
place they granted to Christianity.

But if the essential quality of romantic art is absolute subjectivity,
the thought and art of the Middle Ages, on the contrary, seem to be
marked by an objectification of intellectual and moral reality. This
was apparent even in religious thought, which one may say was
deeply materialistic. The representations of the Christian world—the
Last Judgment, with its weighing of virtues and vices; the book in
which everyone was inscribed, the *Liber scriptus . . . in quo totum con-*

tinetur [The book written down . . . in which all is contained], spoken of in the Dies Irae and the exempla; the interventions of the devil and intercessions of the Virgin and saints; the geography of heaven, hell, and purgatory; the earthly paradise at the farthest limits of the earth, beyond the dessicated tree; the bliss of paradise, in which all would have their place according to a strict hierarchy, and the torments of hell; the semiconfusion between a pilgrimage or crusade toward the earthly Jerusalem and progress toward the heavenly Jerusalem, illustrated in the area of romance fiction by the voyage toward Sarras at the end of the *Quête du Saint-Graal*—this was all material. The objectification of spiritual realities, of course, was not opposed to flights of subjectivity, but it kept the latter from moving about freely in the sphere of ideas. Everything arose from tangible givens, and any idea going beyond them or, even more, opposed to them was felt to be a paradox.

In the same way, secular authors who invited the reader to discover the *meaning* of their work or to submit its allegorical signifier to decryption were conscious of requiring an inordinate effort by not limiting reading to deciphering the literal sense; it is striking that the same word designated the materiality of writing and its immediate meaning, as the careful insistence and the knowing tone of their prologues indicate. The quality this effort required was often defined as subtlety—the meaning of a work was *soutil*; only a *soutil* mind could discover it—thus once again significantly likening the highest intellectual penetration to the faculty of grasping the impalpable. The intellectual adventure began immediately beyond literal meaning, almost beyond the physical materiality of the text, just as the fictional adventure began once one passed through the gates of Camelot; like the fictional adventure, it was studded with landmarks to keep the mind from roaming wherever fancy took it. As for allegory, its very principle was a materialization of intellectual and moral concepts. In general, literature furnishes us with numerous examples of the objectification of ideas and feelings. It is remarkable that in the debate about universals the influence of Platonic thought resulted in the sort of materialization of the concept suggested at times by the realist position, whereas nominalism denied to abstractions any reality beyond the particular.

But these features take on meaning only in comparison and contrast with the essential characteristic of medieval consciousness: exaltation of the individual. That was obviously a product of Christianity. Not only did the incarnation of God as man give every man infinite value but also—despite the quite strong feelings of the ecclesiastical community, marked by a theatrical or cruel rejection of the excommunicated and heretics; and despite belief in communion and the intercession of saints—medieval religious feeling was almost exclusively preoccupied with individual salvation and the individual relationship between each man and God. Thus, almost all exempla were devoted to recounting the unhoped-for salvation or deserved damnation of a particular individual. Monastic vocations were usually described not as a call to spend one's life in prayer for the salvation of all those whose activities in the world or negligence turned them from God but simply as a notably sure way to achieve personal salvation, sheltered from the temptations of the world, at the price of the life of renunciation and austerity demanded by the order.

This is the idea, for example, that one finds expressed around 1170 in the *Livre des manières* by Etienne de Fougères and, a little later, in the *Poème moral*, which agreed with some sermons of the period in half reproaching monks for seeking a cheap salvation by avoiding the dangers of life. The same idea—without such reservations, of course—appears in the writings of Saint Bernard when he contrasts monks crossing the turbulent river of life on a bridge with married people swimming across it at the risk of drowning. On the other hand, the evolution of the doctrine of penitence from the Carolingian period to the beginning of the thirteenth century increasingly favored devoting attention to individual psychology and introspection. It is known that the fixed-rate penance of the early Middle Ages, which provided a standard penalty automatically applied to each type of sin, was succeeded by variable penance, which was, within certain limits, left to the confessor's discretion provided he evaluated the penitent's responsibility by taking into account psychological or social factors and circumstances; at the same time, the practice of hearing confessions favored introspection. Starting in the twelfth century, absolution depended on sincerity of repentance, which was a psychological notion, although here again it was defined materially by the criterion of tears. In 1215 the symbol of this evolution was the canon of the Fourth Lateran Council, which made annual confession obligatory. Thus, the progress of psychological analysis in the Middle Ages was linked to the passion for the individual at the heart of the Christian faith.[15]

In the realm of secular literature, this passion for the individual is particularly striking if we look at the model of the fictional hero. It has often been said that medieval romance was a bildungsroman. It followed a young knight through adventures that revealed him to himself and, at the same time, were a sign, a materialization (once again), at times almost a symbol of inner adventure, discovery of himself, which he arrived at after facing moral conflicts in which values like honor and love were at stake. Hegel himself was particularly appreciative of this aspect of medieval literature, and it is the chapters he devoted to the romance of chivalry and the notion of honor within the context of his analysis of romantic art that are deservedly well known.

Finally, when we look at the plastic arts we cannot avoid thinking of the theory developed by Ruskin. In *The Stones of Venice* he distinguished between so-called servile ornamentation, for whose realization the executant submitted entirely to orders he received, and ornamentation in which the executant's freedom could be exercised even at the price of lesser formal perfection. The first type of ornamentation characterized the art of Egyptian, Greek, or Roman antiquity. Here slaves sculpted, in rigid conformity to an inviolable model, capitals or ornaments that were always identical, whose repetition produced an effect of cold regularity and soulless perfection prefiguring, in Ruskin's view, modern industrial art. They were denied all creativity, which was reserved for those responsible for the noble tasks of architectural planning and sculpture. But medieval art, which was Christian, considered the freedom of each soul and granted the possibility of self-expression to all, even the most humble. That produced the asymmetrical, anarchic ornamentation of Romanesque and Gothic churches, its profusion in the most surprising and least visible places, the fantastic and unexpected character of their sculpture, which was not always perfect but always vigorous.[16] Of course, these views reveal how naïve Ruskin was and how often his systematic mind slightly missed the point. But are they so absurd in themselves? After all, the image of an artisan who offered the best of himself and the best he could do, even if it was nothing much, and whose efforts and intentions were counted to his credit, was not foreign to the spirit of the Middle Ages and their religious feeling: that was the moral of the well-known fabliau *Le Tombeur de Notre-Dame*.

Christianity affirmed that man was created in God's image and God was interested in every man's salvation. It was a religion of inwardness based on a personal relationship between man and God, anxious to plumb the deep recesses of consciousness. It seems quite natural for the period of its tightest grip on thought and feelings to have been marked by an expression of subjectivity in art. But Christianity's relationship to literary subjectivity goes beyond this analogical deduction, being more fundamental. Each in its own way, symbolic and classical art in the Hegelian sense served as mediators of the perceptible embodiment of religious or metaphysical truths. The gods of paganism existed through their iconographic representations and mythological literature. But in Christianity neither religious truth nor metaphysical ideas were revealed through the forms of art. Art, the perceptible expression of truth, was suited to paganism but was surpassed by Christianity, which was beyond the mediation of the perceptible. From this perspective art was like a stage to be surpassed, and we can understand how, for Hegel, the triumph of Christianity and, at the same time, the romantic era whose beginning it marked made art a past "that has lost its authentic truth and life for us and resides in our *representation* more than it affirms in reality the necessity that formerly belonged to it."[17]

The emergence of French literature can thus be seen to coincide with a point when art had to recognize it held no other truth than the subjectivity it embodied. That awareness defines literature. Showing that absolute subjectivity seeks embodiment in form conversely amounts to saying that the literary texts of the Middle Ages can be read as attempts to fix in language—and, it must be acknowledged, possibly on language—a subjectivity's desire, and its representations.

So the infancy of French literature—that is, both the historical time of its emergence and the rise of the concept of literature in the French domain—was marked by an awareness of subjectivity. Why focus a study that aims to show this on the age of Saint Louis (1214–70), spanning the middle of the thirteenth century, and not on the brilliant beginnings of French literature in the twelfth? To tell the truth, my study does not take the thirteenth century, emblematically designated as the age of Saint Louis, as its strict chronological framework; rather, it considers that a threshold period. By granting new importance and significance to the place of the subject in a work, it led to a new conception and distribution of literary forms, modifying those established during the preceding century, and made French literature aware of itself through the incorporation of critical reflection into its activity. The widespread recognition of subjectivity (as previously defined) in literary expression—or in expression that thereby became specifically literary—was essentially a thirteenth-century phenomenon.

It has sometimes been claimed that the reign of Saint Louis was great in all areas save literature. The thirteenth century saw the erection of cathedrals; the development of cities and of their economic strength; the founding of universities; the appearance and triumph of the mendicant orders, which occupied a major place in the spiritual and intellectual life of the times; the strengthening and expansion of royal power; and the reorganization, through the great edict of 1254, of its administration.[18] But the great impetus that spurred twelfth-century French literature seems to have lost momentum around 1230, precisely when Saint Louis ascended the throne, after reaching a pinnacle, at the beginning of the century, distinguished, amid the flowering of exceptionally numerous and varied works, by the appearance of the great prose romance cycles. Later, certain forms, like the courtly lyric, died out; others hung on through repetition. The *Roman de la Rose*, probably the most representative work of the thirteenth century, was begun by Guillaume de Lorris around 1225 and completed by Jean de Meun around 1270; its two parts thus framed Saint Louis's reign without really belonging to it.

Nonetheless, this impression of relative emptiness is in part an illusion, not only because the period did, after all, produce great names like Rutebeuf or Adam de La Halle but for other reasons as well. On the one hand, at times the fascination with origins made philologists add unjustified years to the texts they edited. As editions and studies appear based on new sources, some of these texts have been shifted from the first twenty years of the century into which they once were lumped and have been assigned to a later date. On the other hand, we must not forget that twelfth-century French literary manuscripts are extremely rare. We read twelfth-century works in manuscripts belonging to the thirteenth. Whatever the means of transmission of works between the date of their composition and the earliest preserved manuscript— this point remains a mystery—it was in the thirteenth century that French literature, including that of the previous century, enjoyed real written distribution and began to derive its sustenance from the book. It should be stated as well that in general it was in the thirteenth century, and not the twelfth, that texts in the vernacular ceased to be like islands in the midst of a sea of Latin texts. The thirteenth century was the first truly French-speaking period in the domain of writing, as we can see from the development of the use of French outside the specific field of literature: in history with the *Grandes Chroniques de France*; in law with the appearance of *coutumiers* written in French, like the *Livre de justice et de plet* or the *Coutumes du Beauvaisis* of Philippe de Beaumanoir, or the *Livre des métiers* of Etienne Boileau. The development of French prose is certainly linked to this spread of writing in the vernacular. For the first time a large body of French texts had to be mastered, organized, itemized, and distributed. Paradoxically, this new abundance contributes to an impression of stagnation. For the creative exploration of the twelfth century was followed by a period of critical synthesis thanks to which some transformations took place that will occupy our attention.

This situation typified not only French literature but all of intellectual life. The thirteenth century was one of summas. Thus, after the innovations—indeed, audacities—of theology in the first half of the twelfth century, after the conservative reaction of the century's end, Saint Thomas Aquinas gathered, sifted, unified, and rethought previous advances in his *Summa contra Gentiles* (1259–64) and *Summa Theologica* (1267–74). Around the same time, Vincent de Beauvais, also a Dominican, composed his triple *Miroir (Speculum naturale, historiale, doctrinale)*, a vast encyclopedia whose goal was to assemble all knowledge concerning the sciences of nature, history, and dogma. It was also around 1260 that Brunetto Latini wrote the first encyclopedia in French prose, his *Livre du trésor*. This taste for summas can be seen in manifold ways in French literature, in the writing of the great prose romance cycles or the drift of the *Roman de la Rose* between Guillaume de Lorris and Jean de Meun: the lesson of love concealed by the first poet behind the narrative argument was transformed by the other's pen into an encyclopedic dissertation on affairs of the heart as well as many other things.

The century of critical synthesis was also one of spiritual display, but of an introspective, indeed, anxious sort. This type of religious feeling marked the Cistercian spirit as early as the twelfth century, but it developed most notably in the thirteenth with the mendicant orders, especially the Franciscans, who, despite their institutional break with traditional monasticism, carried on many aspects of the Cistercians' sensibility. Dom Jean Leclerq noted that the Cistercians, like the mendicants, recruited adults and were not, like the Cluniacs, content with preparing children entrusted to them from early childhood for cloister life.[19] Those wearing their habit did so as the result of a personal conversion, after they had already learned the ways of thinking and feeling of the world. This condition no doubt predisposed them to pay attention to more conflictive inner impulses. Later I will have occasion to cite the celebrated passage in which Saint Bernard expressed emotion at his brother's death, with commingled indulgence and restraint in the face of this "fleshly affection," for which he reproached himself without trying to negate it. The evolution of the doctrine of penance has already been pointed out; to which one should add the endless calculations on individual salvation; the personal, emotional link that everyone was invited to maintain with Christ's humanity through the cult of the Virgin; the veneration of the manger and the infant Jesus, particularly by the Franciscans; the increasing number of treatises or, to put it another way, manuals of contemplation intended to let anyone achieve a mystical state by associating every hour of his day with scenes of the earthly life of Christ and the sufferings of His Passion—all this presumed a rigorous, emotional, and tormented attention to the self whose literary consequences will be assessed to the limits of autobiography. Thus, the mingling of intellectual and religious currents summoned literature to reflect upon the self.

Finally, thirteenth-century literature was affected in its world vision and basic images by the urban civilization developing at the time. Twelfth-century poetry was rural, and romances knew nothing of the city but the built-up area surrounding the castle.[20] The knight merely passed through its streets. At most he lodged in a burgher's house before heading, once he had taken up quarters, straight up to the lord's residence, where adventure awaited him. This literature thus obeyed the hierarchical order of the castle's plan and topography. It was interested only in the summit: the lord and his court. That was where the hero's destiny summoned him and where the poet would find his audience. The summit provided literature not only with an ideal audience and a setting but also a self-image and its very raison d'être. Pre-urban twelfth-century literature in its various forms—poetry, chanson de geste, romance—considered itself literature of the essence, of the revelation of meaning hidden beneath the multiplicity of the real, the absolute: the absolute of love, the quest, the crusade, fidelity, salvation. If the literary work happened to pass through the streets of a town, it did not wander about in them but went straight up to the castle, where it would find the revelation of this meaning.

When it discovered the town at the start of the thirteenth century, literature discovered a space with several centers, meanings, and hierarchies. Each category and trade had its street, its neighborhood, its center. Power was dispersed among the commune and the lord, the king and the bishop, the bishop and the abbot or the chancellor of the university in a legalistic jumble contrary to the clear order of the princely court. The town was teeming and heterogeneous—these were its necessary attributes. One got lost in it. It was not subordinated to a single power or place. By taking this as its setting, literature discovered dizzying fortuities and relativity. The town initiated it into the disorganized multiplicity and complexity of reality and thereby hinted at those of the spirit. Absolute love was replaced by petty love stories rooted in the circumstances of life and the space of the town. Misery and disenchantment were the lessons of the labyrinth of streets in which one became lost: the streets of Arras through which the leprous poet walked in his *Congés*; streets of brothels and taverns where wine, dice, and harlots ruined the narrators of *dits*, the heroes of fabliaux, the characters in plays—yet also defined them by their way of life, the vices they were captive to, like the variety of rascals that oozed from the streets of Paris, whom Villon later enumerated in their monotonous variety, all mingled together in the ballade's refrain: "Tout aux tavernes et aux filles" [Everything to taverns and women]. Streets—the crossroads for encounters, adventures, incidents—defined the literary self by anecdote, whereas a century earlier it sought to forge itself according to the abstract perfection of a general idea with which it was commingled.

Thus, the thirteenth century saw the rise of a literature in which reality ceased to be the emblematic reflection of an idea yet shaped everyone's condition and contained its own meaning in itself—or its own absurdity. Its disorderly multiplicity was preferably evoked by urban space in the new literature, that of Arras and Paris, of personal poetry, fabliaux and, later, *nouvelles*, farces, and even mysteries.

The urban masses thus awakened individual voices in literature, defined in relation to them, immersed in them, produced in them, driven to despair by them, without the help, point of reference, or model of princely courts and their hierarchy. That is when the image —destined for such great success—was born of the poet who passes his destiny by and misses it in the movement of the throng ("The deafening street howled around me"),[21] who feeds his perversity on the monstrous spectacles that this throng offers him ("Look at them, my soul, they are really horrid"),[22] who assembles at random the shattered bits of reality and disparate voices heard in "Monday, rue Christine," that he does not try to bring under control.[23] Not that we should try to modernize the Middle Ages through anachronisms. But their preoccupation with the new sounds of the city can indeed be read as concern for their own modernity.

Thus, from whatever angle we consider it, French thirteenth-century literature was characterized by critical expression of subjectivity. In the following pages we shall see literature turning to discourse of the subject and lyric poetry to fictional narration of the self, with literary forms as a whole informed by the subjective feelings of time, life, and consciousness. These movements signify the emergence of the very idea of literature as we have defined it earlier. It is therefore only fitting to focus our attention on the period during which they evolved. The most beautiful medieval texts may have been those of the twelfth century, but literature was invented in the thirteenth.

PART I

Subjectivity and Narrativity

A Change in
Literary Consciousness
The Language of Romance

Literature, at least in its narrative forms, was born as an expression of myth. Inevitably, it gradually undermined belief in its concrete truthfulness as it grew aware of itself and of its power over the material it treated. Throughout much of Greek literature one might read the story of a conflict between the poet who, by reflecting on his condition and his art, discovered that the truth of his work was his own and the truth of the subjects granted him, backed by religion. This conflict ended in a secularization of literature, at times concealed and at other times visible. The emergence of the author per se and of his self-awareness within literature defined both the point where it deserved the name and the time when the work's truth was only what it was granted by the author, who had the sole *authority* to define its nature and bore responsibility for it.

A time came when new reasons had to be found for believing in literature, belief in myths having been altered or weakened. Thereafter people doubted that words really told the truth they claimed to know—not directly, however, in medieval literature but through other words, a written text, writing, which they referred to and insisted they were following with scrupulous fidelity without, however, ever thinking of reproducing it word for word, of being *it*, until the day when *it* became *them* and when, reading "ce dist li contes" (thus says the story), one had to understand it was the story being written that said so. Neither the urge to imitate nor respect for authority was ever pushed to its logical consequence: that would have meant transforming the author into a copyist and modestly fusing the text with his model or, if the latter was imaginary, impudently proclaiming that the text was his model. There were only utilitarian forgeries then: forged bulls of ancient popes, forged royal Carolingian decrees; there was no Ossian. Indeed, the text could invent a fictional source for itself, but it could not claim to be that source.[1] But when a model did exist, there was a line between scrupulous adaptation and transcription, pure and simple, which was not crossed and defined the locus of literature. Fidelity to the past belonged neither to the plagiarist nor to the ethnologist; it consisted of submitting the past to constant, respectful elaboration. But, through an inverse logic, one day the text became its own model, thus offering a guarantee of the most perfect sort of fidelity: to itself. At the same time, it discovered the nature and power of literature: its own. Literature no longer had as its humble mission to speak the truth about a past that would be forgotten without it. It had felt that past as burning, desirable, and dangerous to know; suddenly it realized that, if it was burning, that was because it was not the past: literature alone projected the present that filled or surrounded us into the past, by projecting it into words. Henceforth this intimate present could use disguises other than that of the past to *come forward masked*;[2] in the thirteenth century narrative literature began to treat contemporary subjects. Above all, after this discovery the text had a right to be its own source; without tricks, coy flirtations, precautions, it would need no authority other than its own. It was authorized. But did it henceforth contain any truth other than itself? That is questionable.

There is another question concerning its effect. If the nature of its truth changed, the credence it was to be given also changed. If the objective truth of what the text said was no longer believed, how could the text itself be believed; that is, how could we be swept along by it? The procedures of literary discourse, which had continued to be studied and applied, took on new importance and deserved new reflection. If the text could not invoke the authority of another text in order to be listened to, if it could be authorized only by its author, the author had to assert himself, he had to put his self on the line, and that had been virtually unknown in literature until then. The two elements thus combined made the representation of the author at work essential literary material and, in some cases, a criterion of the work's credibility. Or, rather, the various modes of that representation defined the nature of its truth each time, along with the kind of credibility the work laid claim to. In the field of romance, the consequence was the appearance of subjective novelistic forms: the allegorical romance or the *dit*. Literature perhaps—certainly the writer —existed only from the time this dual doubt was instituted.

Thus, all commences with literature's scrutiny of the past, according to whether it was considered to be myth, History, or fiction. French literature of the Middle Ages did not deal with myths per se. On the one hand, as an heir to classical antiquity it did not exhibit the characteristics of a primitive literature. On the other, Christianity forbade acceptance of myths as true. It could seek justification by claiming to preserve true memory of the past; its relationship with historiography must then be examined. But, as we have stated, this claim was generally based on the use of previous works and, in the case of the romance, literary elaboration came under the heading of imitation or translation. Finally, the point at which literature recognized that its material was fictional was, as we have just seen, also when the author made his appearance. That, par excellence, was the time of romance, a secondary mode of literary expression in the dual sense of its arriving late and being grafted onto other literary practices, the product of a very particular kind of literary activity born under circumstances that were no less so.

French romance appeared around 1150, fifty years after the chanson de geste and troubadour lyrics.[3] As the first vernacular form meant to be read and not sung, it presumed a more intellectualized exercise of literature. The rhythmic and sound effects, the echoes of repetitions and variants on which the impression produced by the chanson de geste largely depended, disappeared from the romance and gave way to pure narrativity. Replacing the chanson de geste's strophic structure and assonanced *laisses* with a linear, indeterminate succession of octosyllabic rhyming couplets, romance abandoned both melody and the purely physical aspect of poetic language's effectiveness and focused attention on the narrative's content.[4] However, it invited its readers to reflect on its overall composition precisely because it was offered for individual reading, which progressed at its own pace and could seek to control the work's entire material, whereas listeners to the chanson de geste, subject to the division that the performer imposed upon it, could embrace only the portion uttered in one session of recitation.[5]

Finally, the chanson de geste's claim to orality was indicated within the written text by the inclusion of a speaker who professed to be the narrator, addressing his supposed audience and vaunting his performance. Moreover, the convention of oral recitation implied that the "I" designated the performer, since the listener could refer it only to the individual pronouncing it. In romance, on the contrary, the "I" could refer only to the author. It could be only he enumerating his previous works in his prologues, revealing his method of composition, and addressing a dedicatee. One consequence of the writer's persistent intervention in the prologue was that all marks of personal statement, all the artifices by which discourse attracted attention to its own working out, would naturally be referred by a reader to the author. Reading a romance thus confirmed its nature as intellectual reception, since the author's presence was first imposed on it through the definition of a project or a process within the order of literary creation. By integrating reflection into the writer's task, romance by the same token defined the reader's task.

The first French romances were adaptations of works of Latin antiquity: Statius's *Thebaid* for the *Roman de Thèbes*, the *Aeneid* for the *Roman d'Enéas*, the compilations of Dares the Phrygian and Dictys for the *Roman de Troie*, that of the pseudo-Callisthenes for the *Roman d'Alexandre*. Their authors were proud of being able to let contemporaries who did not know Latin benefit from their knowledge of ancient literature. That was their glory. They were conscious of being craftsmen, in the literal sense, of the *translatio studii*. One understands why the word "romance," which naturally and customarily designated the vernacular Romance language and all expression in that language, specifically came to designate a literary genre. The word "romance" drew its meaning from implicit but permanent opposition to the word "Latin." It was necessary to specify that people were expressing themselves in "Romance" since they could have expressed themselves in Latin. Is it so surprising that the word "romance" became specialized as the designation of a genre based on compiling and translating Latin texts? The romance was called romance because it was close to the Latin both in its sources and in the intellectual activity it presupposed. In the twelfth century the word might actually designate any text translated from or inspired by a Latin model; for example, the lives of saints—which have been shown to be structurally close to the first romances and, like the latter, acted as popularizations—or other edifying works.[6] In the prologue to the *Roman de Troie* Benoît de Sainte-Maure can be seen, within the space of two lines, to use the common expression "mettre en roman" (to put into Romance), which is to say to translate from Latin into vernacular, and then the word "romance" to designate the work resulting from such translation (ll. 32–39). The evolution of the word thus illustrates Bakhtin's idea that romance was born of a reflexive attitude toward language.

In a word, at the start a writer of romances was a translator:

> Le latin sivrai et la letre,
> Nule autre rien n'i voudrai metre
> S'ensi non com jel trüis escrit.[7]

> I shall follow the letter of the Latin text:
> My intention is to add nothing
> More than what I find written.

At the outset of the history of the romance, later to consecrate the writer's independence and authority, literary creation thus seems to have been suffocating within the narrow area of translation, all the narrower because respect for "historical truth" was added to fidelity to the Latin model:

> Maistre Wace l'a *translaté*,
> Qui en conte la *verité*.[8]

> Master Wace translated it,
> And he tells of its truth.

From the start, however, these very constraints defined the original activity of the romance writer, based on philological competency and the discrimination of historical criticism. In his own view, his effort was one of criticism and had no other value than its own activity and materials. He sought to disguise neither his effort nor his index cards. The value of the finished romance was nothing else than its *fashioning into romance*. The romance was less a literary genre than a method of work, a form of analysis of the past and its sources, an intellectual exercise, a fashioning into romance in which romance form was not its aim but its consequence.

Thus Benoît de Sainte-Maure explained in the long prologue to the *Roman de Troie* why Dares was a more dependable source than Homer concerning the Trojan war, how his long-lost work was rediscovered and translated into Latin, and how Benoît himself in turn translated it into French. The writer's value lay in faithfully adapting the source that was most faithful to historical truth. He was not only a translator but a historian. The first French romances considered themselves to be the first works of history written in French, whereas the first French chronicles, of a later dated, actually were memoirs, as we shall see. True contemporary history, extricated from the memoirs' narrow field of vision, was written by authors who finally reached it by starting from the past: Wace writing the *Roman de Rou* after the *Roman de Brut*, and Benoît de Sainte-Maure the *Chronique des ducs de Normandie* after the *Roman de Troie*. When the latter reproached

Homer for implausibly having the gods intercede in his story, he was in his own way showing a concern for historical truth absent from such contemporary Latin poems as *De Bello Trojano* of Joseph of Exeter and the *Alexandreid* of Gautier de Châtillon, which made greater use of mythology than their classical models.[9]

What kind of history was fashioned into romance? Considering the group formed by the *Roman de Troie*, *Enéas*, and Wace's *Brut*, we note that the three romances are linked by their retracing of successive foundings owed to the same lineage: Aeneas fleeing Troy and reaching Latium and, later on, Brut (Brutus) leaving Latium for England. As we have stated, following *Brut* Wace wrote the *Roman de Rou*, the history of the Dukes of Normandy from Rollo on, before stepping aside, faced with competition from the *Chronique des ducs de Normandie* by the author of the *Roman de Troie*. These authors were therefore writing the history of what in their view was most fundamental, the origins of the English monarchy, going back to the most illustrious episode of antiquity. The retrospective genealogy with which the *Roman de Rou* opens is significant in this regard. They made Henry II Plantagenet, to whose court all were attached, heir to a prestigious past, capable of rivaling the Carolingian past in the chansons de geste, whose glory served the king of France.[10]

The scope of this project did not prevent the author's share from being considered modest; if we are to believe him, he was merely a translator, whose only intervention supposedly was stripping the ancient works of their mythological dross and reestablishing historical truth. In fact, rather than reduce his importance, this apparent timidity increased it and assured his authority. By emphasizing the respect he had for his model and his concern for truth, he drew attention to the work in progress more than to the finished work, that is, to his own efforts and therefore to himself. But it was precisely by displaying these meticulous attempts at research, translation, and adaptation that the author emphasized what was specifically his own. He was too scrupulous to attribute what was his to his sources or to disguise the fact that he had added "a few good words," as Benoît de Sainte-

Maure confessed. He thus opened the door to personal creation at the same time as he made it benefit from its model's authority:

Ceste estoire n'est pas usee,
N'en guaires lieu nen est trovee:
Ja retraite ne fust ancore,
Mais Benooiz de Sainte-More
L'a contrové e fait e dit
E o sa main les moz escrit,
Ensi tailliez, ensi curez,
Ensi asis, ensi posez,
Que plus ne meins n'i a mestier.
Ci vueil l'estoire comencier:
Le latin sivrai e la lettre,
Nule autre rien n'i voudrai metre,
S'ensi non com jol truis escrit.
Ne di mie qu'aucun bon dit
N'i mete, se faire le sai,
Mais la matire en ensivrai.
(ll. 129–44)

(This story is not hackneyed, and it is not to be found all over: it had never been told before, but Benoît de Sainte-Maure discovered it, elaborated it, and set it down; he wrote out all its words with his own hand: he hewed, polished, posed, and arranged them so well that there is no need to add or subtract a thing. I shall now begin the story; I shall follow the letter of the Latin text; my intention is to add nothing to what I find written. I do not say that I shall not add a few good words, if I can, but I shall limit myself to the substance of my model.)

The poet, who prided himself on the originality of his subject and supplied his name at the same time as he was underscoring this, proclaimed at once his fidelity to the Latin model, the extreme care he had taken in writing his text, and the share of this perfect text that was peculiarly his. Thus suggesting that the effect of his work was a displacement of authority, which shifted from the source to the romance, he also shifted from his subject's originality to that of his work. After observing that the story of the Trojan War had never previously been told (in French, we must assume, though at this point he was not being specific), now he was suddenly claiming full paternity, from its general idea to its practical execution. He implicitly compared the words of the text to building blocks: if just one were withdrawn, the whole thing would collapse. He thus based his authority on the quality of his language and style, which rendered the text inviolate. He was growing conscious of the power and importance he was endowed with by literary expression, which was his, his alone, and was everything. In this way he imposed his presence and lent to his function as translator an authority that would not be his if, as he pretended to assert, only the story's truthfulness mattered.

In fact, only the unified form of the romance gave coherence to material borrowed from different sources, whose mode of reference to reality varied widely: ancient epics, Late Latin pseudohistorical compilations, Medieval Latin chronicles. These disparate sources, giving rise to romances of uniform composition, did not convey equal truth. By the same token, the truth of the romances changed, though their form remained identical and, as they became more numerous, even grew rigid as it acquired the features of an identifiable genre.

Indeed, the great dynastic tableau stretching from the Trojan War to the Anglo-Norman kings obliged the romance writers—as soon as they had left the Mediterranean basin for Britain and antiquity for the High Middle Ages—to replace their ancient sources with contemporary chronicles, in particular Geoffrey of Monmouth's *Historia regum Brittaniae*, of which Wace's *Brut* was an adaptation. In this way they shifted from romances of antiquity to Breton romances, which were to enjoy great success. No one, it would seem, cast doubt on the historical truth of the ancient sources. The romance writers vouched for that, irrespective of the liberties they might take. If, on that score, the writers of Breton romance had retained the confidence of the authors of romances of antiquity, the only difference between them would have been their subject, which was practically nullified by narrative continuity leading from the Argonauts to King Arthur. But this, in fact, was not the case. The Breton romancers were almost as openly skeptical about their material as were Giraud de Bari or William of Newburgh, the historians of Henry II's court, who derided the *fabulae* reported by Geoffrey of Monmouth.[11] In *Rou* Wace related his disappointing pilgrimage to the fountain of Barenton (ll. 6373–98). In *Brut* he depicted

> . . . la Roünde Table
> Dont Breton dient mainte fable
> (ll. 9750–51)
>
> . . . the Round Table, of which the Bretons tell many a tale

explaining that storytellers and *fableurs* had said so much about King Arthur that truth could not be distinguished from falsehood; everything had taken on an air of fabrication (ll. 9785–98). Thus he deliberately undermined the authority that exact preservation of the past conferred on him. He obligingly (and unnecessarily) emphasized how much his romance owed to imagination—both his own and that of his predecessors. Was that not taking pride in fiction and not in truth, as in the romances of antiquity, as he himself did in his prologue?

We spoke at the outset of the importance in defining the status of the writer of the point at which literature viewed itself as fiction. We have now seen that this point was reached almost from romance's very first appearance: *fashioning into romance* brought out and emphasized the *romance writer*'s effort and choices. But history, regarded as genuine, still had to be replaced with a story recognized as dubious. This dubious story was Arthurian matter, as opposed to the matter of antiquity. But that still was not enough. *Brut* came before all the romances of antiquity, with the exception of the first version of the *Roman d'Alexandre*. Indeed, it claimed to be a romance of antiquity. For the truth of the past to give way to the truth of romance, which only the writer vouched for and of which he was, in a word, the author, greater importance had to be systematically given to Breton legend. Untruth, which Wace slipped into the midst of his romance, would have to be praised, secretly refuting his prologue's claims, the basis of all prologues, and the justification of a literary method.

That is precisely what Chrétien de Troyes did. He wrote only Breton romances, and his prologues—except to *Cligès*, which was only half Breton—scoffed at the truth of his references and sources. If he claimed, in the prologue to the *Chevalier de la charrette*, that he limited his role to shaping a subject imposed upon him, he was alluding not to the story's truth but only to its meaning. Even more striking is the prologue to *Erec et Enide*. For the first time a novel did not claim to derive its value from its source but, on the contrary, from the latter's weakness. The romance writer's merit was in recognizing the use that could be made of an "adventure story" (l. 13), of no great interest in itself, that anyone else would have scorned. He turned it into a work that would be remembered until the end of time or, with the poet playing on his own name to undermine the apparent "boast" with a modest belaboring of the obvious, "till the end of the Christian era":

> Des or comancerai l'estoire
> Qui toz jors mes iert an mimoire
> Tant con durra crestïantez;
> De ce s'est Crestïens vantez.
> (ll. 23–26)

> I am going right now to begin this story, whose memory
> will be preserved forever, as long as Christianity endures:
> that is Chrétien's [Christian's] boast![12]

The novelty of this attitude is obvious. The author was turning not to a past that his work was supposed to recall but to a future that would recall his work. In no way was his ambition to perpetuate true recollection of the past by using a sure source whose authority would be reflected on his work. Indeed, he considered it beneath him to specify whether his story was true or fictitious. His only concern was to inform readers that his source was insignificant, that his romance had no truth other than the meaning it produced, no authority other than his own—that he, the writer, was its only author. He put himself in the limelight, he pointed to himself, he boasted: "De ce s'est Crestïens vantez."

By the start of the *Conte du Graal*, Chrétien was no longer referring to any source, even to call it second-rate, except—very laconically—the mysterious "book" of Duke Philip of Alsace, concerning which he did not suggest what relationships might exist between him and his work. Furthermore, from the very first lines he claimed to be the originator of everything. It was he who was sowing the seed of the romance:

> Crestïens seme, et fet semance
> D'un romans que il ancomance.
> (ll. 7–8)

> Chrétien sows—it is his seed—a romance that he undertakes.[13]

Chrétien did not clearly indicate the truth of his novels. But to gain the reader's support, he did have to suggest that somewhere in his work there was a truth upon which his authority was based. Actually, he did so in two complementary ways: by insisting on the fact that his romances made people think and had a lesson to impart, on the one hand, and, second, that their meaning sprang in great measure from the organization given the events they recounted. Thus he suggested that the sequence of adventures was both exemplary and symptomatic: exemplary of the tests to be faced by a young knight, the category to which all his heroes belonged, in order to find his rightful place in the world and achieve internal balance and fruition; symptomatic precisely of the internal adventure that the outward ones both provoked and signified. Thus, for the reader the hero was less a model than a reflection, as ambiguous, complex, and hard to decipher as himself, one whose deciphering could nonetheless help in his own. But the reverse was also true, and that was a second affirmation of the romance's truth: the reader was invited to understand the characters and judge their truthfulness according to the experience of his or her own feelings. Take *Cligès*, where the reader was called upon to witness the effects of love:

> Vos qui d'Amors vos feites sage,
> Et les costumes et l'usage
> De sa cort maintenez a foi,
> N'onques ne faussastes sa loi,
> Que qu'il vous an doie cheoir,
> Dites se l'en puet nes veoir
> Rien qui por Amor abelisse
> Que l'en ne tressaille ou palisse.
> (ll. 3819–26)

> You who have experienced love, who keep faith with the customs and uses of his court, who have never violated its law, whatever might happen to you as a result, tell me if one can see the object of which one is enamoured without trembling and turning pale before it.

A reflection more than a model; a constant give-and-take between reader and character, the former called upon to witness the truth of the latter, who resembles him: in such a romance, the past the story was located in no longer was an essential element in itself. Knowing it as such no longer mattered. It was no longer considered true in itself. Truth had undergone a dual shift: from past to present, where it had to appear to be guaranteed, in the disguise of past fiction, by the reader's recognition, and from the material to the psychological world. At the beginning of the *Chevalier du lion*, in apparent contradiction to the above proposition, Chrétien declared that he would rather speak of the past than the present. But that was because the men of the past were more worthy than today's men, and their love was more sincere (ll. 26–32). The past's truth, what made it worthy to supply material for the romance, was no longer one of facts but of love. It did not inform but taught. It was worthy of attention because it was a lesson for the present. We have arrived at the point of recognition that the past's fascination derived from its being a mask of the present, to which the supposed distance of time lent a significance that was both enigmatic and gripping.

From then on the shift in the author's consciousness of his work and the reading he offered of it was irreversible and definitive. As early as the 1180s, with Gautier d'Arras, and the beginning of the following century, with Jean Renart, when a reaction set in against the "lies" of the Breton romances, the "truth" those authors called for was no longer that called for by the first romances of antiquity. By then it was admitted that a romance was its author's own business. There were no more claims for its truth being nothing but the facts it related. As a result, the notion was no longer self-evident, as in literature of a historical bent like the romances of antiquity. It had to be defined, a new problem. Chrétien de Troyes based an author's freedom and authority on the whims of fiction; as we have seen, he did not openly express concern. The definition of truth appeared in his work only as an implicit corollary to his reflection on the meaning of romance. But his successors, who made a show of rejecting his "lies," were by that very fact forced to explain their idea of truth, as did Gautier d'Arras in *Ille et Galeron* and Jean Renart in the prologue to *Escoufle*.[14] Their criticism bore upon the composition of the literary work and the impression it produced, not upon its relation to external reality. A few years later, in the prologue to *Guillaume de Dole*,[15] Jean Renart spoke no longer either of historical truth or of *lies* or *meaning*. The entire prologue was meant to praise the notion of inserting lyric pieces within a romance, and to bring out the harmony between the two. It was solely about literary construction and cohesion; that was the writer's only concern. Not only did Gautier d'Arras's and Jean Renart's so-called realism not in the least have rehabilitation of the historical referent as its effect, but it did away with what one may call the psychological and spiritual referent at the heart of Chrétien's romances. With them, romance became an art not of historical or psychological or allegorical depth but of surface, drifting, slippage.[16]

Thus, in the French romance's first century of existence, the truth that it claimed to express gradually turned away from the referent and increasingly focused on its nature as a literary text. In this evolution the passage from the romance of antiquity to Breton romance played a more than negligible role. We shall perhaps be criticized for analyzing the transfer of authority to the author rather than the eruption of his subjectivity into the romance. That would be an easy task with respect to Chrétien de Troyes or Jean Renart. But in reality it is evident that the demand for the imaginary was in itself an affirmation of the "I," since in the formation of the literary "I" the *imaginary* plays the role of the *image* in the formation of the psychological "I." We can apply to it what Lacan says of the mirror stage: "The function of the mirror stage proves . . . to be a particular case of the function of the *imago*, which is to establish a relationship between the organism and its reality—or, as it is stated, between the *Innenwelt* and the *Umwelt*."[17]

What romance adventure was for the hero—a mirror in and through whose reflection his *I* was defined—the romance itself was, as a literary activity, for the author.

But from a less general and more historical perspective, the invasion by subjectivity was another matter, a sequel to the one just mentioned, and another period, the age of Saint Louis, to whose threshold Jean Renart has brought us. We have already stated that this period, which was characterized by the organization and theorization of knowledge in the development of Western culture, was marked by uncertainty in the field of literature, so that the proliferation of forms as well their fecundity led to hesitation as to which paths to take, and at times obliterated the ones already staked out. This uncertainty favored critical activity, an increase in aesthetic experiments, a search for new points of view, and in particular a redistribution of lyric and narrative forms. We shall soon see that the fictional confession or introspection offered by the *dit* accustomed readers to seeing narrative literature turn toward a display of the subject or, rather, the display of the subject turn toward narrative literature. The same result was reached by different paths in the allegorical romance, whose importance increased as a result of the *Roman de la Rose*. The decomposition of the mind into personified psychological elements, their encounter with personifications of another sort, the almost universal presence of a narrator, the frequent association of allegory with dreams—in a very special way turned allegorical romance into a romance of the subject. Furthermore, a romance of the subject is, by definition, a romance of the present; through it romance literature ceased to be necessarily a literature of the past. We shall return to these points at greater length.

With the appearance of the great prose cycles in the first third of the thirteenth century, a sizable portion of romance production started up a very different path that led it back eventually, at the end of the Middle Ages, to the claims and historical packaging that characterized the earliest romances. By contrast, with objective narration now embodied in prose, the current represented by verse romance flowed in the opposite direction, toward the new subjective poetry, itself increasingly prone to narrativity. The *Roman de la Rose* appears to be exactly contemporaneous with the prose *Lancelot*. In the latter, the sight of a rose, reminding Lancelot of Queen Guinevere and his desire to reach her, gives him the strength to tear out the bars of the prison in which Morgan le Fay has locked him up.[18] Daniel Poirion has demonstrated that this scene contains the argument of the *Roman de la Rose*.[19] The same image, incorporated into the development of the adventure romance, was also the entire space of internalized romance. In their own way, romances like *Guillaume de Dole* or the Provençal *Flamenca* considered themselves just as deliberately a narrative illustration and development of typical situations and obligatory motifs of lyric poetry present in Jean Renart's romance, studded with numerous chansons. By the end of the twelfth century, a fair number of romance writers were taking advantage of the opportunities their stories gave to speak of themselves, their desires, and their love life. Some, like Huon de Rothelande in *Ipomedon* and *Protheselaüs* or the author of *Flamenca*, indulgently imagined themselves in the erotic situations that their heroes were put into or fatuously compared their own amorous prowess with what was attributed to them. Others, like the authors of the *Lai d'Ignaure, Floriant et Florette*, and particularly *Parthonopeus de Blois*, strayed even further from the argument of their romance; their heroes' amorous triumphs led them—in either a light or a melancholy vein—to recall their own loves, which, despite their fidelity, had brought them only suffering and rebuffs.[20]

Joufroi de Poitiers,[21] a romance whose hero was inspired by the picturesque character of Count Guilhem IX of Poitiers, Duke of Aquitaine, is an extreme case of lyric emotion's intrusion into romance storytelling. In a ninety-line prologue, the poet addresses the reader concerning his amorous misfortunes—before even informing him that the poem he is undertaking is a romance and presenting its subject. Then, throughout the romance, he interrupts his story some ten times with thirty- to fifty-line interludes, in which he returns to his unfortunate loves and elaborates on the reflections they inspire in him. The memory of his amorous woes thus serves as a counterpoint to Joufroi de Poitiers's cynical, risqué tale of brief, easy feminine conquests. The writing of romance is presented in this way, implicitly but clearly, as a consequence and not a translation of the poet's personal emotions, expressed directly from time to time. This expression was nonetheless subject to the universalizing idealization and abstraction that were the rule in courtly lyricism, so that we cannot say the poet's subjective story is in response to the romance tale whose hero is Joufroi de Poitiers. It must be recognized, however, that *Joufroi de Poitiers* is a work unique in its genre, not to mention that it was left unfinished. That romance alone cannot bear sufficient witness to the encounter between narrative and the subjective, whose path we shall follow from another point of departure: lyric poetry.

But it was not really alone. At the end of his romance[22] the author of *Parthonopeus de Blois* reveals the sobriquet of the lady of his thoughts, to whom he has alluded several times during the course of the work. That sobriquet is "Passe-Rose." He is considering another book project dedicated entirely to her: "Faire en porroie un autre livre."

It would be the internalized romance of an "I" in love with the beauty who, as her name implies, surpasses the rose: the *Roman de la Rose*. Pierre-Yves Badel, noting that the "I" is one of the marks of autobiographical dream, links it with "the current, evident in adventure romance from *Parthonopeus de Blois* on, which made romance writers interweave fiction with allusions to their own love lives."[23] The adventure romance thus conceived its own future for itself in the form of a transformation into romance of the self.

From Lyric Poetry to Personal Poetry
The Ideal of Love and the Anecdote of the Self

The romance of the self, exerting its fascination on adventure romance pervaded by its author's subjectivity, was also the form toward which lyric sensibility evolved. The thirteenth century saw the birth of a personal poetry playing on narrativity. In a parallel movement, the chanson yielded to recited poetry, as the figure of the poet took shape and gained prominence. The modern notion of poetry appeared at the end of this evolution. That notion, although vague, has become so familiar to us that we have difficulty imagining an earlier stage when there was neither poetry nor poets but only chansons and their *trouveurs*.[1]

However, if our grasp of this first stage of medieval lyricism is flawed, it is not for lack of being lectured on it. How often have we been told that the lyric poetry of the Middle Ages differed radically from that of later centuries and, in particular, that it was the opposite of the romantic sensibility still coloring our image of the poet today! Indeed, it did not claim to yield the original confessions of a particular and unique personality; but within the limits of a requisite and inviolable form of writing whose codes referred only to itself and excluded almost all external referents, either anecdotal or biographical, it indulged in rhetorical, rhythmic, and melodic variations, arousing in its hearers the double pleasure of familiarity spiced with delicate surprise. The definition of medieval lyricism as formalist poetry, however bold and paradoxical it seemed thirty years ago, has today become the most commonly accepted one, thanks to the work of Robert Guiette, Roger Dragonetti, Paul Zumthor, and their disciples.[2] It applies to the lyrics of the troubadours and *trouvères*, in particular to what they themselves called the chanson, customarily designated, following Dragonetti's lead, as the great courtly lyric, expressing *fin'amor* and the social ideal of *courtoisie*.

A striking gap separates this poetics from the one, from the mid-thirteenth century on, underlying the poetry of Rutebeuf, to choose an eminent example. Before proposing a theory of these oppositions, as Paul Zumthor did in a justly celebrated article comparing a chanson of Thibaud de Champagne with a *dit* of Rutebeuf,[3] we immediately note that Rutebeuf's poem is distinguished from Thibaud's chanson by having the air of an anecdotal, biographical, personal confession. Its other essential trait is the disappearance of music. Sung poetry, which is a poetry of rhetorical formalization and ethical generalization, contrasts with recited poetry, which is a poetry of the anecdote of the self. What necessity links these two antithetical pairs together? Why should one poetics combine song and generalizing abstraction and another, in contrast, recitation and anecdotal confession?

If we compare the mode of preservation of troubadour poetry with that of the *trouvères,* the system described here on a diachronic plane also appeared on the synchronic plane. The songbooks of the *trouvères,* that is, the manuscripts in which their lyrics were anthologized, bore musical notation more often than those of the troubadours. In the former, staves were usually drawn—at least room was provided for them—even when the melody was not transcribed. However, not even this was true of certain troubadour songbooks, which were quite carefully, indeed, lavishly executed. This was by no means the rule but rather a pronounced enough tendency for us to know far more *trouvère* than troubadour melodies; some of the latter have come down to us solely through the manuscripts in langue d'oïl[4] in which they were transcribed. They have thus more often preserved what, beyond all else, allowed the audience to appropriate a poem for itself. For melody invited the manuscript's users to take an active role as interpreters. Through their singing they could not help making the words of the poem their own and identifying with the subjectivity expressed in it.

On the other hand, in songbooks in langue d'oc,[5] which were never or only rarely notated, each troubadour's poems were preceded by his biography (*vida*) and commentaries on his works (*razos*), which were also biographical, a practice unknown in their langue d'oïl equivalents. *Vidas* and *razos* linked the poems to the author's persona, just as melodic notation linked the poems to the audience. It is no accident, therefore, that these two apparently unconnected phenomena were more or less mutually exclusive, the reason being that they revealed two polar opposites of poetic reception: distance and assimilation. The *vidas* and *razos* increased the distance between the reader and the subjectivity expressed in the poem by giving it biographical roots, whereas music or, more precisely, the fact that the poem was offered for musical interpretation reduced that separation.

The troubadour and *trouvère* songbooks, most of them copied at the end of the thirteenth and in the fourteenth centuries, bring together lyrics from the twelfth and first half of the thirteenth centuries. They reflect a belated reception of pieces dating from the previous generation or century. Through the intervention of the *vidas* and *razos*, those of the troubadours—often copied in Italy, thus adding a cultural gap to the time gap—invited anecdotal and biographical readings no longer corresponding to the aesthetics of courtly lyricism. Their usual indifference to melody confirms this separation. The *trouvère* songbooks seem more respectful of this aesthetics, in part perhaps because of the interest in musical questions in northern France. But it was also in langue d'oïl that the literature of their time developed a poetics of the anecdotal expression of the self that, adopting new forms, made it unnecessary to graft it onto traditional lyricism.

How did this new poetics see the light of day and challenge that of

39

the great courtly lyrics, whose principles seem completely opposed to it? The courtly lyric professed to be a confession of love, of course, but only in appearance. The poet proclaimed he was in love; quite obviously there is no point in wondering whether the proposition was a true one. It does make sense, however, to define the role played in the poetic system by these protestations of amorous sincerity, which created the illusion—though only an illusion—of a confession. The confession was merely apparent, for the poem's systematic tendency was toward generalization. It neglected to reveal the circumstances of love, privileging considerations of the nature and effects of love, its demands, its ethic and, more fundamentally, rhetorical variations on the expression of love. The confession was illusory, not only because of the generality of its aim but, in particular, because the poem was closed upon itself; not only because the proposition "I love" exhausted its contents but, even more, because its aim was to explain why that proposition had poetic creation as its necessary corollary, and poetic creation was the equivalent or reciprocal of that proposition rather than its consequence. Each of the two propositions—"I love" and "I sing"—merely referred to the other. The "I," as Zumthor has said, was simply the grammatical subject of processes expressing the qualities of love and song. The poem was condemned to repeat indefinitely that it existed as a poem because love existed. Feelings were expressed only in general conformity to the amorous model or, in other words, were externalized only as a uniform expression of the poetic model.

Thus the parlor game of which poetry of that time consisted was, more than anything, a word game. Beyond all else, to enjoy poetry meant to pay attention to the poet's effort. The chanson attracted attention to its own working out, at times explicitly in the initial and final stanzas, always implicitly by deriving its effects from subjecting discourse to a traditional norm and its variations in relation to it. In the process, it emphasized the poet's persona, to which the "I" of the poem, though omnipresent, could not really claim to refer because of the generalization and externalization of its aim, thus requiring the image of a poet at work before that of a poet in love.

Nevertheless, as has often been noted, the great courtly lyrics professed to be "sincere." This claim of sincerity was most persistent among the poets furthest from personal confidence or anecdotes, like Gace Brulé or Thibaud de Champagne. Thus, the former wrote:

Grant pechié fait qui de chanter me prie,
Car sans reson n'est pas droiz que je chant,
Qu'onques ne fis chanson jour de ma vie
Se fine amor nel m'enseigna avant.[6]

He who requests me to sing is quite wrong, for it is not right for me to sing without reason; I have never written a song unless true love first taught it to me.

Of all courtly lyric's favored commonplaces, the one that consisted of affirming that only a sincere lover could be a good poet was among the most frequent. Its best-known expression is found in the troubadour Bernard de Ventadour, but it appeared in the north still more often. The poet's affirmation of his love's sincerity does not contradict the formal character of the poetic play defined earlier. But, more than the preceding analysis might lead us to expect, it seemed to emphasize a real, personal experience of the poet as lover. In addition, it often turned up in a quite particular context. We know that the troubadours and *trouvères* of the first generations generally began their chansons with a "springtime stanza" celebrating the renewal of nature—the bursting of buds, love, and the singing of birds, the blossoming of flowers—which let the lover state he was in harmony with this amorous rejoicing or, on the contrary, complain that he alone was excluded from it. Springtime, an invitation to love, was thus an invitation to singing, and the amorous poet used this dual invitation as his reason for composing a poem.

A time came, however, when the beginning of spring went out of fashion and was no longer appreciated, as the *vida* of troubadour Peire de Valeria attests:

Joglars fo del temps et en la saison que fo Marcabrus, et fez vers tals com hom fazia adoncs, de paubra valor, de fuillas et de flors e de cans et de auzels. Sei cantar non aguen gran valor ni el.[7]

> He was a jongleur of the time and in the season of Marcabru; he wrote poems, as they were written then, of little value, about leaves and flowers, songs and birds. His songs had no great value, nor did he.

Like many *vidas*, this one had as its aim to play to the crowd, which explains the terseness and severity of its final judgment of the man and his songs. That is also the reason for the joke that consists in modifying the customary formulation "he was from Marcabru's period" to read "he was from Marcabru's time and season," the peculiar quality of the poets of that *time* being indulgence in developments— deemed ridiculous now—concerning the new *season* and the *weather*.[8] Aside from such quips, the text is not explicit about the reasons for the disfavor into which springtime verse had fallen.

For their part, the *trouvères* were more explicit. If, in a kind of paralepsis, they willingly indulged in recollection or review of springtime motifs, it was often merely to proclaim that their deep and enduring love owed nothing to the fleeting emotions of springtime, or occasionally to condemn "Maytide singers," whose skin-deep sensuality was the ephemeral fruit of a season and whose amorous complaints were superficial or even feigned. Such was already the meaning of the "winter stanza" in the works of Bernard de Ventadour and many others, which sometimes took an opposite tack to the traditional motif. There is no lack of examples:

> Amis Harchier, cil autre chanteor
> Chantent en mai volontiers et souvent;
> Mes je ne chant pour fueille ne pour flor,
> Se fine Amor ne m'en done talent,
> Car je ne sai par autre ensaignement
> Fere chançon . . .
> (Raoul de Soissons)[9]

> Harchier, my friend, other singers sing in May, gladly and unceasingly; but neither leaves nor flowers make me sing if true Love does not make me feel like it, for I cannot write songs under the effect of any other inspiration . . .

The refusal to subject love songs to seasonal influence and thus link "the pleasures and the days"[10] could only accentuate the tendency toward abstraction and generalization characteristic of the great courtly lyrics. It renounced the greening-songs' picturesqueness, at times tinged with fanciful nuances, in which all of nature came to life and answered the poet, whether he encountered the daughter of the nightingale and the siren clothed in leaves that turned green when the weather grew damp or accompanied with his citole the nightingale singing "Sanderaladon / Tant fet bon / Dormir lez le buissonet,"[11] or two girls offered his horse "Flours et violetes / Et rozes novelles / Sus un eschaiquier."[12] True, this renunciation was tempered by the device of paralepsis. But by considering that genuinely felt love alone was worthy inspiration for great courtly lyrics, by emphasizing the independence of their feelings vis-à-vis springtime and winter motifs and, even more, by proclaiming that it was not springtime that evoked love but love that transformed everything—even winter—into springtime, the *trouvères* were once again drawing conclusions from the confusion between "I love" and "I sing," equating the ideal of poetic expression with the ideal of love.

The generalizing abstractness of the courtly lyric was thus not a consequence of language turning back upon itself and a denial of any referent extraneous to the statement but rather a sign of confusion between the latter and the consciousness in which it was worked out and cited as proof of the poet's sincerity: in order to be credible, he had to prove that love was impervious to the risks and happenstance of the external world. Thus, in terms of events only rhetorical ones were left to the poem; paradoxically, a concern for amorous sincerity, that is, for conformity between love and the song, resulted in emphasizing the figure of the poet not as lover but as author.

Renouncing springtime motifs was also a way for the poet to attest his disdain for a too facile poetry and the vulgar audience that favored it. Take, for example, Thibaut de Champagne:

Feuille ne flor ne vaut riens en chantant
Que por defaut, sans plus, rimoier
Et pour fere solaz vilaine gent

Qui mauvés moz font souvent aboier.
Je ne chant pas por aus esbanoier,
Mes pour mon cuer fere un peu plus joiant.[13]

Leaves and flowers have no value in songs. They are there
only because of inability to rhyme, nothing else, and to
amuse boors who are made to bark with unabated joy by
wretched words. I do not sing to please them but to cheer
my heart up a little.

We should note that with *boors*, lovers of springtime poetry, the
poet contrasted not a public whose taste was more refined but rather
his own heart. He was singing for himself alone, to give himself a little of the *cheer* that was a lover's virtue. The search for poetic perfection had as its object not communication with even a limited circle
of connoisseurs but satisfaction of the self.

At the end of the preceding century a somewhat analogous attitude was apparent in certain troubadours who were proponents of
trobar clus (hermetic poetic composition), which they felt revealed
the poet's true qualities and what could be called his genius. As the
chanson's complexity drew attention to its author's skill, it invited his
performers to show scrupulous respect for the text, thus guaranteeing
its correct transmission. That is what Peire d'Alvernha seemed to be
saying in a *sirventès*.[14] By contrast, there was Guiraut de Bornelh, an
enemy of *trobar clus* who, in the *tenson* pitting him against Raimbaut
d'Orange,[15] showed indifference to the deformations to which bad
performers might subject his songs. Finally, the elitist concern underlying the theory of *trobar clus*—contrary to the position of
Guiraut de Bornelh, who was happy for his poem to be easily understood and easily sung by everyone, even ordinary people at the fountain—when carried to the extreme resulted in a sort of turning back
upon itself that cannot but recall the attitude of Thibaut de Champagne in the stanza quoted earlier.

Ulrich Mölk, speaking of Peire d'Alvernha's use of the expression
"amor de lonh, amor londana" (love from afar, far-off love), which
appeared in Guilhem IX's works and played a significant role in
Jaufré Rudel's poetry, has offered the opinion that the audience of the

Count of Poitiers and the Prince de Blaye consisted of a small circle of initiates. Peire d'Alvernha, for his part, took up the idea of far-off love precisely in those poems claiming to bring to light a new, internalized concept of love that seemed like folly to other troubadours and required dense, obscure expression. He thus went further along the trail that Guilhem IX and Jaufré Rudel had blazed. He found in *trobar clus* "the form of expression suited to the experience of a love understood as personal property. . . . The small circle that, in the case of Guilhem and Jaufré Rudel, included the aristocratic poet and his aristocratic audience in contrast to the many people excluded, was in Peire's case limited to its center, constituted by the artist's self: from a small number we have passed to a single being."[16] Similarly, imitating one of Marcabru's poems, Peire d'Alvernha completed the satire of bad love (*amar* as opposed to *amor*) by expressing his own heart's preference, a completely internalized, secret, and nostalgic love.[17]

The *trouvères* did not practice *trobar clus* or generally cultivate obscurity. They did not have the resource of hermeticism to demonstrate the high aims of their amorous selves and the solitary pride of their poetic selves. If they renounced the images of springtime, which were deemed vulgar, all that remained to them—and they gloried in them—were rhetorical, metrical, and melodic refinements to exalt in disembodied form the amorous, poetic self that also sought to impose its presence from behind the abstract "I" of their works.

Thus, a tension was created within the courtly lyric. The circularity of the chansons, since they pointed to nothing but themselves; their denial of links with a particular subjectivity or anecdote; the formal poetics of variation, limited within an immutable framework relying on the audience's literary memory, upon which the savor of the chansons depended; the presence of melody, through which they were turned over to their performers—all this allowed the audience to take total possession of a poem and locate its own subjectivity behind an "I" having little to do with that of the poet. At the same time, however, the poet rejected facile imagery that might awaken the strangest echoes in a broad public, posing as his poem's sole beneficiary. He drew attention to his effort and his talent as proof of his love, proclaiming his sincerity. In short, he seemed to be suggesting that there was room for a biography of the poet, that is, for another fiction that, unlike the poem's, would be biographical, located outside the poem, whose scrupulously respected rules excluded it.

As it happens, this suggestion seems to have been heard in the course of the thirteenth century. The *vidas* and *razos* created a romance of the self felt to be concealed behind the poem's "I." The anecdote of romance and the poem's universality were articulated discretely without intermingling. In the north, the text in langue d'oïl closest in spirit to the *vidas* and contemporaneous with them was a true-life romance dating from the end of the thirteenth century, which claimed to recount the life of a twelfth-century *trouvère*, quoting his chansons and inserting them into the story line. This was the *Roman du châtelain de Coucy et de la dame du Fayel*, which treated the quite common folkloric tale of the devoured heart, also present in the *vida* of troubadour Guilhem de Cabestanh. Generally speaking, the fashion begun by Jean Renart shortly before 1230 involving studding a romance with lyric pieces, whose success continued to grow till the end of the Middle Ages, presumed an analogous relationship between the particular circumstances of romance and the affective generalization of lyricism.

But anecdotal presentation of the self behind the abstraction of the lyric "I" took on its full meaning only when it dealt with the poet himself. This is precisely what happened in French literature of the thirteenth century, and it drastically altered the concept of lyric poetry. To understand this evolution, we must go back a little way in time and briefly follow a tradition independent of lyricism: unsung poetry of a satirical or moral character.

This was not in itself a tradition in subjective poetry. The edifying or satirical poems of the twelfth century scrutinized the various levels of society and condemned their vices and lectured them, without the poet himself appearing. But a tendency toward emotion was sometimes revealed behind the concern for edification. In the last decade of the century, the Cistercian Hélinand de Froidmont's *Vers de la mort*[18] enjoyed considerable success.[19] In them traditional rhetoric—

expertly handled, it must be said—developed only through a personal sense of death. The first lines sought to portray the poet's experience in the face of death, and death's mark on the life of the poet:

> Morz, qui m'a mis muer en mue
> En cele estuve o li cors sue
> Ce qu'il fist el siecle d'outrage.
> (ll. 1–3)

> Death, you who have enclosed me so I change in this steambath where the body sweats away the excesses it committed in life.

Hélinand became a Cistercian after a worldly life at the French court. The thought of his imminent death and the judgment that will follow impels him to expiate his sins in the austerity of monastic life, to eradicate them, to *sweat* them away in a monastery steambath, as he says. Later on he asks death to go "to Proneroi and Péronne" and greet his friends Bernard and Renaud, so they may take stock of themselves as he has and follow the same path. The last lines of the poem exalt pease porridge, the frugal diet of a Cistercian poet who has renounced gluttony and lust:

> Fui, lecherie! Fui, luxure!
> De si chier morsel n'ai je cure,
> Mieuz aim mes pois et ma poree.
> (ll. 598–600)

> Away, gluttony! Away, lust! I care nought for such costly morsels: I prefer my peas and my porridge.

In itself there is nothing more personal here than in the courtly chansons where a poet told of his love and his lady before dedicating the poem to one of his friends. Hélinand's confessions, from the "steambath" to the porridge, do not amount to much in comparison with the pathetic, didactic, rhetorical flow that they frame, in which they play no part. But it is remarkable for the poet to appear—even discreetly—when the genre did not require it, and to do so at the beginning and end of his poem, as if he were basing his teachings on

47

personal experience of the idea of death. This attitude seems to have struck his imitators and ensured his work's success.

The thirteenth century saw the appearance not only of other *Vers de la mort* but also of poems in which the author told of himself, poured out his feelings, and placed his life on display in the light of his death. These poems confessed their debt to Hélinand in their use of the stanza he pioneered, but they retained the 8 or 10 subjective lines of verse from his work rather than the 590 didactic ones. The circumstances of several other poets' lives and deaths led them to set out on this path as well. Around 1202 Jean Bodel, a *trouvère* from Arras who was the author of numerous works of various kinds, was stricken with leprosy and prevented by his disease from leaving on the Fourth Crusade. He then wrote his *Congés*, a long poem in Hélinand-style stanzas, in which he bade farewell to the world and his friends and meditated sorrowfully on the awful trial that God had imposed on him, sending him to end his days in a leper house at a time when he had hoped to go and serve Him overseas. Seventy years later (c. 1272–73), when Baude Fastoul, another *trouvère* from Arras, also became a leper, he imitated his illustrious predecessor by writing his own *Congés*; this repetition established the farewell complaint of the leper-poet as a literary genre. Finally, Adam de La Halle, leaving Arras (1276–77?) under less dramatic circumstances, composed a third set of *Congés* from Arras.[20]

The first two poets substituted verses on their own death for verses on death. No more general considerations on death's omnipotence and the need for repentance; no more addresses to death, inviting it to greet the poet's friends and remind them of these truths. The leper-poet struggled to see in the horror of his disease and the proximity of death the blessing of a repentance that God had specifically reserved for him. He bade farewell to each of his friends, complaining of his disease and renewing with each one the heartbreak of farewell and the shame of realizing that he had become an object of repulsion. The dense social network of Arras's bourgeois literary community and its *puy*[21] was evoked in contrast to the solitude of the poet, who was excluded and, being doomed to death, cut off from the world of the living. In other words, the particular circumstances of social life served to dramatize the expression of subjective experience. Adam de La Halle's use of Arras society was somewhat different. He condemned it as a whole, subjecting Arras and its inhabitants to lengthy invective and sarcasm before exempting his friends from reproof, taking reluctant leave of them, thanking them for their kindnesses and listing their names in the remainder of the poem. The latter was thus related to both satire and panegyric, but its author thought he should connect it to a real or false autobiographical event: his departure, or intended departure, from Arras, on which occasion he summoned his fellow citizens by name. Without so dramatic a state as the leper's to influence his literary output, he injected the satire into the anecdotal framework of his life and friendships.

Adam de La Halle, like Jean Bodel and Baude Fastoul, was a *trouvère* in the classic sense of the term. But differences in his work demonstrate what had changed by the end of the thirteenth century, compared with the preceding era. As a classic *trouvère*, Adam composed courtly chansons in total conformity with the genre's norms, displaying the same qualities of generalization and idealization they had shown for over a century. But at the same time it was recourse to individualization and particularization of traits, to anecdotes and caricature, that was the basis for the pseudoconfession and appearance of the self in his unsung poetry: a metaphorical appearance in the *Congés* but a literal one in the *Jeu de la feuillée*.[22] Adam himself is the play's main character; he appears surrounded by his nearest and dearest friends, inhabitants of Arras, all designated by name, caricatured, and quite recognizable, playing out a psychodrama of impossible leave-taking in the guise of a comic parade. Finally, Adam de La Halle was a remarkable musician who was responsible for considerable progress in polyphony. The melodies of his courtly lyrics are completely traditional nonetheless. He reserved his innovations for his rondeaux, which he used as a basis for his motets. The balance between music and text was thus upset in favor of the former. The rondeau's text was brief, lacking the courtly chanson's textual dignity; it served its author's literary glory less since it was made up of reminiscences and borrowings. For this reason it was usually anonymous, and its authorship was claimed by an author like Adam only because he was renewing its music. In fact, when a motet was performed, the listener had his attention absorbed by the polyphonic composition and more easily turned to it from the texts because their superposition made them hard to understand.

Adam de La Halle's works thus marked the breakup of the lyric synthesis constituted by the *trouvères'* poetry, which survived only in the few courtly lyrics that he composed. Melody, to which polyphony lent new complexity and technicality, was almost sufficient unto itself and relegated the minor texts it set to the status of bit players. Thus was proclaimed the divorce between poetry and music that marked the fourteenth century. At the same time, recited poetry took over, in opposition to the great courtly lyrics, replacing generalization by anecdote and idealization by satire. Accounts of circumstances and events and the grotesque exaggeration of traits defined a particular self that sought to reveal itself in a poetry that was no longer lyrical but personal, related not to the lyric but to the *dit*.[23]

More than anyone else, Rutebeuf, who was active from about 1250 to 1280, embodied this shift in poetic language. His *dits* appeared as a caricature of the self and society, an enterprise of ideological destruction—of courtly ideology in particular—through a concrete imaginary world.[24] His poetry points up the fact that the *dit*, a genre formless in itself, was defined by a display of the self in the face of others and society. Once melody disappeared, which had allowed the audience to appropriate the poem for itself, the poet sought not to compensate for this process of appropriation by other means but rather to make it impossible by imposing his presence. He talked of himself and recounted his life, although it would obviously be futile to ask how much truth was contained in these false confessions. He spoke of his dreams and the allegorical visions he had been favored with. He named himself and glossed his name frequently and at length, piling up etymological jokes. He talked with his audience as the poets of Arras had talked with those they were taking leave of, and Hélinand had talked with death. Finally, *annominatio*, which for

Zumthor serves as the definition of the *dit*, constantly imposed the poet's presence. Thus, his poetry often gave an impression of self-display, of a dramatic monologue conceived entirely for the sake of the effect that it sought to produce on the audience. The latter perceived it as an open confession, improvised under the influence of ill humor or discouragement, during one of those moments when people forget their self-respect, no longer able to keep up appearances, and can do nothing but laugh at themselves sadly or bitterly. *A Poor Man's Soliloquies*, more or less—the pseudonym of Jehan Rictus[25] proves the debt he felt he owed the Middle Ages—or perhaps the equivalent of a music-hall or café-theater "one-man show." Unlike courtly poetry, this poetry of daily life had no need of sincerity as a precondition, even though the former was far more abstract and obeyed rigid formal rules. It aimed solely at a concrete dramatization of the self. It was poetry of a specific, recognizable reality, though one that wore a disguise, just as the self exposing both it and itself was specific and wore a disguise.

It also underscores the importance assigned to both theatricality and the comic in the new thirteenth-century poetics. French theater arrived rather late, took a long time gaining independence from Latin liturgical drama, and remained an underrepresented genre until the end of the thirteenth century. Jean Bodel's *Jeu de saint Nicolas*, the first play written entirely in French—including prologue, stage directions, and headings—was originally staged in Arras around 1200. Adam de La Halle's *Jeu de la feuillée*, the first secular play, also from Arras, dates from around 1280. Between the two, aside from the brief farce *Le Garçon et l'aveugle* (after 1266) and Rutebeuf's *Miracle de Théophile* (c. 1270), we find works offering only sketchy dramatization. Of this type was *Courtois d'Arras*, a modernized variant on the parable of the prodigal son, or *Aucassin et Nicolette*, which seems to have lent itself to a sort of mimed recitation. This lengthy infancy of the theater, urban and peculiarly identified with Arras, displays two important characteristics from this point of view. On the one hand, genuine theatrical plays seem rare because we give the genre a modern definition and expect texts entirely acted out by several characters, without a reciter, narrator, or conventional author figure to deform or destroy the mimetic illusion. Instead, we find a whole series of works of various kinds based on the *performance* of a reciter, supposedly fused with the poet, and on his virtuosity in assuming one or several parts, a virtuosity that he exploited, never letting us forget it even as he became someone else: the person he was supposed to be in real life. The *Jeu de la feuillée*, an extreme and exemplary case of self-representation's shift toward dramatic representation, was a genuine theatrical play, according to our standards, but one whose main character was the poet playing himself, mimicking his *congés* and defining himself through the network of social relationships that determined and stifled him.

Thus, there was no discontinuity between *dit* and theater; more precisely, the theatricality of the *dit* embraced and unified all of that protean genre's variants. The constant play of *annominatio*, the puns, etymological figures, effects of alliteration and paronomasia, ambiguities, unexpected or obvious rhymes—all this dazzling and disconcerting paraphernalia was already *mimicry* by the poet, claiming his *dit* for himself, imposing his presence on it, at the same time that he underscored the display's distance. In the various *dits de l'herberie*, of which Rutebeuf's was the best known, what was funny was not so much the charlatan's patter as its reproduction by the poet who played him and played *with* him, the alternation of verse and prose underscoring the side effects of literariness. It is no accident that the three names of thirteenth-century dramatic authors that have come down to us are those of the three founders of the poetics of the *dit*.

A second characteristic of French drama in its beginnings seems completely fortuitous and insignificant: the more or less systematic presence of tavern scenes. The *Jeu de saint Nicolas* is a religious play whose action is set in the "kingdom of Africa," containing painful reflections on the crusades' apparent failure, on suffering and death, and on conversion and salvation. Nonetheless, a good deal of the play takes place in a tavern much like those in our own country, in which the king of Africa's courier plays dice for drinks after quarreling with the innkeeper; Auxerre wine is consumed; shabby crooks get drunk, gamble, and fight, getting excited over a fabulous "job" that fails thanks to the saint's intervention, and are thrown out into the street in the early morning, leaving their cloaks behind as security for their debts.[26] The main part of *Courtois d'Arras* unfolds in a tavern, in which Courtois drinks his inheritance away with prostitutes who gull him. The *Jeu de la feuillée*, too, ends with a tavern scene, signifying Adam's definitive confinement within the miserable routine of Arras life and the meager warmth of drunkards' friendships, after half-hearted attempts to depart for a new existence. As it happens, the image the poet invented for himself in the personal *dit*, which achieved such success from Rutebeuf to Villon that it became a stereotype, was of an impecunious and weak-willed character, a prisoner of his poverty and vices, an indulgent witness to his own downfall due to wine, women, and gambling. If this image was also a quasi-obligatory motif in early drama, it confirms the fact that *dit* and drama belonged to the same type of performance. It is only fair to recognize as well that medieval literature as a whole looked for effects based on *dramatization*. The importance of dialogue in both lyric poetry and chanson de geste and romance, as well as the attention paid to gestures and emblematic poses, were all signs of this.

In the *Dit de l'herberie*, the display of degeneration was meant to make people laugh, as was showing off. Humor went hand in hand with theatricality in the *dit*. By showing himself as pitiful and grotesque, the poet intended people to laugh at the character he was playing and the pose he struck. This choice appears clearly not only in Rutebeuf's and Adam de La Halle's works but in those of many others as well, like the Clerk of Vaudoy, whose writings were so close to Rutebeuf's, or in the *Congés* of the two leper-poets. Jean Bodel portrayed himself as "half-sound and half-rotten," venturing a bitter joke about the white spots on a leper's skin. Baude Fastoul used this procedure systematically. He would take the side of the mockers, look at himself through their eyes, laugh with them, as abjectly as a mortified clown, at the mutilated and grotesque creature he had become: his skin was no longer worth anything; not even shoemakers wanted it. He no longer needed pointed shoes to house the stumps that remained of his feet. He was hoarse all year round and could accompany a minstrel playing the tambourine with his whistling. God had made him lose the game by giving him "the rot," that is, "rotten luck" but also a disease that made him rot while still alive.[27] It was the same tone in which Rutebeuf before him and Villon after him expressed their wretchedness.

The laughter thus provoked was different from what was usually found in the remaining literature of the period and the preceding century. In the twelfth century—apart from a smile of benevolent complicity and the light humor of certain romance writers—laughter was frequently the laughter of superiority, which excluded the speaker and which a reader could understand but not share in. Roland's laughter, an insulting reply to Ganelon's anger, does not make us laugh. Nor does King Mark, who, upon learning that Frocin has revealed his secret—"Mark has horse's ears"—laughs or smiles, draws his sword, and cuts off his dwarf's head.[28] Merlin's laughter is an enigmatic sign of his powers. Elsewhere—in the fabliaux, for example—the narrator invited his audience to join with him in laughing at the victims, thus sharing with him in the superiority of laughter. In the personal *dits*, on the contrary, although that kind of humor was not absent, the "I" representing itself was a humiliated and offended one and elicited laughter at its own expense. It was upon him, the undesirable who bore all the ills and flaws, that the audience was invited to unburden itself, to relieve its own woes at the same time that it recognized them. The identification with an abstract and solemn ideal of the self, defined by the ideal of love proposed by courtly poetry, gave way to the distance of derision. The figure of the poet broken by life's disorders became dominant, offering up his weakness to ridicule. Humor was thus not present merely by chance in this poetry. It was a means chosen to give the "I" coherence and discourage listeners from appropriating it for themselves, as songs had accustomed them to do.

Around the *dit*, the romance of the self, a new division of genres was taking place, determining poetic form at the end of the Middle Ages. Abandoning melody and the required strophic structure of the courtly lyric, stretching endlessly according to its fancy as it drew from subjectivity the matter of its supposed fancies, the *dit* was well situated to receive everything that was discursive in the poetry of the troubadours and *trouvères*—the *canso*, the *sirventès*, and dramatic song—and expand it with all the concrete incidents, without necessarily giving up courtly ideology. By the same token, it reduced the object of lyricism as such to pure affective impressions that settled more and more for the few verses drawn into themselves of the rondeau or virelay. If lyric poetry is "the unfolding of a cry," the *dit* took on for itself the justification of that cry and left its echo to the fixed-form poems henceforth comprising the bulk of lyric poetry. Guillaume de Machaut and many poets who came after him in the fourteenth and fifteenth centuries took advantage of this opposition. The amorous fiction, subjective and particular, and the internalized romances toward which courtly romance writers were already turning were developed in the *dit*, within which were inserted fixed-form poems intended to express lyric emotions, which soon were no longer always sung. Moreover, even though no *dit* wove its narrative web through the latter, they tended to be organized into collections that were supposed to be homogeneous and to trace just by means of their sequence the stages of an internal or amorous adventure. Examples of this are not lacking, from Christine de Pizan to Charles d'Orléans. In this poetry the rhythms—possessing an autonomous existence independent of all melody and thereby more easily perceived by modern ears than the poetry of the troubadours and *trouvères*—gained new value as the plays on language inherited from Middle Latin poetry, from which Rutebeuf had systematically profited, gained new meaning. Thus, the last *trouvères* paved the way for the *Grands Rhétoriqueurs*.[29]

But the evolution just described, starting with the transition from song to recited poetry, takes on fuller meaning when situated in a much broader perspective relative to the establishment of a verse-prose system, which also occurred in the thirteenth century. Like all literatures in their beginnings, early French literature knew no prose and was entirely in verse until the end of the twelfth century. Prior to that date, the only prose monuments are juridical documents or sermons. Literary prose appeared in the form of narrative, not oratorical prose, as in the case of Greek and Latin literature. The first years of the thirteenth century saw the flowering of the earliest prose romances, which initially all dealt with the Grail matter made fashionable by Chrétien de Troyes's last, unfinished romance. This link between prose and the Grail matter, which seems fortuitous, was perfectly clear to contemporary eyes. The translator of the *Philippide*, a Latin epic dedicated to the glory of Philip Augustus, declared that he would write in prose based on the model of "the book of Lancelot, in which there is not one single word of verse." A century later Guilhem Molinier, stating that he would limit his *Leys d'amors* (which we shall soon discuss) to the study of verse and ban prose works from it, gave as an example and emblem of the latter the *Roman du Saint-Graal*. This association of prose with the Grail was certainly a consequence of the association of prose with the religious. Prose romances appeared at the time when Grail literature took on a mystical tinge, when worldly glory and courtly love ceased to be exalted and were marked with the stamp of sin, when Galahad figured as a new Christ of chivalry who had come to complete the work of redemption. This juxtaposition was no coincidence. The only models of French prose that the pious authors of these romances had at their disposal were religious texts: sermons, edifying treatises, hagiographic accounts translated from the Latin. Moreover, prose served to express the sacred in Latin; it was the language of exegesis and preaching and, in the eyes of the Middle Ages, the language of the Bible itself. In a word, prose was the language of God. Conceiving it, as did Isidore of Seville in connecting *prosa* with *pro(r)sum* (*Etym.* 38), as a mode of direct expression in a *straight line*—as opposed to the meanderings of verse, which was subject to metrical constraints—was an implicit recognition of its more perfect appropriateness to the idea, not disguised or distorted by circumlocutions and ornamentation. In the Platonic atmosphere of medieval Christianity, that denoted superiority. It was hard to imagine God's word being bent to the trivial rules of verse.

Nonetheless, it is obvious that religious scruples and the model of Latin prose are not enough to account for the success of prose, which rapidly became the privileged and, by the end of the Middle Ages, virtually the only mode of narration. The idea that it was more direct and less ornate than verse, as well as less difficult—a false idea, of course, but one fostered by the definition that it was given by the first encyclopedia in French prose, Brunetto Latini's *Livre du trésor* (c. 1265)—designated it as the language of history or accounts intended to be direct. By the end of the Middle Ages, its use facilitated a reuniting of history and the romance. Finally, its development was definitely linked with that of individual reading and a certain relaxation—or perhaps even trivialization—of the practice of reading.

In the face of this spread of prose and its characteristics, verse henceforth tended to define itself by opposition and contrast, thereby receiving a new meaning and, at the same time, a new unity it had never possessed. Verse production as a whole, precisely because it was in verse, ended up by being considered a coherent category. This evolution is noticeable in the fourteenth century in Guilhem Molinier's *Leys d'amors*.[30] That Provençal grammatical and poetic treatise formalized and systematized the rules applied by twelfth-century troubadours, with the aim of preserving them. Before the appearance of literary prose, the troubadour songs were in no way confused with the rest of verse production, stemming from a very different spirit and conventions and not always sung. But two hundred years later the system no longer functioned in the same way; without realizing it, Guilhem Molinier used categories that no longer corresponded precisely to those of the troubadours. He quite naturally excluded didactic and novelistic verse production from his scope, without even feeling a need to justify it. However, he included under the name of *rimas novadas* unsung poems in rhyming couplets that were totally extraneous to the troubadours' traditional production.[31] In particular, whereas his purpose was to define the different genres according to formal criteria based on metrics, he conceived *trobar*, taken as a whole, as an expression of affectivity: "declarar e expressar son desirier e sa voluntat" (to declare and express one's desire and will) (I, 11).

What characterized poetry in his eyes was thus the expression of subjectivity through that of desire; the difficulty for him arose as a result of his being imbued with this notion in formulating rules for troubadour poetry, which was based on other principles. He codified formal poetry at a time when the notion of formal poetry was disappearing—or at least undergoing the profound transformation described earlier—with poetry henceforth divided between subjective discourse in the *dit* and a codified cry of affectivity in fixed-form poems. Verse romance in the sense of the early Middle Ages in France had no place in this perspective: it was not connected with poetry, being a mode of literary narration. It fell outside Guilhem Moliner's two criteria for poetry: the avowed one, namely, "fixed form," and the partially avowed one, the expression of subjectivity. But instead of an opposition between verse romance and lyric poetry, in reality there was a new opposition between verse and prose, the only explicit one, since Guilhem Molinier made it clear at the very beginning of his treatise that he would speak only of works in verse, excluding prose works like the *Roman du Saint-Graal*. His definition of *trobar* referred to this opposition, and the admittedly vague idea that prose was narrative and verse affective. It was also because of this opposition that he incorporated *novas rimadas* in his treatise. Naturally he defined them according to purely metrical criteria, as nonstrophic forms, in contrast to strophic lyric forms. But it is quite true that they in fact corresponded to langue d'oïl's *dits* and shared with fixed forms two modes of expression that differ from subjectivity, within a system that henceforth included them both and was no longer solely lyrical but poetic. It was because prose increasingly monopolized narrative that verse tended to define affectivity as its specific domain and would henceforth be almost systematically associated with a notion corresponding to the modern usage of the word "poetry." That was a new reason for verse romance to be associated with the expression of subjectivity.

This new division is illustrated in an especially visible way by the troubadours' songbooks, in which the *vidas* and *razos*, written later, alternate with the older songs that they comment on. This is why we once again find the texts that served as its point of departure at the end of this analysis. Having related them to the preservation or absence of melody, thanks to them we can see the opposition between verse and prose transformed into an opposition between poetry and prose. Now we can understand how they offered an anachronistic reading of the troubadours' songs based on a poetics different from theirs.

The *vidas* and *razos* not only claimed to illuminate the song and define the "I" expressed in it through the poet's biography; by that very fact they presupposed that the song's source was doubly outside itself. On the one hand, the song was presented as the fruit of anecdotal circumstances surrounding its composition, without which it would not exist or would be different. On the other, it was considered incomprehensible, or imperfectly comprehensible, to someone who did not know those circumstances. It was necessary to look beyond the song for the secret of its composition, as data authorizing its reception. The generalizing abstraction and formalism of the great courtly lyrics were interpreted as a flaw that necessitated arranging outside the poem those elements that it was not able to incorporate but that were essential to it, without which it could not stand on its own. This procedure consisted of reading the great courtly lyrics while applying the principles of a poetics that did not belong to them—in a word, that of the *dit*. The foregoing discussion has sought to indicate the representation of self in the *dit* but has proposed no principle that would permit us to account for the totality of works laying claim to that extremely vague form. But the principle exists, and Jacqueline Cerquiglini has demonstated it brilliantly. Not only has she demonstrated that "the *dit* is a discourse putting an 'I' onstage, the *dit* is a discourse in which an 'I' is always represented. In this way the *dit*'s[32] text becomes the *miming* of speech." She has also explained the law of the genre's composition:

> We call *dits* all texts whose source of composition is an external one coming from elsewhere. And thus [we see] innumerable texts whose principle is numerical: *Dit des cris de Paris, Dit des douze mois, Dit des trois signes*, etc., texts with

an enumerative structure; the same for texts whose principle
is assemblage—the assembling of lyric pieces and letters in
the *Voir Dit*, for example. . . . The principle of distancing . . .
can refer not only to the source of the text's composition,
but to its meaning. We can then grasp the privileged relationship of the *dit* to parody, or quite simply to the traversal
of literary models.[33]

Both *vidas* and *razos* treated the lyric as a *dit* because they inferred
from the use of the first person that lyrics were "a discourse representing an 'I'." They presumed an "external source" for them; judg-
ing, with good reason, that the text did not designate it clearly, they
compensated for this lack by inventing one, even using signs chosen
arbitrarily from within the text. The structure thus built up contrasted so violently with the lyric that they were led to lay explicit
claim to this contrast. Quite often they did so through the use of derision or humor. The *vida* of Peire de Valeria has furnished us with an
example of that. In particular, they did so through recourse to prose,
which marked them as having nothing to do with the lyric., Through
their explanations they could justify this *dit* that was not a *dit*. But
they could play no role in representing the "I," no matter how feebly
sketched it might be in their view. In relation to it, they could be
written only as something other than a poem. The *dit* was less in opposition than in succession to the lyric, as the lyric, treated as a *dit*
and stripped of its music, succeeded itself. It was by opposition to
prose narration, whose development was contemporary with its own,
that it associated the representation of the "I" with verse writing in a
revelatory fiction. That association was to define poetry for some
time to come.

PART II

Subjectivity and Time

Viewing the evolution of romance and of poetry separately, as we have done, was both a necessity and a device. It was a necessity because the two literary forms were obviously based on different conventions, differing invention and imagination, and even a different social practice of literature. The romance writers appear to have been professional men of letters, whereas lyrics were integrated into the grand game of courtly society and whoever observed the rules could try his hand at them. However diverse or inconsistent the contents of a thirteenth-century manuscript may have been, it never mixed narrative and lyric works. The trick was to consider only romance and lyric poetry among all literary forms and, with respect to each, to treat only those aspects that prompted reciprocal interactions in the course of their respective evolutions, which in extreme cases even led to their commingling and redefinition. That is to say, the use of this trick was more apparent than real: it merely consisted of anticipating the results of the demonstration. Since the latter—to oversimplify— aimed at showing the intervention of subjectivity in romance narration and the evolution of lyric subjectivity toward narrative expression, the points dealt with all concerned the presence of the author in his work and, more specifically, his mediation in its reception. To this

end we employed various pairs of antithetical terms that should be recalled as we summarize the results obtained before proceeding from
the author's presence to the present of the work. In the case of French
literature, the emergence of works dealing with contemporary subjects, which corresponds approximately to the turn of the thirteenth
century, was not a superficial, chance phenomenon but the expression of a significant evolution of literary activity and its meaning.

The first terms we considered, in connection with romance, were
those of truth and fiction. We have seen romance laying claim, at the
start, to referential truth and purporting to relate true facts, known
thanks to a reliable source faithfully adapted. But very soon authority passed from the source to romance itself, with the writer no longer
posing as competent historian and philologist but as author. Henceforth he suggested that the romance, as he constructed and wrote it,
possessed a truth and meaning that were not only independent of the
historical truth of the facts reported but became more evident as
those facts admitted to uncertainty and fictitiousness, since romance
was then free to give them meaningful organization. One might consider a question of this kind totally extraneous to the preoccupations
of lyric poetry. We have seen that such was not the case, and that the
problem of truth lay at the heart of courtly poetics, which presupposed an identity between the truth of love and that of poetry and
made sincerity the touchstone of amorous and poetic perfection. Not
only was that experience not incompatible with the universalizing
formalism of the great courtly lyrics; it was even one of its causes,
since it imposed on the poem an abstract idealization of love and precluded deriving effects from incidents and contingencies that should
not affect it. But during the course of the thirteenth century this aesthetic gave way to another concerned with the creation of realistic effects thanks to wordplay, abandoning the sincerity of generalization
and idealization in favor of the illusion of concrete reality. As in the
case of romance, it meant that the poet no longer subjected his poem
to external truth existing in itself but rather induced a readers' faith
in the fiction he created through the effects of the text.

This dual evolution was thus not based merely on an opposition between truth and fiction but also on a shift from the source's authority to that of the poet, a process through which the romance writer acquired a status that brought him closer to the lyric poet. Once factual truth was no longer a criterion for the work's interest— or at least not the only one—the latter's truth as well as its allure, whether it was romance or a lyric, was based on shared sensibilities or, if you prefer, the intersubjectivity of author and audience through the mediation of a character, either the hero of a romance or the figure designated by the "I" of a poem. The unique quality of the adventure and the love was compensated for and rendered credible by the common experience of the audience, appealed to either directly or from the angle of abstract or allegorical generalization, exemplarity, or proverbial or aphoristic formulation. These traits appear in both romances and courtly lyrics or personal poetry of an anecdotal sort. The poet's authority derived from the fact that he was speaking for the audience. This was particularly evident in the noncourtly lyric genres but, in truth, was universal. He held up to his audience a mirror in which its own image, taking shape, defined his "I."

Thus, the importance of a third pair of antithetical terms, the general and the particular, emerges. At first glance the development of romance and of lyric poetry appears reversed from this point of view. Increasingly romance sought for itself the general meaning of a lesson, to the point where it no longer found justification in reporting true facts. Starting from the general formality of the great courtly lyrics, lyric poetry evolved toward the personal anecdote. But at the source of this dual evolution was an analogous reflection concerning the two points defined earlier: the truth of the work and the authority of the poet. At the end of the thirteenth century, the need for universality was no less great in personal poetry than in lyric poetry, since in any case its satisfaction was necessary for the audience to be touched by the fortuitous incidents of a particular subjectivity and to recognize itself in them. But instead of that universality extending to the form of poetry itself and the nature of love, the new poetics—

which now seems quite normal to us—sought a means to make it understood through the particular, as narrative literature was constrained to do by its very nature.

The series of terms considered up to this point offers a certain consistency, allowing us to analyze the forms of the author's presence as it was displayed in his work and the sort of credence that was expected of the reader each time. It was not the same with the opposition between past and present.

On the one hand, this opposition has seemed important to us in terms of romance, yet almost antecedent to the others, since the facts reported in the first examples of narrative literature were always those of the past. Thus, referential truth was always a truth of the past, whereas internal truth or truth of meaning, which the works would soon claim, is by definition a truth of the present, the actual product of the work and the distinctive mark of its author. On the other hand, the opposition between past and present does not seem apt when applied to lyric poetry, whose very subjectivity defines it as a genre of the present. And yet it exists, once again calling into question the place of the author's self in the poem. If in romance the poet's authority prevailed over the authority of the source, that fact, as we have just seen, was a sign that the present's authority and meaning prevailed over those of the past. In the poetics of the *trouvères*, the mediation between the "I" of the poem and the receptor's subjectivity passed either through the universality of the great courtly lyrics or through individual or allegedly collective—even *historical*—memory supplying the material for noncourtly genres. In other words, universalizing idealization and the distance of the past served an equivalent function in literary communication. If, instead of these two mediations, the poem refers to an anecdote of the self, we are dealing with a new association of factors: the present, the concrete, the "I" of the poem. This combination refers solely to the poet's self and no longer to the subjectivity of the receptor, whose place was allowed for in courtly universalization by an illusory projection into common memory of the amorous fantasy. One sign of this change was the disappearance of music, a means of appropriation of the poem's subjectivity by the performer.

Whether narrativity invaded what had been lyric poetry or subjectivity arose in romance, in either case literature was being fashioned by a present of the self. While the glamor of the past was being exercised as much as ever in romance and chanson de geste, twelfth-century French literature was becoming a literature of contemporaneousness in terms of its new forms, characteristics, and evolution. This is not just a matter of speculation as to the nature and meaning of the works. As we have said, the mere fact that narrative literature could deal with contemporary subjects was something quite new in itself. It is therefore justifiable to attempt to define the signs and the impact of this characteristic.

Periods and Dates in
Literary Works

The Middle Ages, it has often been said, cared little for historical ex-
actness and tended to envision past ages in their own image. They
did not classify history among the major intellectual disciplines,[1]
which in their view were essentially speculative. This is reflected in
the study syllabus, which began with language sciences and ended
with theology—the natural consequence of a world vision concerned
entirely with the signs of God and the roads to salvation. Nonetheless, it would be wrong to deduce from these observations, which are
too superficial to be entirely correct, that the Middle Ages were a period of chronological uncertainty caring little about time and dates,
as incapable of representing the perspective of the past as that of pic-
torial space. Christian revelation was injected into history, and the
progress of the liturgical year imposed a measurement of time. The
science of the "computus," determining the date of Easter each year
and from it the other movable feasts of the liturgical calendar, was
considered essential. The computus was one of two or three books
councils and synods recommended that all priests possess, along with
the New Testament and a few homiletic commentaries. Even in the
vernacular, "tables to calculate the date of Easter" soon became quite
common. Thus, the activities of secular life could be situated in a

year's progression thanks to the celebrations of events in Christ's earthly life.

The succession of years was determined just as carefully. A major concern of the first Christian historians was to establish a concordance between the history of the Hebrew people handed down by the Bible and that of Greece and Rome. That is why Eusebius of Caesarea, before undertaking his *Ecclesiastical History*, wrote a work entitled *Chronological Canons and Summary of the Universal History of the Greeks and Barbarians*. By combining biblical history with that of classical antiquity, these historians were expressing a desire for continuity and chronological consistency. Until the eighth century, events were dated from the founding of Rome. The Venerable Bede was the first to date them from the birth of Christ, a custom that soon became prevalent.[2] Not only were there more and more annalists from the Carolingian period on, but many of them placed a kind of summary of universal chronology, dating from the beginning of the world, at the head of their works, or tried to draw up a chronological, synoptic table of the royal dynasties of the West, starting with the Roman Empire. Of course, inaccuracies and contradictions often abounded. But some writers engaged in meticulous comparison and cross-checking to verify the dates that tradition had handed down to them, thus rectifying many errors and at times achieving results that modern science has not repudiated; that, for example, was the case of the eleventh-century Reichenau monk Hermannus Contractus.

These few general remarks are intended solely to remind us that the Middle Ages were interested in historical methods and the task of the historian and perceived the importance of measuring time, determining dates, and precisely assessing the depth of the past. Thus, the place allotted to time and the past by fictional literature; the accuracy or, conversely, the vagueness of chronology; the insistence on the distance of the past or on foreshortening effects and syncopes that brought it closer to the present or mingled the two—all these were the result of deliberate will and were packed with meaning. They should not be ascribed, without further examination, to the spontaneous force of literary and intellectual habits and attitudes. Just as it was not a natural product of the sensibility of the times, any possible lack of chronological precision was not proportional to distance in the past. Whether narrative fiction was situated in the distant past or in the present or recent past, its date could be specified in relation to historical referents, real or imagined, or left vague. Thus, its precision or lack of it did not stem from the fact that the action was situated nearer or farther away in the past but, once again, was the result of a conscious choice.

Twelfth-century narrative literature was still a literature entirely of the past. Action took place in the time of the Trojan War, or Charlemagne, or King Arthur, or simply "long ago." At the turn of the century, the development of the fabliau and other generally brief narrative forms with unspecified limits— courtly short stories, moralizing tales, exempla—marked the appearance of a literature whose grammatical time remained the past but whose main appeal was not bringing back to life a distant period but rather offering a meaningful reflection of the contemporary world, either caricatured or idealized. At times a date emerged from the recent past, going hand in hand with the author's testimony or involvement. Thus, the author of an exemplum vouched for the event related by indicating the year when it took place or, failing that, when he heard it from the mouth of a trustworthy witness. Since the poem supposedly recounted his own story, the poet would lend weight to this convention by citing a date: "En l'an soissante" (In the year sixty), as in the *Mariage Rutebeuf* or, later, "L'an quatre cent cinquante-six" (The year four hundred fifty-six), as at the beginning of the *Lai de Villon*. Progress toward the present in this literature thus appeared at the same time as a progression toward the "I." Generally speaking, it is likely that internal dating of the work and, indeed, even in the case of the distant past, the need to supply exact dates can be interpreted the same way.

By situating their action in the age of Charlemagne or King Arthur, the chansons de geste and romances were not so much providing a chronological indication as defining a literary form, that used for dealing, respectively, with the matter of France or of Britain. So one never finds an introduction such as "In the time of Charlemagne" or "In King Arthur's time." The time was understood. The poet merely indicated that at the time his story began, Charlemagne was leading such and such a military expedition, or King Arthur was holding court one Whitsun day at Camelot. Naming the sovereign who was emblematic of the literary genre was sufficient:

> Del roi Artu et de ses houmes
> Est cis roumans que nos lisoumes.[3]

> King Arthur and his vassals
> Are the subject of the romance we are reading.

It should be noted that the only verb tense in these two lines is the reader's present, while the laconic and natural association of the words "romance" and "are reading" gives a more modern tinge to the two notions in this thirteenth-century text than in the uses a few decades—at most barely a century—earlier, which has been analyzed in a previous chapter. The poet—and, in this sense, "the novel we are reading"—designated his source, but its nature and the use he made of it are blurred by the vagueness of the plural and the passivity of reading, especially if we compare these few words with the laborious explanations on the same theme at the start of Benoît de Sainte-Maure's *Roman de Troie*. But, according to the modern formula, "the novel we are reading" is also "the romance that is going to be read," which the poet was offering to his audience, with whom he identified by placing himself on the side not of the production but of the reception of his work. In a way that is fleeting but so revealing, at the very moment it announces that it will deal with the past, with King Arthur and his vassals, the romance emphasizes intersubjectivity in the present of the commingled poet and reader.

Starting with the present of the work being written or read—or, more precisely, with the present of the person writing or reading the work—and going back to the past which provided the work's material was a process already followed by Wace in 1160, in a text that dates itself, at the start of the *Roman de Rou*:

Mil chent et soixante anz out de temps et d'espace
Puiz que Dex en la Virge descendi par sa grace,
Quant un clerc de Caen, qui out non Mester Vace,
S'entremist de l'estoire de Rou et de s'estrasce,
Qui conquist Normendie, qui qu'en poist ne qui place,
Contre l'orgueil de France, qui encore les menasce,
Que nostre roi Henri la cognoissë et sace.[4]

The space of time of a thousand one hundred sixty years
had gone by since God, in his grace, was incarnated in the
Virgin, when a clerk of Caen named Master Wace undertook to write the story of Rollo and his line, who con-
quered Normandy, whether we like it or not, against the
pride of the French, who continue to threaten them: let
our King Henry be aware of it.

Starting at line 17, there is a genealogy of the dukes of Normandy
from Henry II Plantagenet back to Rollo; this therefore appears to be
a kind of explicit and exemplary development of the procedure. The
present in which the work was rooted was thus intended to be historical and political: the threat that the neighboring French were
bringing to bear upon Normandy, as they had never ceased doing
since its conquest by Rollo—a threat that King Henry II would be
wise not to forget. But before this historical and political present appears the personal one of the poet. The date, given solemnly and at
length in two lines, is the one on which he began his work. The very
turn of phrase underscores the enterprise's importance with special
pomp, since these eleven hundred and sixty years are represented as a
space separating two dates: Christ's incarnation and the one on which
Wace began writing the *Roman de Rou*. It was in connection with this
date that the poet presented himself, carefully setting forth his name
and city.[5] Thus, the date was meant not to justify the work's historical ambition, as the text's drift would lead us to believe, but to draw
attention to its time of composition in order to emphasize its author
as a person.

Nevertheless, it is true that the whole romance was based on an idea of historical continuity evidenced by the retrogressive chronology of the opening. That continuity was asserted, from the origins of the matter of Britain, by the nature and the very title of Geoffrey of Monmouth's work *Historia regum Britanniae*; and we have seen how ancient and Breton matter were organized into a vast historical fresco whose end result was the Anjou dynasty. Designating the Arthurian world as fictitious resulted in a break in continuity. From then on, references to it served as literary, not chronological, markers. The personal relationship between the author's or the audience's present and the past of the subject dealt with, masked by historical continuity even as it was being displayed in the *Roman de Rou*, appeared to be completely obvious from a reading that Jehan, the author of the *Merveilles de Rigomer*, noted in passing without feeling the need to dwell on it. But the changes experienced by the Arthurian world during increasingly synthetic modifications and amplifications of the Grail material gave rise to a new chronology. This no longer stretched from Aeneas to Henry II Plantagenet via Brutus, Arthur, and Rollo but from Christ to Perceval or Galahad or, more precisely, from the first Adam to the new Adam (Christ), and then to the new Christ (Galahad). The lineage it traced was that of Joseph of Arimathea. At the beginning of the *Estoire dou Graal*, Robert de Boron defines the past in which his story begins as being prior to the Redemption:

> A icel tens que je vous conte
> Et roi et prince et duc et conte,
> Nostres premiers peres Adam,
> Eve no mere et Abraham,
> Ysaac, Jacob, Yheremyes
> Et li prophetes Ysayes,
> Tout prophete, toute autre gent,
> Boen et mauveis communement,
> Quant de cest siècle departoient,
> Tout droit en enfer s'en aloient.[6]

> At the time of which I am telling you, kings, princes, dukes and earls, our first father Adam, our mother Eve, Abraham, Isaac, Jacob, Jeremiah, the prophet Isaiah, every

prophet, everyone else, the good and the bad together,
when they left this world went straight to hell.

The new Arthurian chronology was thus mixed in with the universal chronology of mankind, since the crucial date for it was the one that served as a starting point for counting the years, the date of the Incarnation and Christ's birth. For this reason not only were successive generations from Joseph of Arimathea to Perceval and Galahad scrupulously indicated but the events relating to the adventures of the Grail were sometimes also dated to a precise year. Indeed, the measurement of time, starting with the Incarnation of Christ, took on particular meaning in the case of these complements to Christic revelation, the manifestations of the wonders of the Grail. At the beginning of the *Histoire du Graal,* a prologue later added to the *Lancelot-Graal* cycle, a recluse declares that on Good Friday of the year 717 he received from Christ a little book that must be read in the language of the heart and the mouth, which he started to transcribe two weeks after Easter. The story that follows is thus an account of transcendent truth through the mediation of an "I" inserting it into human time, the time that has passed since the Incarnation, liturgical time, the time of a life. It cannot, however, be said that the perspective of these romances was historical, like the romances of antiquity or the *Roman de Rou,* save with Mordred and Galahad replacing Brutus and Rollo. It was not historical for two closely related reasons. The first is that the synthesis of the Arthurian universe constituted by the Grail romances enclosed this world within itself, whereas the enumeration of the successive sovereigns from King Arthur to the Plantagenets established a continuity between modern Britain and Arthur. The apogee represented by the revelation of the Grail and the choice of its elect precluded any sequel, at least any enduring one. The apocalyptic collapse described in the *Mort le roi Artu* thrust the Arthurian world back not only into other times but into another place. The sense of irremediable loss was so keen that some authors intensified it retrogressively by imagining a pre-Arthurian golden age already lost when the adventures began, as the author of Perceval's

Elucidation did in evoking the fountain fairies and their disappear-ance, or as the account of Balain's dolorous stroke suggested more confusedly. The other reason was even more directly inherent in the Grail material, which became involved in the most essential myster-ies of the Christian religion, whose revelation it claimed to be seek-ing. For all that, it was not gospel. The Church never accepted the slightest word of it. And if some, like the author of the *Quête du Saint Graal*, had fairly solid theological training—though we must not exaggerate its depth—for that very reason they were in a position to measure how far they had strayed from orthodoxy. Their readers probably knew as well. Their interest in this material certainly was not confused with direct and positive conviction of its historical truth, as called for by the episodes of Christ's life, rooted in their his-toricity by the initial formula dear to vernacular texts of the period: "At the time when Our Lord walked bodily on the earth . . ." Not that Grail literature was not instructive, but its power of instruction was in its meaning and not in its historical truth. The Grail romances were romances of meaning. The belief they called for was belief in the truth of meaning, and in the allure of the lost world within which that meaning was revealed and concealed. They thus called for a dual archaeology of knowledge, seeking a universe that had disappeared and a hidden meaning that was the meaning of life and of Christian eschatology. But these revealed themselves in another, different, and closer incarnation—forgive the play on words—suited to the fulfill-ment of the chivalric dream. It was the same for their chronology. The dates they mentioned were mixed with those of History, but they created a parallel and different chronology. More than the chronology of history, it was the true chronology of mankind since it did not just settle for starting at Christ's birth but drew meaning from it. This chronology of meaning and the romance imagination, as opposed to a chronology claiming to be historical, was thus a sign of the literary project and of the romance writer's presence. It had the same effect as the temporal indeterminacy that, in other romances, underscored the demands of fiction as such and encouraged a search for its meaning.

If it is true that words are "a presence composed of absence," by creating another temporal determination of the past the present speech of writers of romances evoked an elsewhere of time and meaning and called for the search for its truth between that past and its present.

The particular case of the Arthurian romances and, among them, the even more particular one of the Grail romances must not make us forget a general rule of narrative literature of that period: action was situated in an indeterminate past—usually a distant one—but located geographically with some precision, a feature that might relate this literature to the form of legend if other aspects did not stand in the way of the comparison. In such and such a region there once lived such and such a character: that is the beginning of a tale, not a romance. Indeed, a prologue of from thirty to a hundred lines allowed the author to intervene in his own name each time, before beginning his story. It could be a dedication or a statement of his literary methods and principles. In this way Jean Renart meditates on the notion of fictional truth in the prologue to the *Escoufle*, and in that to *Guillaume de Dole* he presents the technique of lyric insertions. In the first lines of the *Roman du comte d'Anjou* Jean Maillart enumerates a series of literary genres—Arthurian romances, chansons de geste, assorted lyrical pieces—all of which he challenges as lies and fables, contrasting them with his romance, which he boldly presents as both instructive and true. The author of *Joufroi de Poitiers* is still more intrusive. The ninety lines of his prologue are a long, amorous plaint in which he recalls the ill-requited fidelity with which he has served Love, complaining that his lady still calls him "Sir," not "dear, sweet friend." The rest of his account is continually interrupted by his amorous laments.

This presence of the author at the start of a work whose action was situated in the distant past might be nothing but yet another illustration of the formula proposed earlier in defining the process of romance: start from the present of the work being written and go back to the past that furnishes the work's material. But that past was always quite lackluster. It was no longer identified with a glorious, mythical age, as in Arthurian romance. It was noted only by a brief adverb—"once," "long ago"—or even by just the verb tense. This vague brevity, as we have said, contrasted with the precision of geographical indications. It also often contrasted with the way the author flaunted himself in the prologue, and with the contemporary realities that the romance never failed to depict. This unobtrusive past seemed more than ever like a mask for the present. So the shift to an acknowledged present was made almost imperceptibly, particularly in the context of brief narrations, the form that fictional literature on contemporary subjects first adopted.

What has just been said of romance also applies to the Breton lay. Marie de France expounds her literary project in the general prologue to her *Lais* and the one to *Guigemar*, whereas each story, if it is not set in King Arthur's time, begins with mention of a very vague past and a quite precise place (Brittany) and its towns (Nantes or Saint-Malo). Of course, it is neither surprising nor significant to find the procedures of romance in the Breton lay. Their use is no more surprising—though it is more meaningful—in brief texts often designated as lays but with nothing Breton about them, which to us seem to be some kind of courtly short stories of undefined typology. For with the disappearance of Brittany—whose mere name was evocative of a marvelous, chivalric long ago—an additional element that could orient narration toward the past, the only past surviving being the narrative past, also vanished. The rest is all present: the author, who designates or names himself in the prologue and defines himself by his literary project or his works; and the story, illustrating contemporary mores, virtues, and vices.

In the *Vair palefroi* of Huon le Roi, the *Lai de l'ombre* of Jean Renart, the *Châtelaine de Vergi*, no "long ago" comes to temper the proximity of familiar provinces with its imprecise distance. These knights of Lorraine, Champagne, or Burgundy were contemporaries and neighbors of the author, who introduced himself at the same time, and of the reader, whose life was so like theirs that he was invited to profit from their stories, to love with as much constancy as the knight from Champagne, to show as much delicacy and presence of mind as the knight from Lorraine, to be as wise yet more discreet than the Burgundian.

The same kind of introduction—even the same terms introducing the author and his project, his story's past and location—thus appeared in all narrative literature. But their meaning varied and evolved. Always similar, at times they signified a projection into the past, at others a reflection of the present, this even when they introduced works as close to each other as a romance and a lay or a Breton and non-Breton lay. The formal stability of this literature was an illusion masking significant changes.

This can be seen even more clearly when we observe that these same formulas were common in fabliaux. Often the poet introduced himself as *author*, like Gautier le Leu:

> Puis que je me vuel apoier
> A conter ne a fabloier,
> Je vos doi bien faire savoir,
> Se *li leus* a tant de savoir
> C'on doive autorissier ses dis,
> D'une aventure qui jadis
> Avint en la terre d'Ardane
> A quatre liues pres d'Andane.[7]
> (ll. 1–8)

> Since I want to start telling fabliaux, I must inform you, if *a wolf* is learned enough for his words to be accepted as authority, of an adventure that came to pass in the Ardennes, four leagues from Andenne.

Or again:

> Gautier, qui fist de Conebert
> Et del Sot Chevalier Robert,
> Nos aconte d'une aventure
> Qu'il a fait metre en escriture,
> Qu'il avint deus vilains de Rasce
> Qui s'en alevent en Tierasce.[8]
> (ll. 1–6)

Gautier, who told the story of Conebert and the one about the silly knight Robert, tells us of an adventure that he set down in writing and that befell two villeins of Rache who were going to Thiérache.

There is the same *Cligès*-style mode of presentation in the writings of Jean Bodel:

> Cil qui trova del Morteruel,
> Et del mort vilain de Bailluel
> Qui n'ert malades ne enfers,
> Et de Gombert et des deux clers
> Que il mal atrait en son estre,
> Et de Brunain la vache au prestre
> Que Blere amena, ce m'est vis,
> Et trova le Songe des vis
> Que la dame paumoier dut,
> Et du leu que l'oue deçut,
> Et des Deux Envïeus cuivers,
> Et de Barat et de Travers
> Et de lor compaignon Haimet,
> D'un autre fablel s'entremet.[9]
> (ll. 1–14)

> He who invented the story of the porridge, the one about the villein of Bailleul who died without being the least bit ill, the one about Gombert and the two clerks whom he let into his house, to his misfortune, the one about Brunain, the priest's cow, which Blerain took with her, I believe, and who also invented the dream of pricks that obliged the lady to indulge in handling, the story of the wolf who was tricked by the goose, the one about the two envious wretches, the one about Barat and Travers and their comrade Haimet: that one is beginning a new fabliau.

As these examples demonstrate, the story always belonged to a past—usually presented as far off—and, in particular, the place of action was indicated, often in the title itself, in an almost systematic and precise way.

These observations, however, must be supplemented and corrected. They must be supplemented because the initial intervention of the poet in the fabliau was not always to boast of his knowledge of poetry or enumerate his works. He might allude—in a less conventional, more disenchanted tone—to the jongleur's trade, which forced him to make rhymes, come what may, and spew out stories without great enthusiasm:

> Ils sont mais tant de menestrex
> Que ne sai a dire des quels
> Ge suis, par le cors saint Huitace!
> Guillaume, qui sovent se lasse
> En rimer et en fabloier,
> En a un fait, qui molt est chier.[10]
> (ll. 1–6)

> The minstrels are now so numerous that I could not say what kind I belong to, by Saint Eustace! Guillaume, who often exhausts himself versifying stories, has made up a really good one.

In six lines the exhaustion of an unfortunate man who was ceaselessly obliged by competition "to make up a really good one" was expressed in a tone that was itself that of the fabliau. Now a fabliau whose poet was its subject was a *dit*, and by definition it was a story in the present. It also happened that an author declared he had heard the story told in the very town where it took place, like Jean Bodel in the *Souhait des vits*.[11] Boivin de Provins was given as both hero and author of the fabliau bearing his name, the latter drawing literary material and profit from the tricks played by the former.[12] In the long prologue to the *Prestre teint*, Gautier le Leu expatiated on misadventures that befell him in Orléans before getting to the account of an event that took place in the city, which he heard there:

> Il est bien droit que je retraie,
> Puis que nus hons ne m'en deloie,
> D'une aventure que je sai
> Qu'avint en l'entree de mai
> A Orliens, la bone cité,
> Ou j'ai par mainte foiz esté.

L'aventure est et bone et bele,
Et la rime fresche et novele,
Si con je la fis l'autre jour
A Orliens ou fui a sejour.
Tant i sejornai et tant fui
Que mon mantel menjai et bui
Et une cote et .I. sercot.
Mout i paié bien mon escot.
. . . Or vos diroi
De cele aventure d'ouen,
Devant la feste seint Johan,
Qu'avint en la cité d'Orliens
Chés .I. bourjois, qui mout grans biens
Fesoit .I. prestre son voisin.
(ll. 1–34)

Since no one keeps me from doing so, it is only right for
me to recount an adventure I know of that took place at
the beginning of the month of May in the good city of Orléans, where I have often been. The adventure is good and
fine, and the rhyme fresh and new: I wrote it the other day
in Orléans, where I was staying. I stayed there so long, I remained so long that I ate and drank up my cloak, an un-
dergarment, and an overcoat: I paid my bill in full. . . .
Now I am going to tell you the adventure that took place
this year before the feast of Saint John in the city of Orléans, at the home of a burgher who showered his neighbor, a priest, with gifts.

The opening lines inextricably mingle the "adventure" that took
place in Orléans, the frequent stays the poet made there—the last of
them being the occasion when he learned about it—and the poetic
quality of the account he would make of it. Before he begins, he recounts his own adventures in Orléans in such abundant detail that
the development is too long to be quoted here in its entirety. As he
does so, he paints his own portrait and sketches in the character of
the high-flying, penniless vagabond poet under whose features he
hoped the audience would see him. This character, well known to us,
is the one portrayed in the *dits*. Gautier le Leu, who happened to be

a jongleur in real life, touched on confessional poetry topoi of his times, just as the author of *Joufroi de Poitiers* introduced himself through the traditional image of lover and poet in the great courtly lyrics. But here his own character and that of his characters, their adventures and his own, were all interwoven and brought together in Orléans.

They were all interwoven, in particular, because the story he told had taken place only a short time before his own stay in the city. He stressed this and gave a large number of chronological markers: it happened this year (l. 30), before the feast of Saint John (l. 31), at the beginning of the month of May (l. 4). We are far from the indeterminate or "long ago" past of romances. In this fabliau everything is contemporary: the poet's adventures; the one he recounts because he heard it in the very city where he had his own; and, finally, his poem, whose "freshness" (ll. 8–9) he boasts of as if it were some perishable commodity. It is all in the present and it is all present through his character and experiences. The action of fabliaux was thus not always pushed back into the past, like that of romances. The fabliau of the *Prestre teint* was not the only one that specifically mentioned an immediate past. Others situated the adventure "not long ago,"[13] and Watriquet de Couvin, in *Des Trois dames de Paris*, paralleled with the "wonders" recounted by the most celebrated jongleurs of the past the quite fresh and recent ones that were the subject of his story, which he dated from Epiphany 1324. This late date, in relation to the period of the genre's development, also allows us to understand why the author contrasted his story's recentness with an already archaic literary tradition.

Generally speaking, it is clear that the fabliau was a genre of the present. Quotations like the preceding ones merely confirm the obvious. On the one hand, the fabliau's humor was to a great extent that of satire, which is effective only when applied to the contemporary world. On the other hand, present time lent more spice to the generally racy or scatological news items comprising the genre's essential matter. Lines 4–7 of the *Trois dames de Paris* are proof of this, showing the town all abuzz with the misadventure that had "recently" befallen those ladies. But it is remarkable for this present to be openly asserted and no longer concealed behind an illusion of "long ago"; at the same time, the poet no longer represented himself in the guise of a philologist, like the authors of romances of antiquity, or as a courtier, man of letters, or preacher, but precisely in the guise of a character in the fabliau. Emblematizing this reflection, the *Dit des deux bourdeurs rivaux* showed two jongleurs grappling in a drunken quarrel, hurling their repertoire at each other in a caricature of literary prologues, like barroom Chrétiens de Troyes. In the present, in the sense of daily life, the fabliau character and the poet's own persona, which he portrayed in the *dit*, tended to fuse, as the dividing line between the two genres was unclear. There were numerous fabliaux whose heroes were jongleurs. The *dit* of the *Trois chanoinesses de Cologne* of Watriquet de Couvins, which shows an obvious thematic kinship with the fabliau of the *Trois dames de Paris*, illustrates this confusion even better than the *Prestre teint*, in which that characteristic appears only in the prologue, or *Boivin de Provins*, in which the author's identification with the character occurs in extremis and is not confirmed by the narrative's form. On the contrary, Watriquet presents himself right from the start and throughout as the hero of the adventure he is recounting, which is nothing but a fabliau. Authors succeeded perfectly in creating the illusion that this dual character—the one in the fabliau and the "I" of the *dit* who resembled him—was their own, to the extent that generations of readers have confused Villon with the "poor little schoolboy" of the *Testament* and have sought Rabelais's features in the portrait of Panurge, imagining them both to have lived in the world of fabliaux. This illusion was the belated fruit of a literary system that might be called literature of the present, surrounding the fabliau and the *dit* in the thirteenth century and embracing them both, since both produced the same illusion.

This system, based on a sense of the present, was once again faced with the question of truth. This was all the more the case because if the fabliau and the *dit* were at times close enough to be confused with each other, the former, derived from the word "fable," was above all defined as fiction, whereas the latter, as treated by the authors of the time, often implied a claim to truth. Even independent of any reference to the *dit*, the realism characterizing the fabliau, to put it crudely, found it hard to adapt to the fable as such. So incisive a mind as Jean Bodel's was aware of this difficulty. He raised it on two occasions at the start of a fabliau, each time resolving it with a jest. That is the case at the opening of the *Vilain de Bailleul*:

> Se fabliaus puet veritez estre,
> Dont avint il, ce dist mon mestre,
> C'uns vilains a Bailleul manoit.
> (ll. 1–3)

> If a fabliau can be true then it so happened, as my master
> has told me, that a villein lived in Bailleul.

By giving hypothetical form to the first line and emphasizing that the association of the words "fabliau" and "truth" is almost an oxymoron, the poet suggested that a fabliau could scarcely be true even if he wished it to be. For that reason he would act as if the one he was about to relate was indeed true. The affirmative tone of the second line constrasts with the hesitations of the first, as an illogical consequence of which it is presented. Finally, that respectable though vague and indirect source, the "master," adds to the mixture of certainty and doubt. It is as if we were hearing once more in a very different context the hesitations of Wace concerning the Arthurian world and its being "not entirely a fable, not entirely true."

The question is debated at greater length at the opening of the fabliau *Des sohaiz que sainz Martine dona Anvieus et Coveistos* (The wishes that Saint Martin granted to Envious and Covetous):

> Seignor, aprés le fabloier
> Me voil a voir dire apoier;
> Car qui ne set dire que fables
> N'est mie conteres raisnables
> Por une haute cort seirvir,
> S'il ne set voir dire o mentir.
> Mais cil qui del mestier est cers
> Doit bien par droit, entre deux vers,
> Conter de la tierce meüre,

Que ce fu veritez seüre
Que dui conpaignon a un tanz
Furent, bien a passé cent anz . . .
(ll. 1–12)

My lord, after this fabulation I want to try and speak the
truth, for he who knows only how to tell fables is not a
reasonable storyteller, worthy of offering his services to a
noble court, if he cannot tell the truth as well as lie. But he
who is adept at his craft must, as is only normal, between
two "green" stories, know how to tell a "ripe" one.[14] So it is
the honest truth that once there were two journeymen, a
good hundred years ago . . .

Lines 3–6 recall fairly closely Jean Renart's words of about the
same period in the previously cited prologue to *Escoufle*:

Car ki verté trespasse et laisse
Et fait venir son conte a fable,
Ce ne doit estre chose estable
Ne recetee en nule court . . .
K'a cort a roi n'a cort a conte
Ne doit conteres conter conte,
Puis que mençoigne passe voir.
(ll. 14–21)

For anyone to go beyond or abandon the truth, and trans-
form his story into a fable, should not be admitted into
any court. . . . For a storyteller must not tell a story at either a king's or a count's court, once lies surpass the truth.

Jean Bodel was not so categorical. He did not require the storyteller always to tell the truth, but to be able to do so from time to
time, between two lies. This blithe indulgence for fabliau writing in
general, to which he recognized he had often conformed, combined
with the claim of truth for the particular story he was about to tell,
shows that the poet was once again sensitive to the contradiction between the *fable* inherent in the fabliau and the need for truth to en-
hance the story's interest. He protested that his story was true, of
"definite truth"; but did he want us to believe him, since he simulta-

neously admitted that at times he lied and at times told the truth in a two-to-one ratio? Did he want us to believe him in specifying that the story took place over a hundred years earlier? A hundred years was not the past of King Arthur or Charlemagne, so long ago that it constituted an elsewhere. It was a measurable past inscribed in the real time of real life, and real-life criteria of truth applied to it. The precise numbering of the years reinforced the story's credibility, but their extent weakened it. The chronological indication "a good hundred years ago" echoed the hesitation between truth and falsehood shown in the prologue, as in the first lines of the *Vilain de Bailleul*.

So where was the truth in a genre that, by its own admission, wavered between complete fable and half-truth? Where was the truth in the two or three fabliaux of Jean Bodel that begin with the formula "I recount in this fable . . . "? Their truth was of two kinds. On the one hand, it lay in the fabliau's realism and in that respect was related to its nature as a contemporary genre; as we have just seen, setting the fabliau at an identifiable time meant proclaiming its truth, and pushing that time into the past meant placing it in doubt. On the other hand, it lay in the lesson to be drawn from the fabliau, which made it a fable in the modern sense of the term. Jean Bodel was not quite sure how the story of the *Vilain de Bailleul* ended. However, he was sure of its moral:

> Ce ne vous sai je tesmoingnier
> S'il l'enfouïrent au matin;
> Mais li fabliaus dist en la fin
> C'on doit por fol tenir celui
> Qui mieus croit sa fame que lui.
> (ll. 112–16)

> I could not vouch to you that they buried it the next
> morning; but the fabliau says at the end that we should
> consider any man who believes his wife more than himself
> to be mad.

The exemplum was a genre that, even more than the fabliau, based its truth on the lessons it bestowed and also claimed referential truth for the reported facts, at the same time vouching for it by their insertion in time and the personal testimony its author could give. The preachers and spiritual writers of the twelfth century were generally satisfied with instructive anecdotes drawn from Holy Scripture, the church fathers, the *Dialogues* of Gregory the Great, compilations like the *Disciplina clericalis* of Peter Alfonsi or, in a completely different genre, the *Physiologus* and the innumerable scientific works, bestiaries, and lapidaries that stemmed from it. According to their view, the truth of the stories was guaranteed by the antiquity and authority of the *liber* in which they were found. By contrast, though they did not fail to recognize that exempla were subject to the needs of preaching, their thirteenth-century successors treated them as an autonomous literary genre by assembling original collections, organized according to a didactic plan, to give them their own coherence and autonomy (the virtues and vices for Caesarius of Heisterbach or the seven gifts of the Holy Spirit for Etienne de Bourbon). Far from advancing the antiquity and authority of a written source as a criterion of truth, they often emphasized the fact that the event occurred quite recently and that they learned of it either directly or simply through the agency of a trustworthy witness. It was difficult, of course, to present as entirely new a method implemented six centuries earlier in the *Dialogues* of Gregory the Great. However, it is true that it had lain dormant during the immediately preceding period, and that its rediscovery in collections of Latin exempla and, to a lesser degree, vernacular collections of Marian miracles had a meaningful place in the general evolution of literature at the time. Here is an example taken from Caesarius of Heisterbach:

> Cum hoc anno essem in Hademare, villa dyocesis Treverensis, modo grangia domus Eberbacensis et dictis missis starem cum abbate meo ante otium ecclesie, allocutus est nos quidam miles dicens: "Domine, referam vobis grande miraculum, quod contigit in hoc loco."[15]

> This year, when I was in Hadamar-on-the-Elz, a town in the diocese of Trier, formerly the property of the [Cistercian] abbey of Eberbach, as I was standing before the

church door with my abbot [Heinrich von Heisterbach]
after saying mass, a knight spoke to us, saying: "My lord, I
am going to tell you of a great miracle that occurred in
this place."

The story was thus nothing but hearsay, based solely on the word of
the knight, who was speaking to the author on his own, not being
otherwise known to him. But Caesarius tried to substantiate it by
surrounding it with as many verifiable details as possible in order to
disguise the fact that it was not so in itself: the quite recent time—the
time of the account, not the event; the well-known place, indicated
with an abundance of details, circumstances edifying in themselves—
he had just said mass; the presence of someone above all suspicion,
his own abbot—though it was not he who vouched for the story. The
result of all these efforts was that the author represented himself in an
anecdotal, detailed prologue, as was done by the authors of several
dits or fabliaux.

The fact that the exemplum was in reality a very common folktale,
as was often the case, as well as the role of personal testimony and
contemporary reference in the treatment its reuse gave rise to, can be
seen more clearly still:

Alius autem deportatus fuit ad domum matris in feretro,
multis vulneribus confossus, et ipsa fuerat imprecata. Hoc
autem, cum factum esset recens, et predicaretur in dicto cas-
tro, dicta mater mihi retulit cum lacrimis, petens peniten-
ciam pro dicta imprecacione; et hoc idem vicinia testabatur,
quod infra decennium, ut estimo, factum erat. Cum ego
predicarem crucem apud Verzeliacum contra hereticos Albi-
genses, dictum fuit mihi a pluribus qui illum hominem ibi
viderunt, ut dicebant, et multi in pluribus locis dixerunt
mihi eo tempore hominem vidisse qui habebat maximum et
horribilem bufonem in facie . . . [16]

Another man was brought back to his mother's house on a
stretcher, pierced by many wounds; it was his mother herself who had cursed him. Since the event was recent, and
on the occasion of a sermon that had been given in that

castle, the mother recounted it in tears, requesting a penance for the curse; the testimony of a neighbor woman confirmed that the deed had occurred less than ten years earlier, by my estimation. When I myself was preaching the crusade against the Albigensian heretics in Vézelay, many people said they had seen a man there who, according to what they said, had an enormous and horrible toad on his face; many told me they had seen him about the same time in various places.

There follows the well-known story of the man with the toad. A miser was furious at having to provide for his old father. The latter showed up one day as he was sitting down at table to eat a chicken served in a covered dish. When his father asked him what the dish contained, the son answered that it was a toad. After his father left, he lifted the lid: the chicken had been transformed into a toad: it jumped up onto his face and remained stuck there until he had accomplished a lengthy penance and been overcome by sincere repentance. This story figured in numerous collections of exempla and, later, in folktales.[17] In particular, it is found in the works of Caesarius of Heisterbach. Etienne de Bourbon seized on what today would be called a cock-and-bull story[18] if it weren't about a chicken and a toad, lending it the weight of truth by mixing it as far as possible with his own personal experience and testimony. He inserted it into a series of exempla dealing with the effects of curses uttered against unworthy children by their fathers or mothers. He immediately preceded it with the story of an event whose veracity he could guarantee: the mother of a young man who was gravely wounded as a result of her unwise curse had told it to him herself. The facts were still recent—she could not talk of them without weeping—and she asked him for a penance in order to expiate the drastic consequences of her intemperate language. It took place in her own castle, where he had come to preach, the same castle to which the poor man had been brought back to his mother on a stretcher. Our author even took the precaution of gathering testimony from a neighboring woman, who confirmed that the facts dated back less than ten years. We note that the story was framed by the insistent observation that the facts were recent ("cum factum esset recens; infra decennium . . . factum erat"). From there Etienne de Bourbon went on to the toad. But, unlike the rest of the chapter, the transition did not depend on the similarity between the exempla and the lessons stemming from them. It was based on the activities of Etienne de Bourbon himself. He encountered the mother of the young man on the occasion of a sermon. Speaking of sermons, when he was preaching in Vézelay against the Albigensians . . . And what happened in Vézelay? Did he see the man with the toad? No, but several people said they had seen him there, and around the same time he was encountered all over. It must be said that, in a somewhat different version of the exemplum, the hero, a fine young man, had a penance imposed by a bishop upon him to travel around France with a toad on his face. The witnesses that Etienne de Bourbon encountered were the characters of this variant, who had seen the unfortunate traveler all over. Beyond that he refused to commit himself, and he referred to their testimony ("ut dicebant"). Thus, the whole story's believability and impact rest not so much on the testimony of the author, who in any case was evasive, as on the author's representation of himself as an actor in his own story. Etienne de Bourbon was credible because he showed himself leading his life as a Dominican—traveling, preaching, hearing confessions— only a few years after the misadventure of the son cursed by his mother and at the very time the man with the toad was encountered. There is a functional equivalence between closeness in time and the author's presence in his account. Etienne de Bourbon's seems quite discreet in a sentence like the following, which lacks any indication of date:

> Item audivi ab abbate Johanne Bellevile, viro sancto, quod in quadam abbacia, quam ipse mihi nominavit, quam exprimere nolo, ne eos videar annotare male, accidit quod, cum monachi essent simul congregati in coro suo, tonitruum maximum insonuit.[19]

> Similarly I heard it said by the holy abbot Jean de Belleville that in a certain abbey, which he named to me but whose

> name I do not want to mention in order not to seem to be
> pointing a finger, a terrible noise was heard while the
> monks were gathered in the chancel.

Belleville-sur-Saône was our Dominican's home. So his refusal to name the abbey in question, like the reasons he gives for it, not only draws attention to the role he played in the transmission of abbot Jean de Belleville's story but also shows that the event was recent enough for the monks' susceptibilities to be ruffled by his divulging their name. Similarly, Caesarius of Heisterbach was completely absent from an introduction like the following:

> Anno gratie MCCXXIII circa penthecosten contigit, quod
> dicturus sum. In Hasbania villa quadam dyocesis Leodien-
> sis femina quedam sacerdoti suo veniens ad confessionem,
> recitavit illi hystoriam satis mirabilem.[20]

> What I am about to relate occured in the year of grace
> 1223, around Whitsuntide. In La Hesbaye, a town in the
> diocese of Liège, a woman came to confess to her priest
> and told him a quite extraordinary story.

The year 1223 was probably the one in which Caesarius wrote his work. Offering the story as absolutely contemporary validated it sufficiently in his view for him not to need to get mixed up in it any more. Here, as elsewhere, the present of the event, the present of the account, the present of the author, his presence—all combined or substituted for one another in eliciting the reader's belief.

Thus, a demonstration of moral truth, the exemplum's lesson, proceeded through affirmation of the referential truth of the anecdote illustrating it, an affirmation based on the author's personal involvement. The author's part involved dating the exemplum in relation to the present of his own life. The link connecting these three elements—the work's truth, the present of the narrative, and the presence of the narrator—which the fabliau lets us clearly discern appeared even more explicitly and necessarily in the exemplum.

In addition, the organization of the account, in which the author relates a story that he has heard himself, results in his acting as both narrator and narratee. In the first role he imposes his own subjectivity, in the latter he mingles it with his public's, which means imposing it in an even more insidious and urgent way by suggesting to all the impression that the account supposedly made on him and the credence he granted it, and by actualizing them in the present of his own account.

Nonetheless, we may recall that the writer of romances imposed his presence on his work by admitting it was fiction and by claiming the truth of meaning for it at the expense of the truth of historical referent. The presence of the author now seems to us to be linked to the concern for referential truth elsewhere. But in each case this presence corresponds to a will to experiment and a desire to test the truth: testing historical truth, using the methods of philology and history, for the writers of romances of antiquity; measuring the internal truth of an account and its characters, using the yardstick of a reader's personal experience, for Chrétien de Troyes; illustrating a social axiom, a moral maxim, God's interventions in the world, for the authors of courtly stories, fabliaux, pious tales, miracles, and exempla. The difference is that Arthurian romance created its own meaning in the immanence of its writing, whereas the other genres sought consonance of preexisting meaning and an account justifying it. That account could be recognized as fictitious even while asserting its exemplarity—in this sense the fabliau was more exemplary than the exemplum—or else it could claim literal truth. In both cases it turned outward, as opposed to inward-directed romance accounts as Chrétien de Troyes and his successors in the Arthurian domain conceived them. That is why the author represented himself in it, as the very presence of the contemporary world; conversely, dating it in the present was a sign of his involvement in the work.

It should come as no surprise that this characteristic appeared with particular acuity in the transition from lyric to personal poetry. We have seen that individual experience subordinated to universalizing idealization, the only conveyor of meaning in the great courtly lyrics, became the vehicle of meaning in recited poetry of the thirteenth century. The troubadours and *trouvères* had gone so far in the name of amorous and poetic sincerity as to challenge the springtime *incipit* that had been the rule among the earliest of them and was a kind of dating—albeit illusory—since it referred only to the cyclical return of the seasons and not to the unfolding of the lives of men in general and the poet in particular, merely claiming to be a mode of expression of amorous feeling. Then their successors began to date the anecdote on which the poem was based by specifying the year, the season, the day of the week, the hour of the day—even their age. The year and the day located the poem in contemporary time as it was experienced by all; the season and the hour located it in poetic time, whose meaning was conventionally perceived by the poet and his audience; the poet's age located it in the unfolding of his own life and imposed the subjective point of view.

That is why the beginning of Villon's *Lai*[21] indicates the year and the season at the same time as the poet's name:

> L'an quatre cens cinquante six,
> Je, Françoys Villon, escollier
> . . . .
> En ce temps que j'ay dit devant,
> Sur le Noel, morte saison.
> (ll. 1–2, 9–10)

> The year four[teen] hundred fifty-six,
> I, François Villon, a student
> . . . .
> At the time I just mentioned,
> Toward Christmas, the dead season . . .

whereas the first lines of the *Testament* give his age:

> En l'an de mon trentiesme aage
> Que toutes mes hontes j'euz beues . . .
> (ll. 1–2)[22]

> In the thirtieth year of my life
> When I was beyond all shame . . .

We know that the sentence begun this way has no main clause and never ends. It is immediately interrupted by a wave of bitterness, suffering, and pity that sweeps through the poem and constitutes it, being not the regular syntactic consequence of the first two lines but their development, the fruit of age and shame. Still, Villon's work is merely a belated illustration and result of the poetic sensibility emerging in the thirteenth century, whose manifestations we have examined earlier in the new poetic forms to which it gave rise. Although the great courtly lyrics had not yet been completely silenced, there is no lack of examples of a poetry that, attempting to translate the incidents of the self, sought to base its subjective flowering on the contingencies of time.

Few poems of the Middle Ages are as well known as Rutebeuf's *Griesche d'Yver*,[23] particularly its opening lines:

> Contre le tens qu'arbre desfueille
> Qu'il ne remaint en branche fueille
>   Qu'il n'aut a terre,
> Por povreté qui moi aterre,
> Qui de toutes pars me muet guerre,
>   Contre l'yver,
> Dont moult me sont changié li ver,
> Mon dit commence trop diver
>   De povre estoire.
> Povre sens et povre memoire
> M'a Diex doné, li rois de gloire,
>   Et povre rente,
> Et froit au cul quant bise vente:
> Li vens me vient, li vent m'esvente
>   Et trop sovent
> Plusors foïes sent le vent.
> Bien le m'ot griesche en covent
>   Quanques me livre:
> Bien me paie, bien me delivre,
> Contre le sout me rent la livre
>   De grant poverte.[24]

In the season that strips the leaves from the trees so not a leaf is left that hasn't fallen to the ground, felled by poverty that strikes me from all sides, in wintertime (but that would take another verse),[25] I begin my quite pitiful *dit*: a

> poor story. Poor sense and poor memory were given to me
> by God, the king of glory, and poor wages and a cold ass
> when the north wind roars: the wind buffets me, an ill
> wind whips me, and I often feel the wind's repeated blows.
> Bad luck indeed had promised me all it brings: it pays me
> right, it pays up what it owes, for a penny it gives me back
> a pound of deep poverty.

No troubadour's or *trouvère's* lyric has ever approached the renown of this *dit* in modern times, evidently because the tone of familiar and disillusioned confession corresponds to the idea of poetry our present time has far better than does rhetorical virtuosity applied to the expression of general truths about love. And the rhythm of recited poetry must be perceived by modern ears better than that of a song whose meter and tempo, if not its melodic line, elude us. Besides, these triplets—whose third line falls with weary terseness, its incomplete rhyme remaining in suspense until the following triplet —have an easy, loose-limbed rhythm that seems to match the poet's going with the flow, drifting along in destitution and moral paralysis.

In addition, this introduction grants a significant place to the presumed season of the poem. Its composition is determined by two circumstances, one temporal—the time when the trees lose their leaves (l. 1), namely, winter (l. 6)—and the other causal—poverty (l. 4). The text binds the two circumstances together tightly through a series of interweavings and correspondences. First it presents them in alternation: the season, then poverty, then the season again, then the association of the two givens:

> Et povre rente,
> Et froit au cul quant bise vente.
>
> . . . and poor wages, and a cold ass when the north
> wind roars.

It plays on the prepositions "pour" (for) and "contre" (against), which in normal usage are antithetical but in this case are not far from synonymous: "Contre le tens qu'arbre desfueille . . . Por povreté . . . Contre l'yver" (In the season that strips the leaves from the trees

. . . By poverty . . . In wintertime). But in the end it makes the poet a dupe of these equivalences, since "for ['contre']" a penny "bad luck ['la griesche']" gives him back a pound—seemingly a profitable deal—but a pound of poverty. In particular, it links the two circumstances, winter and poverty, from the point of view of both poem and poet through its use of equivocal rhymes. Thus, in the first four lines they suggest a similarity between the bareness of the trees whose leaves fall to the ground ("à terre") and that of the poet whom poverty fells ("aterre"). Indeed, in the remainder of the poem the need for and the lack of warm clothes are expressed insistently not only in lines 13–14 (quoted earlier) but explicitly in lines 53 and 63 and lastly in the final development, which is a long metaphor spun out—pun intended—on the theme of cloth.

More interesting still, because they involve the mode of poetic composition, are the equivocal rhymes of lines 6–8. The expression "mout me sont changié li ver," which is at least well documented if not commonly used, means: "my situation has changed a great deal." But here the superimposed play of rhymes requires a "literal" meaning: "my verses [i.e., those that I compose, my poem] have changed a great deal." Indeed, to read only "poverty and winter have changed my situation a great deal" does not give a very full meaning or one closely related to the immediate context: the next line deals not with the material situation of the poet but with the *dit* he is beginning. And what is the nature of this *dit*? It is "trop divers," that is, "very different" as well as "quite pitiful." Very different from what? From a summertime *dit* of course, since it is "diver":[26] the equivocal rhyme makes that obvious. Retrospectively, the rhyme "l'yver" (the winter) and "li vers" (the situation or the verses) designates what winter "changed": the "verses" or "the situation" of the poet. But it is possible that this "li ver" connotes "vers" of another sort. Think of other poems by Rutebeuf. For example, take the opening of the *Voie du Paradis*:

> Mi marz, tout droit en cel termine
> Que de souz terre ist la *vermine*
> Ou ele a tout l'yver esté,

Si s'esjoïst contre l'esté.
(ll. 1–4)

In mid-March, precisely at the time when the *vermin* that have been underground all winter long issue forth and rejoice for the summer.

Or consider the *Dit d'hypocrisie*:

Au tens que les cornoilles braient
Qui por la froidure s'esmaient
Qui seur les cors lor vient errant,
Qu'eles vont ces noiz enterrant
Et s'en garnissent por l'iver,
Qu'en terre son entrei li *ver*
Qui s'en issirent por l'estei . . .
(ll. 1–7)

At the time when the crows caw, uneasy because of the cold swooping down on them (they bury nuts and put them away for winter), when the *worms* have gone underground, whence they came forth for summer . . .

The changing seasons are thus indicated by a change in behavior of the worms ("li ver"): "l'hiver, li ver de terre" (in winter, the earthworms) go back underground, and the verse ("li ver") of the poet takes wing.

Returning to the *Griesche d'Yver*, the poem remains marked by the paradox that makes it "a monstrous child of sterility," as Reboux and Müller[27] would say in the manner of Baudelaire, a fruit of winter and poverty. It has a "poor story" both because the poet has but a "poor mind" and a "poor memory" and because he has but "poor wages": it is a story of poverty poorly told. This pitiful harmony between the poem's form and its content, between its subject and its poetic working-out, is underscored by the poet as a kind of jest and boast. Nevertheless, the lack of "mind" and "memory" is not referred to merely by chance. The poet claims not to have sufficient intellectual resources to invent or recall a fine, splendid story, a "rich story"; his intellectual poverty compels him to settle for describing his own life, a poor man's life, a "poor story." The topos of modesty thus serves to create an illusion of his aim's truthfulness.

At the same time, it is perhaps in this harmony of form and content that the survival of the *trouvères'* poetics is best observed in the poem. A demand for sincerity restricted the great courtly lyrics to generalization and abstraction because the introduction of concrete incidents in the poem would have allowed us to believe that the love inspiring them was susceptible to such incidents and their risks. We find the same conviction here, although the field of application is reversed: the poetic form has to exhibit the very qualities of what it expresses. Poetry of destitution is necessarily destitute. Poetry of material conditions is subject to the conditions of its working out. Winter, the season of barrenness when the consequences of a passion for gambling make themselves most painfully felt, is the season in which the poet composes a *dit* on the gambler's destitution.

Everything was thus linked. Drawing material for a poem from life's circumstances—which were neither always happy nor always glorious—in the present and in the presence of life as it unfolds or was thought to unfold meant giving up an ideal of perfection that, up to that point, had been not only that of lyric poetry but of all literature: perfection of love; a perfection of poetic form ceaselessly proclaimed or demanded, from romance prologues to the final stanzas of songs; perfection of the self in love. The troubadours and *trouvères* displayed misfortune or dissatisfaction, not unworthiness. Nothing was less Dostoyevskian than courtly poetry: perfection of the epic or romance hero; the narrative perfection of a story that always ended happily. The legend of Tristan and Iseut, whose protagonists were ambiguous and which ended tragically, was treated in a fragmentary manner until the thirteenth century; hesitantly, almost incoherently, with a kind of reluctance that belies the fascination it exerted. It is also true that some lays ended unhappily, but tragic denouements seem to have been a specialty of short narratives throughout the ages. In any case, the essential thing is that all these stories, including Tristan and Iseut's, ended happily for love even if they ended unhappily for the lovers. On the other hand, it was thirteenth-century literature that developed the catastrophic ending of the Arthurian adventures, demolishing the comforting dream of Arthur's survival in Avalon with which Geoffrey of Monmouth and Wace consoled themselves; finally, the thirteenth century endowed poets with dismal biographies, inaugurating the fashion for allegedly biographical and—worse than sad (for sadness can be exalting)—disenchanted poems or stories, along with *congés* and *dits*, blazing a trail later followed by Machaut, Christine de Pizan, Alain Chartier, Jehan Régnier, Michaud Taillevent, Pierre Chastellain, Charles d'Orléans, and Villon; a text like the *Historia calamitatum* or the correspondence of Héloïse and Abelard, even if not a complete forgery, was certainly rewritten and, in any case, circulated in the thirteenth century. This would seem to take us far from the *Griesche d'Yver*. And yet we are quite close to it. Poetry of present life was poetry of an imperfect life; a poetry of eventualities that no longer rejected being rooted in a season but whose season was winter; a poetry of destitution that pretended to accept its destitution and proceeded by small steps in the brief, irregular meter of its tercets.

Being rooted in a season—even winter—obviously was not in itself a brand-new thing for poetry. And if we may understand the shift in poetic form from these roots, it is only on condition of situating it in relation to other signs. It was different, however, when the poem provided a real date, as in *Le Mariage Rutebeuf*:

> En l'an de l'Incarnacion
> Uit jors aprés la nascion
> Jhesu qui soufri passion,
> Et l'an soissante,
> Qu'arbres n'a foille, oisel ne chante,
> Fis je toute la rien dolante
> Qui de cuer m'aime.
> Nis li musart me claime.
> (ll. 1–8)

In the year of the Incarnation, a week[28] after the Nativity of Jesus who suffered the Passion, in the year sixty, when trees have no leaves and birds do not sing, I made the

thing that loves me with all its heart unhappy. Even fools
call me fool.

We have already found this kind of full and rather solemn dating
at the start of Wace's *Roman de Rou*, referring explicitly to Christ's incarnation as a starting point for numbering the years. But here the
context, tone, and use of dating are very different. First of all, the
date is not that of the literary undertaking but of a supposed event in
the poet's life, whose course and meaning—the subject of the poem
itself—have been changed for the worse by it. It is a hypothetical
event since nothing authorizes our treating this effect of realism as
biographical information; Faral, who tried, found himself drawn into
futile, ill-advised speculations about Rutebeuf's wife's change of life,
since the poet tells us that she was fifty years old when he married her
but apparently gave him a child a few years later. This latter bit of
"information" is all the more questionable given that in the passage
of the *Complainte Rutebeuf* in which he supplies it Rutebeuf humor-
ously enumerates all the misfortunes heaped upon him: his wife has
just given birth and his horse has broken a leg (ll. 53–54). Nobody
would think of looking for revelations about Aristide Bruant's life in
the song "A Montmartre" or, rather, "A Montmertre," which nevertheless is brimful of precise dates and whose metric pattern, curiously
enough, is the same one as that used by Rutebeuf:

> L'an dix-huit-cent-soixante-dix
> Mon père, qui adorait l'trois-six
>   Et la verte . . .

> In the year eighteen hundred seventy,
> My father, who adored brandy
>   And absinthe . . .

In any case, Rutebeuf speaks very little of his wife in the *Mariage*
except to say she is old, poor, and ugly (ll. 28–41); thus he does not
have to fear having anyone take her away from him. His real marriage
is with poverty, and it is a solitude. The basic thing is not taking a
wife but losing his friends thereby. The last warmth of tavern and

gambling friendships, even though a false one, is gone. Upon reaching a certain level of poverty, one is looked on as a strange beast and left to one's own devices (ll. 116–22). This is not the information but the lesson contained in the poem.[29]

But to return to dating, the reader is struck, much more than in reading the opening of the *Roman de Rou*, by distortion, suspense, and anomaly in the expression of the date. The indication of the day is inserted in the middle of that of the year, which consequently seems dislocated. We are left with the impression of a rhythm submerging meaning and muddying time through its careless syncopation. The poem's time, marked by its rhythm, subverts calendar time, the time of life, which it expresses. The tempo of the poem itself is stretched on only one occasion: a quatrain replaces the tercets. Surprise and expectation are thus created, since after the second octosyllable we expect a four-syllable line yet get another octosyllable, only following which comes the shorter line. This surprise and expectation correspond to those produced by the statement of the date, which specifies the day (ll. 2–3) after foreshadowing the year (l. 1) but before actually giving it (l. 4).

Another time is added to that marked by this date: the life of Christ, from the Nativity (l. 2) to the Passion (l. 3). The reference to Christ's incarnation, far from being just a detail and marking a simple point of departure for the calendar computus, embraces all of his earthly life—the time of his incarnation superposed on the years since his incarnation—and occupies three lines in the time of the poem, in which it introduces the postponement that has been mentioned. In addition, it serves to designate both the day and the number of the year. The Nativity marked the beginning of the years leading up to 1260, but within the year, each year, the Nativity also served to count the days, here to seven, the seventh day following Christmas, in the twelve hundred sixtieth year after the first Christmas. However, the poet did not write "in the year twelve hundred sixty," but "in the year sixty." Omitting the two digits designating the century, leaving just those designating the year within the century, roots the poem in contemporaneity. Just as he acts as if he were drawing his material solely from particular and immediate incidents of the poet's life—the "poor story" of the *Griesche d'Yver*, to which, for lack of means, he had to limit himself—he appeals neither to past nor to posterity but instead claims to be addressing his immediate contemporaries, for whom "the year sixty" can only be the year 1260. Thus, when Aragon wrote "the tune a passerby whistles around '60 must have made a hit,"[30] a contemporary reader of the poem, written in the 1940s, understood that he obviously meant 1860. In other words, Rutebeuf stated the date at such length, extending the stanza and introducing an irregularity into it, precisely in order to close offhandedly with the cadence of a short line that did not even allow him enough space to specify what century the year of the Incarnation was in, after a beginning that solemnly promised to indicate it. To tell the truth, neither years nor days, the Incarnation, the Nativity, the Passion, nor numbers were there to provide information about the date since everyone knew very well what year "'60" was; rather, it was all intended to plunge the reader into the poem's time.

These superposed and interwoven times—the life of Christ, the years since the Incarnation, the days of the year—all lead to a concrete expression of time,[31] the *incarnation* of time, the weather, seasonal time, winter, of course (l. 5): a time of bareness ("when the tree has no leaves") and a time of silence ("the bird does not sing"). So it is true that the seasonal introduction here defines neither the time of poetic composition, as in the *Griesche d'Yver* and many other poems, nor that of allegorical dream—of fiction explicitly presented as such, as in the *Dit d'hypocrisie* or *La Voie de paradis*, to limit ourselves to Rutebeuf's work—but a time presented as real, marking the date of a specific event, namely, the wedding of Rutebeuf. But it is truer still that this dating is a ruse: both because it is expressed at length, even redundantly ("in the year" is repeated twice), even though, as we have seen, it is incomplete; and because its length has as an aim and consequence not precision but a mixing, a swirling of times, from which only the poet's winter finally emerges. It is also a ruse because the date given is loaded with a symbolism too meaningful to be unintentional. For the feast celebrated a week after the Nativity is the Circumcision, an operation too evocative of castration for it not to seem ill-chosen in connection with a wedding. It is also a significant date because it coincides with the Feast of Fools.[32] Finally, it is an impossible date since, as Faral observed, "in principle the Church would not conduct weddings during the period from Advent to Epiphany."[33] The date confirms our impression that this supposed wedding is a nonwedding, a wedding of want and *indigence*, a solitude.

Besides, who could this creature be, this "rien" (thing) that loved the poet with all its heart and had been made unhappy by his wedding (ll. 6–7)? Could it be "everyone," all those who loved him, as Jean Dufournet, who referred "rien" (thing) to "toute" (fem., all), interpreted it? This would be so alien to the linguistic habits of the time that such an interpretation is implausible. Was it his wife, whose misfortune he supposedly caused by marrying her? That is not really in keeping with the rest of the poem, from which it is evident that it was rather *she* who caused *his* misfortune and that she was a shrew who, far from "loving him with all [her] heart," made him dread the time when he had to go home and face her (ll. 105–12). Or was he speaking ironically in claiming she loved him? But then the preceding line would have to be taken ironically, too, which seems difficult. May we not assume that the only person who loved him sincerely was himself, and could the two lines not signify "I have caused my own misfortune," which is indeed the central idea of the poem? Similarly, later on, when he describes his wife as old and ugly, he seems to be taking that ugliness upon himself as the fruit of age:

> Et si n'est pas gente ne bele;
> Cinquante anz a en s'escuele,
>   S'est maigre et seche:
> N'ai pas paor qu'ele me treche.
> (ll. 35–38)

> And she isn't even charming or beautiful; she has fifty years in her platter, she is skinny and bony: I have no fear she'll be unfaithful to me.

Around the same time—it is hard to decide which of the two poems preceded the other—similar formulas are to be found in the *Dit des droits* of the Clerk of Vaudoy, whose works presented a kinship with Rutebeuf's that then seemed evident enough for both to figure in the same manuscript on at least one occasion:

> Li Clers de Voudai vous acointe,
> De son bordon use la pointe,
> N'en a mes que la manuele.
> De la pointe orrez la novele:
> *Trente et set anz en s'escuele*
> A conversé mignote et cointe.
> Or est tornee la roele,
> Si s'en veut partir comme cele
> Qui des or mes s'en desacointe.
>
> De la pointe dirai m'entente:
> La pointe si est ma jovente
> Qui de moi se veut départir.
> Se j'ai quarante anz ou cinquante,
> Bien est droiz que je me repante
> Et du jurer et du mentir.[34]
> (ll. 4–18)

The Clerk of Vaudoy introduces himself, he wears out the tip of his staff, nothing is left but the handle. Listen to the story of the tip: *it has thirty-seven years in its platter*, that is how long it has lived, sweet and charming. Now the wheel has turned, it wants to separate from the staff and take its leave.

I am going to tell you the meaning I give the tip of the staff: the tip of the staff is my youth, which wants to leave me. If I am forty or fifty years old, it is certainly normal for me to repent both having sworn and lied.

In a tone that cannot help but suggest the Arras *Congés*, an impression reinforced by his use of the Helinandian stanza, the poet explains that the time has come for him to repent and that he hopes to win God's mercy and avoid damnation by bearing the infirmities of age as a penance. However, only the first five stanzas are personal in tone; the remainder of the 468–line poem is devoted to the moralizing teachings announced by its title, each stanza from the seventh on beginning with "Droiz dit que . . . " (Justice states that . . .). We may note, in the passage cited, that the poet used the same familiar expression as Rutebeuf to deplore the passing of his youth, the wearing down of his pilgrim's staff on the road of life, whose tip (youth) has disappeared: "It has thirty-seven years in its platter," "She has fifty years in her platter." Although he admits to thirty-seven years, later he talks of forty or fifty as a hypothesis, as an advanced age when it is time to retreat into oneself. Admitting his age now that he is no longer young means admitting his physical or psychological indigence. Noting his age means depicting the image of self in his poem that gives it its meaning. But the identical device used in both poems is not directly relating to the poet the age defining him, and thereby his alone, even though it could be someone else's. In a double rhetorical ricochet, the Clerk of Vaudoy's thirty-seven years are those of the tip of his staff, which is his youth. Should we say that Rutebeuf's wife, unlike this staff, is not an allegory but a real person? In any case, the effect is the same in the sense that the projection, the shock rebounding against the poet's image, is the same. Rutebeuf's irony was to entitle a poem devoted to his own solitude—whose date and the manner in which it was stated revealed its meaning and key in this respect—*Le Mariage Rutebeuf,* if the title, attested to by two manuscripts, was really his.

The date, supposedly referring to an event in the life of the poet, in reality defined the poetic enterprise, as is the case in numerous other examples that could be cited. Thus, we see Watriquet de Couvin playing on the date and the ambiguity of rhyme to introduce a "ditié tout nuef" (a brand-new *dit*) and introduce himself through the play of signifiers:

> En l'an mil .CCC.XV. et nuef
> Commença .I. ditié tout nuef
> Watriqués de matere nueve.[35]
> (ll. 1–3)

In the year one thousand three hundred fifteen, plus nine,
Watriquet began a brand-new *dit*, on a brand-new subject.

Think of all the occasional ballades that Eustache Deschamps later wrote to celebrate royal births, many of them almost entirely devoted to reflection on a date.[36]

A still more striking example can be found, in the same year (1266), which has a symbolic value for us since it was the first of Saint Louis's reign, whose apparent literary barrenness was the point of departure for one of our reflections. At the start of the *Besant de Dieu*, a moralizing poem based, as its title indicates, on the parable of the talents,[37] Guillaume the Clerk of Normandy very typically expounded his literary project in a long preamble. The reader will forgive our citing a lengthy excerpt:

> Guillames, uns clers qui fu normanz,
> Qui versefia en romanz,
> Fablels e contes soleit dire.
> En fole e en vaine matire
> Peccha sovent: Deus li pardont!
> Mult ama les desliz del mond
> E mult servi ses ennemis
> Qui le guerreient tut dis.
> . . . .
> Mes issi avint, ceo fu veir,
> Qu'il jut un semedi al seir
> En son lit e se purpensa
> De cest siecle qui si passa,
> Qui est si fols e decevanz
> E pensa qu'il aveit enfanz
> E sa moiller a governer
> Et ne lor aveit que doner
> S'om ne lui donout por ses diz.
> Donc pensa qu'il ert malbailliz
> Se le somoneor venist
> Qui idoncques le somonsist
> Et qui deïst: "Levez, levez,
> Seignors qui estes atornez,

Entrez as noces od l'espos,
Car ja sera close a estros
La porte qui ne overa mes!"
Donc pensa qu'il esteit malvés,
Qu'il n'aveit oile ne clarté
Ne nule ovre de charité
Ne vesteüre covenable
Por venir a si haute table
E par devant si bon seignor
Qui li aveit fait tant de henor
Qu'i li out son besant baillé,
Qu'il n'aveit pas multeplié.
. . . .
Pur ceo que ceo ne puet faillir
Qu'il ne voille au revenir
Acontes oïr de chescun,—
Ja n'en serra esparnié un,—
Pensa Guillaume qu'il fereit
Vers consonanz ou l'en porreit
Prendre essample e bone matire
Del monde haïr et despire
E de Nostre Seignor servir
Tant comme l'ome en a leisir.

El contemple qu'il fit ces vers
Aveit la mort geté envers
Le rei de France Loïs
Qui ert eissu de son païs
Por autrui tere purchacier.[38]
(ll. 75–163)

Guillaume, a Norman clerk who wrote poems in the vernacular, used to tell fabliaux and short stories. He sinned
many times by treating frivolous and vain subjects, God
forgive him! He loved the pleasures of this world and
served the demons who assailed him daily. . . . But it came
to pass—this is the truth—that he lay in bed one Saturday
night and reflected that this world is foolish and deceiving;
he also told himself he should look after his children and
his wife, and he had no other resource for them unless he

was paid for his poems. So he told himself he would be in a bad position if at that very moment the exhortation rang out for him: "Rise up, rise up, you who are ready,

Go to the wedding banquet with the bridegroom, for soon the door will close tight, never to open again!" He told himself then he would be condemned, he had no oil for his lamp and no light, no charitable deed, no fit garment to sit down at so great a table, before so good a master who had done him the honor of giving him his talent: and he had not multiplied it. . . . Since the master will not fail to come back and ask everyone for an accounting—none will be spared—Guillaume told himself he would write poems that would supply an example and teaching, to hate and spurn the world and serve Our Lord as long as one could.

At the time he wrote these lines death had struck down King Louis of France, who had gone forth from his country to lay hold of another man's lands.

This didactic poem, aimed at propounding universal teachings, presented itself as the answer to a question of the poet's individual conscience, an answer that lay less in its content than in its nature as a religious poem. The poet, who until then had composed light and worldly works that seemed reprehensible in God's eyes, thought it time to use *ad majorem Dei gloriam* the talent He gave him for "writing poems in the vernacular" to write a moralizing work. This is the general sense of the passage. If we examine the time of conversion itself, a Saturday night when the poet, lying in bed, took stock of himself (ll. 91–116), we see that, far from drawing a general lesson from it, he insisted on the fact that the dilemma he was caught in was the result of his own individual situation. On the one hand, he viewed life as transitory; he should thus turn to God. On the other, he was responsible for his family, a wife and children, and the only trade he knew was the poet's; if he was to feed his household, he really had to continue exercising it and writing works that were appreciated, in order to make money. The solution he arrived at, of course, was to write religious works. But the situation was not ideal. It was a compromise with circumstances. It would no doubt have been better for him to devote himself entirely to God, to enter a monastery—whatever. But you had to write to make money for your own. So at least write to please God.

Writing was not in the realm of the ideal. It was in the realm of the material—lowly, as they would have said in classical usage—necessities of everyday life. This dual, equal condemnation to poverty and writing, which Rutebeuf sometimes emphasized to the point of making it the only subject of his poems, was presented here as self-evident, as a definition of the writer necessarily reflected in the image of him presented in the poem.

In speaking of himself, Guillaume gave two temporal indications. His reflections on the way to save his soul while continuing to exercise his trade as a poet, for lack of something better, came to him on a Saturday night. And he wrote his poem just after the death of King Louis of France, that is to say, Louis VIII († 1224). On a Saturday night, because "Lou samedi soir faut la semainne" (Saturday night ends the week), as Gaiete and Oriour's "chanson de toile" said: the week was over, the monotony of the days of toil was broken. Something new could happen: for Gaiete a love affair; for Guillaume to take stock of himself, examine his conscience, reflect on the necessities of life and the obligations of salvation, at a time of repose and silence, the eve of the Lord's day, "un samedi al seir / En son lit" (lying in bed one Saturday night). Louis VIII's death justified the poet's conversion by showing the force with which God's hand struck the guilty. In the eyes of Guillaume, who was Norman and therefore hostile to the king of France, the latter sought to satisfy his greed and extend his domains through injustice and violence by rekindling the Albigensian crusade and invading the South of France. Punishment was not long in coming: he died, and any beggar in his realm who happened to be stouter than he was now took up more ground, since his grave was bigger than the king's. The poet developed this theme for fifty lines or so by employing the traditional arguments of the *contemptus mundi*, using it as a transition between the personal nature of the prologue and the body of his poem. Meditating in bed on the brevity of life and the vanity of the world, he was encouraged to turn to God, and invite his readers to do the same, by the most important contemporary event, one so important that its mere mention was enough to date his poem, furnishing him with both his introduction and his first example: the death of the king of France.

The year, the day of the week, and the time of day were thus all drawn back toward the poet himself, all taking on meaning with respect to his own spiritual and literary progress. The poem's lesson and the figure of the poet took shape through the contours of the present. Resigning oneself to destitution and to writing, to the destitution of writing, arose from a conviction that one could not escape this present time. Writing was neither a way to master time nor a way to escape it. It was part of the contingencies and compromises required by daily life.

This quality characterized the literature of the thirteenth century in all its new forms. It often depicted needy jongleurs and clerks; its actors indulgently pretended to be one or the other. They posed as needy poets: a farthing was a farthing, as the author of the *dit* bearing that title put it so wittily.[39] The needy poet wrote out of necessity even though he was "often weary of telling tales and writing poems," like the author of the fabliau *Du prestre et d'Alison*; even though he yearned for the silence of the cloister like Guillaume the Clerk of Normandy; even though he had only "poor sense and poor memory" like Rutebeuf. In other words, this poetry presupposed similarity— even confusion—between the image the poet gave of himself and the characters he created, whose story he recounted. It did not make the distinction between "I" and "he" a criterion for discrimination among literary forms. The same *need*, the same contingencies, the same constraints of circumstance, the same urgency of the present moment determined poetic creation, the figure of the poet, the nature of the poem. The latter underscored this by showing the same causality, with its source in incidents of reality, at work in both its content and the principles of its composition. That is why the character of the poet resembled the characters in the poem, and why both were often supposed to be prey to material or psychological indigence, at once an extreme case and an exemplary representation of the weight of contingencies and forced submission to the incidents of reality. The dramatic quality of all this literature presumed the same depiction of the subject, whether or not he was supposed to represent the author. Whether the work was represented as personal confession, moralizing or entertaining tale, or allegory, the same principle was at work. The author of one of the Artois *dits* of French manuscript 12615 in the Bibliothèque Nationale combined the following in his prologue: a confession that he was forced to talk rubbish in order to earn a living, like that of *Du prestre et d'Alison*; the realization that he should give this foolishness up to win salvation, like Guillaume the Clerk of Normandy; and a concern for telling the truth, like Jean Bodel:

> Signor, je vif de trufoier,
> Se trufoie ui com trufoie ier,
> En maint liu ere mal venus:
> Ja mais ne voel metre men us
> En dire trufe ne mençoigne;
> Je ne truis prestre qui m'engoigne
> De me trufe, sans repentir;
> Por çou n'ai cure de mentir,
> Ains dirai pure vérité.[40]

> My lords, I live by talking rubbish. If I did today as I did yesterday, I should be ill-received in many places: henceforth I give up speaking rubbish and lies; if I do not repent, I shall not find a priest to give me absolution. That is why I do not care to lie but shall speak the utter truth.

At the beginning of another *dit* in the same collection, the poet, moved by the same scruple as his colleague, stated that he had conceived his poem as a work of penance and composed it during Advent and Lent. He thus paid as much attention as Rutebeuf to the time of poetic creation, related to the liturgical year and inner conversion, of which liturgical time was merely the representation. Was it conceivable that the poet should really interrupt his *dit* between Advent and Lent, at the time of Christmas and Epiphany?[41] All liter-

ature obeyed the same basic principles, which were to be found neither in an ideal of feeling, as in the poetry of the troubadours and
trouvères, nor in a projection of the past mingled faithfully with literary tradition, as in the romance and the chanson de geste, but in a
confrontation of the subject with influences of the external, present
world. From them sprang a truth that had little to do with that
claimed by the literary genres arising in the preceding century.

We may thus hope to justify the particular direction adopted in the
preceding analyses. Whether we are dealing with the shift of narrative
literature, the development of recited poetry of a personal nature, or
fabliaux, in each case the literary forms that appeared or underwent
significant evolution in the thirteenth century maintained a new relationship with time, particularly with present time, that had a decisive influence on the conception of the literary subject. Examining
certain peculiar aspects of this literature should permit a closer and
more precise study of this hypothesis.

The Present Interior
Allegory and Subjectivity

Our guiding hypothesis thus far has been that the irruption of present time and the contemporary world into literature was not an incidental, superficial innovation but the sign of a profound evolution of literary consciousness. Viewed from this angle, the development of allegorical literature is of particular interest. Once it took the form of *psychomachy* understood in the broadest sense, that is, the description of movements and conflicts within moral as well as psychological consciousness, by definition it dealt with the present of subjectivity.

So it is not surprising if the expression of time and dates in the works themselves found its most complete and complex illustration, in relation to the subjectivity expressed in them, in the opening of the *Roman de la Rose*.[1] In the first fifty lines of Guillaume de Lorris's poem the reader is shuttled back and forth so rapidly and deftly from dream to reality and from present to past that he is disoriented without noticing it; the text seems limpid even though it is extremely complicated.

Let us reassemble the intertwined elements that the poet reveals bit by bit. Many people believe dreams are deceptive (ll. 1–2, 11–14). The poet is convinced, for his part, that some come true afterward and are premonitions of events that, in fact, come to pass later on (ll. 3–5, 15–20). He draws this conviction not only from the authority of Macrobius (ll. 6–10) but from personal experience: he had a dream that afterward came to pass in every detail (ll. 28–30). It is this dream that he has set out to recount in verse (ll. 31–33). He hopes that this poem, the *Roman de la Rose* (ll. 34–38), will be appreciated by the woman for whom he undertook it, who is so worthy of love as to deserve to be called Rose (ll. 40–44). One night when he was twenty years old he had this beautiful dream (ll. 21–27). It was the month of May (ll. 45, 47, 84–86) a good five years earlier (l. 46), the time was morning (ll. 87–88), and he was arising (l. 89) . . . Then the account of the dream's events begins.

It can be seen that the disorder introduced by the poet in the exposition of these diverse elements is essentially chronological. He must have attached great importance to time to go to such lengths to confuse it. He begins by evoking a dream, and the circumstances surrounding it, that he had at the age of twenty, before introducing the poem he is now undertaking, giving its title, speaking to his audience, and mentioning the woman it is addressed to; then he returns to his dream, the time when he dreamt it, the season of the year and the time of day he thought he was in during his dream. But there is more than disorder here, almost ambiguity. The following lines

> Avis m'iere qu'il estoit mais,
> il a ja bien .V. anz ou mais,
> qu'en may estoie, ce sonjoie . . .
> (ll. 45–47)

> I believed it was the month of May, a good five years or more before: I dreamt I was in the month of May . . .

can be understood two ways. Either "I believed it was the month of May, five years or more before, and so, in my dream, I was in the month of May," or "I believed (it was a good five years or more ago) that it was the month of May, and so, in my dream, I was in May." In the first hypothesis, at the age of twenty (l. 21) he dreamt he was in

May of the year when he was fifteen. In the second, he wrote his poem five years after having this dream at the age of twenty, that is, at the age of twenty-five. The latter interpretation is obviously more plausible. In any case, the text imposes the idea that love's coming true was unfinished, suspended, interminably stretched out over time, an impression further reinforced by the intertwining and resumptions. Twenty is the age at which Love "prent le paage / des jones genz" (exacts a toll, a tribute, from young men)(ll. 22–23). In other words, it is the age when young men make a sacrifice to love without receiving anything in return. Did the narrator dream he had gone back five years, to the still tenderer age of fifteen? More likely he dreamt but did nothing but dream, and he would have to wait five years to see his dream become reality. That explains his triumphant aplomb: his dream has finally just come true after so many years; he has not believed in vain in the truth of dreams.

Thus, the temporal indications of the text first concern the apprenticeship of love. For everyone, it would seem, this begins at age twenty, and the poet then required five years to go from dream theory to real-life practice. But the poem, like many others we have already cited (which imitated it perhaps), mentions not only the passage of years but the cycle of seasons. That of the dream is the month of May. Not that the poet had his dream in the month of May, but in his dream he thought it was the month of May. He underscores both this impression and its fictitious nature with a repetitive insistence verging on the ponderous. Thus the three lines quoted earlier: "I believed it was the month of May and so, in my dream, I was in May." A long description of the springtime rebirth of nature follows, a development of the traditional spring stanza of the *trouvères*, at the end of which the poet again repeats:

> En icelui tens deliteus,
> que toute rien d'amer s'esfroie,
> songai une nuit que j'estoie.
> (ll. 84–86)

> I dreamt one night that I was in that delightful season
> when the desire for love disturbs all beings.

Repeating that in his dream he believed it was the month of May, whereas in reality it was not, is the same for the poet as saying that at twenty he dreamt of love without living it. For the same reason, he repeats several times that he had this dream while lying in bed one night (ll. 23–24, 86–87), but in his dream it was morning and he was arising (ll. 88–89). The morning of love, like the springtime of love, existed for him only in dreams, still sleeping at night.

The poem's insistence on temporality and dates is thus an insistence on love's suspense. In the present, in which the poet undertakes the account of this old dream, he is driven to this step by a new fact, the realization of the dream and of love—or the beginning of their realization. Since Guillaume de Lorris's poem was left unfinished, it is impossible to know whether the narrator's dream was to end with the conquest of the rose and whether Jean de Meun remained true to his predecessor's intentions when he gave it that conclusion. In truth, it seems unlikely. After emphasizing that his dream came true in all details and giving his account the title *Roman de la Rose*, the poet added:

> or doint Dex qu'en gré le receve
> cele por qui je l'ai empris:
> c'est cele qui tant a de pris
> et tant est digne d'estre amee
> qu'el doit estre Rose clamee.
> (ll. 40–44)

> God grant me grace to see it [the *Roman de la Rose*] give
> pleasure to her who has such merit and is so worthy of be-
> ing loved that she must be called Rose.

In other words, what he called his dream come true was his real love for the lady he called Rose, whom he thereby compared to the rose of his dream and to whom he dedicated the *Roman de la Rose*. Since he affirmed that

> . . . en ce songe onques rien n'ot
> qui tretot avenu ne soit
> si con li songes recensoit . . .
> (ll. 28–30)

> . . . there was nothing in this dream that did not come true
> exactly in accordance with it . . .

the conquest of the rose in the dream would mean that five years later
he indeed enjoyed his lady's intimate favors. Not only would that be
an indiscreet revelation, but it would scarcely correspond to the spirit
of courtly poetry, which was more amorous entreaty than post-tri-
umph gossip.

Moreover, the prayer in lines 40–44 takes on its full meaning only
if the poet still has something to hope for. Only then does it demonstrate the progress of fiction toward reality through the mediation of
writing. Why wait five years before turning the dream into material
for a poem? Because the urgency of writing became evident only once
it came true. But how could it become evident if some deficiency did
not remain for its fulfillment of reality, which was the very reason for
writing and to which the poet implicitly testified by emphasizing that
he was undertaking to write for his lady and was reduced to praying
to God that she might take pleasure in his poem? What could it
mean for her to take pleasure in his poem except to give him the remainder of reality he lacked, even though the dream had entirely
come true. This means there were two deficiencies in the dream: one
of reality and one of completion. When the first was fulfilled five
years later, the writing expressed this in order to make it evident that
the second remained and to request its disappearance. Lines 487–92
say this explicitly:

> Tote l'estoire veil parsuivre
> ja ne m'est parece d'escrivre,
> par coi je cuit qu'il abelise
> a la bele, que Dex guerisse,
> qui le guerredon m'en rendra
> mieuz que nule, quant el voudra.

> I wish to pursue the account of the entire story, I am not
> yet tired of writing; I expect thus to please the beautiful
> lady (God protect her!) who will reward me for it better
> than any other when she wishes.

To state it plainly, as have others before us,[2] there is no reason to suppose that had Guillaume de Lorris's poem been finished, it would have gone much farther than where it was interrupted. A lover who had been able to perceive favorable inclinations toward himself in the object of his love and to win a few favors—in particular a kiss—but still came up against numerous formidable obstacles: that is what the dream would have shown; that is where the poet would have been five years later.

We noted earlier that the tangle of periods and the play of time in the prologue to the *Roman de la Rose* tend to emphasize the conditions of apprenticeship and the suspense of love. The hypothesis just formulated confirms and strengthens this interpretation. The poet tells us that the dream now possesses a matching, corresponding reality. But it has taken five years to go from dream to reality, to know otherwise than in a dream this "tens deliteus / que toute rien d'amer s'esfroie" (delightful season when the desire for love disturbs all beings)(ll. 84–85), to mature and have a real experience of love. What need of this dream did he have now? He still had to recall the dream from his twentieth year, the tribute paid by youth to Love, to subject it to literary elaboration in the light of the new reality of love so that the dream could influence this reality and its course might persist beyond the limits of the dream. It was all a question of time: the emotional and poetic personality designated by the poem's "I" was formed thanks to the conflict and intertwining, reproduced in the text itself, of recollection and the present, of the memory reawakened by writing, with the unfinished reality that memory must help him to pursue, of the amorous dreamer and the amorous poet who were one and the same person and separated by five years.

When Jean de Meun later recalled the romance's destiny through the words of Love, its interruption by the death of Guillaume de Lorris, his own birth, and the conditions under which he was carrying on his predecessor's work (ll. 10496–624), the passage took the form of a prophecy. The romance's plot required everything to take place in the dream Guillaume de Lorris had five years before undertaking the writing of the work: the latter's vicissitudes, particularly Guillaume de Lorris's demise and Jean de Meun's intervention, could appear in it only as a projection into the future. The confusion of character and narrator and the rooting of the account in the latter's consciousness were so strong that Jean de Meun was compelled to respect them. Guillaume de Lorris, whose subjective point of view was the basis of the entire work, revealed nothing in it about his life and himself; he did not even give his name, which we would not know if it were not for Jean de Meun. The latter's subjective investment in the work was quite meager, however, but he gave copious information about himself, his birth, his origins, his education, and the passage of time (not the internalized time of his own life, like Guillaume de Lorris, but the objective time of history, mentioning the forty years separating him from Guillaume). Thus, at the beginning of the century Guillaume de Lorris was still involved to a certain degree in courtly abstraction. By century's end, Jean de Meun, a contemporary of Rutebeuf, was basing his poetic creation on the external circumstances of his life, in conformity with the new poetics we have previously defined at length.

It is not enough to state here that the poem employed the expression of time to create an image of subjectivity, as was the case in previous examples. Everything did not simply occur between the old dream, updated in writing, and present reality, about which nothing is known save that it corresponded to what the dream had shown in all its details. What it revealed was not a pure and simple anticipation of reality. The dream of the *Roman de la Rose* was an allegorical one requiring interpretation. In a kind of parenthesis at the start of Love's speech, the author announced that he would supply the interpretation at the end of his poem. The reader was to wait patiently till then to get an explanation of "dou songe la senefiance" (the meaning of the dream)(l. 2070):

> La vérité, qui est coverte,
> vos sera lores toute overte
> quant espondre m'oroiz le songe.
> (ll. 2071–73)

The hidden truth will then be completely revealed to you
when you hear me explicate the dream.

Unfortunately that promise was not kept, since Guillaume de Lorris's poem was left unfinished. What is clear is that the dream was not
an illusory first version of real events taking place five years later.
Rather, it gave the meaning of those events in advance. The movement back and forth between present and past in the prologue was
thus brought to completion. Present reality lent its weight of truth to
the past dream, but it derived its meaning from that dream. The
truth and relevance of the allegory—that is, its ability to account for
experience, formalize it, and bring out its meaning—were confirmed
by the dream's coming true. Conversely, only interpretation of the
dream and revelation of its "senefiance" would allow us to see its realization in the experience of love. This exchange would take place
thanks to the writing out of the dream, which was in every sense of the
term a reflection on the dream—in other words, thanks to the poem.

The literary process thus made the allegorical universe a subjective
experience of the poet and set it against his equally subjective experience of reality. This sort of intersubjectivity—lacking in any external
referent since the object of the poem was the dream and not the supposedly real love—was emphasized by the fact that the temporal indications in the prologue, though numerous and precise, also lacked
any external point of reference: the poet had a dream at twenty and
loved and wrote at twenty-five, but unlike many other poets (some of
whom were noted earlier) he did not say in what year he dreamed,
loved, and wrote; he did not even say in what season he dreamed,
only what season he thought he was in within his dream. The years
were expressed only in a subjective way, in terms of age and aging.
They had no value other than an emblematic one in relation to the
poet's persona, like seasons for the lover, and the seasons themselves
were dreamt seasons, not real ones.[3]

Here as elsewhere the expression of time is not only used as a re-
vealer of subjectivity but also points up the link between allegory and

subjectivity.[4] The existence of that link is not self-evident, particularly if we observe that it must not be confused with the one that for a long time associated allegory with the expression of psychological realities.

In itself, the latter proposition is, of course, too general. Allegory was not limited to the realm of psychology. In our view, the personifications in ancient literature that were related to allegory, on the one hand, were not limited solely to the realm of emotions, passions, and thoughts; on the other, they were generally the object of religious beliefs, and as such were objectified. In still another respect, allegory underwent a more or less inverse reduction as soon as it was viewed as a literary procedure: Quintilian and his successors considered it merely a rhetorical ornament.[5] However, it is true that it had always been a favored means for describing and even investigating the soul's impulses and inner life. This truth compels recognition no matter how the question is broached. From both a general and a fundamental point of view, it has been known since Dodds's classic work that, as early as Homeric literature, the representation of the gods was a means of accounting for the obscure forces and passions dominating the human soul and explaining by means other than those of rational analysis—which was never successful—the ideas covered by words like *atè* or *thumos*.[6] For example, not only did the myths that Plato used to reveal the nature of love or the soul fall under the category of allegory, giving a concrete image of abstract realities, but his representations of the conflict between the soul and the bodily passions or between the two parts of the soul—one a prey to obscure, irrational passions and the other striving to dominate them—are a point of departure for any *psychomachy*. In fact, he twice illustrated them (in the *Phaedo* and the *Republic*) with the same quotation from Homer, which is significant in that respect: "Striking his breast, he berated his heart in the following terms . . ." (*Odyssey*, XX, 17).[7] This form of thought was to reach Christian literature through Neoplatonism and Saint Augustine, and on such favorable terrain it could not fail to experience tremendous growth. The New Testament had accustomed Christians to decipher parables and to seek truth behind appearances, or, in Pauline language—which, since its first aim was the reception of the Law, by definition applied to any reading—to go beyond the letter and discover the spirit. They were accustomed as well to a representation of the world in which the forces of good and evil were opposed and, again thanks to Saint Paul and, later, according to the interpretation of the historical books of the Old Testament and the Psalms, to a metaphorical description of that confrontation in the form of a combat.

It should be observed from the Platonic perspective mentioned earlier, then in the Augustinian conception of the combat against the forces of evil, and then in the description by Duns Scotus—the first Plato-inspired theologian of the Middle Ages of *bellum intestinum* (internal war)—that not merely the individual soul was at stake. Just as the *Timaeus* first described the world soul and then the soul and human body, the struggle for salvation was played out in history, both that of the world and the Church and that of each human destiny. The parallel is not at all gratuitous. Just as the medieval historians strove in their allegorical works—the *De mundi universitate* (Totality of the World) and the commentary of the *Aeneid* of Bernard Silvestris, the *De planctu Naturae* (Lamentation of Nature) and *Anticlaudianus* of Alain de Lille—to reconcile the chronology of pagan antiquity and the Bible, so the theologian-poets of the twelfth century attempted to unify the Platonic vision of the universe with that proposed by the Bible.[8] When the first of these visualizes the city Aeneas wished to found as an image of the human body, each category of inhabitants corresponding to an organ whose place it occupied and whose function it fulfilled, it is difficult not to think of both the *Republic* and the *Timaeus*. When, in the two authors' works, at the end of a voyage through the celestial spheres Nature needs help—from either the intellectual faculties, in the case of Bernard Silvestris, or faith, receiving from God the gift of a soul capable of bringing life to the inanimate body—in creating man and breathing life into him, it is both Plato's demiurge and the Christian God we see at work. Genius, who appeared at the very end of *De planctu Naturae* before attaining his importance in Jean de Meun's *Roman de la Rose*, was

> the spirit of God, conceived as a demiurgical power that im-
> posed on matter the *figura*, the types, the seals of form. . . .
> Here we recognize a coherent doctrine, rooted both in an-
> tiquity and in the contemporaries [of Alain de Lille]. . . .
> The profound unity of the Western poetic tradition is strik-
> ingly evident here. The ugliness and beauty of images, alle-
> gories, and figures constituted a divine language. This was
> fulfilled in theophany, a direct and intuitive form of knowl-
> edge complementing theology.[9]

Thus, not only did the reflection of the macrocosm in the micro-
cosm, the destiny and functioning of the universe in the individual,
invite us to see in each a transposed meaning of the other. Poetic language also revealed the presence of the divine by making this transposed universal meaning perceivable. Allegory was the favored mode
of expression for the relationships of the soul with the universal principle and with God.

One can thus see that medieval allegory was not limited to personifications, the latter representing only its final coinage. They first
strike us in reading Prudentius's *Psychomachia* (Contest of the Soul)
and Martianus Capella's *De nuptiis Philologiae et Mercurii* (The Wedding of Philology and Mercury), two essential works in the development of the medieval allegorical world. But in the struggle between
the virtues and vices Prudentius seemed to see both that of the soul
and that of the Church throughout its history. Martianus Capella's
works, often grouped together in manuscripts with Macrobius's commentary on *The Dream of Scipio* and the *Timaeus*, were glossed by
numerous commentators in the Middle Ages, including Duns Scotus. Regarding the voyage that led Apollo and Mercury up to the
heavens, to the sound of the harmony of the spheres, in order to win
the hand of Philology from Jupiter, Duns Scotus elaborated on the
dual voyage of the soul through the celestial spheres to become incarnate in the human body and then return to heaven after death.[10]
This is to assign Martianus Capella an importance other than that
granted him in the area of pure literary history for having mingled
the gods of antiquity with the personification of abstract ideas, as was

to be done so often in the Middle Ages, or for having been the first to devote seven books of his works to the seven Liberal Arts, thus becoming, in some ways, the father of the medieval *cursus studiorum*.

We can also see why medieval literary allegory was so deeply rooted in religious thought. It was not because secular literature transposed or adapted to its own domain the methods of biblical exegesis—based on illuminating the three or four meanings of Scripture and, more basically, on the idea that because of man's imperfection divine revelation could occur only through indirect means, either of human language or of human history—that there was nothing in the symbolism specific to Scripture that was not at once "res et signum" (thing and sign), to use Saint Augustine's terminology. All this had in itself nothing to do with the personifications or drawn-out metaphors that allegory, as a literary process, was based on.[11] The Middle Ages distinguished very carefully between the composition of a work of fiction carrying allegorical meaning, allegorical commentary on a text whose letter was true—for example, the Bible—and allegorical commentary on a text whose letter was fictional, like that of Bernard Silvestris on the *Aeneid* and those of Rémi d'Auxerre or Duns Scotus on the *De nuptiis Philologiae et Mercurii*. We have only to read the *Roman de la Rose* and any of the scriptural glosses to observe that there was no connection between them save that both presumed a transposed meaning alongside the literal one.[12] Allegory's roots in the religious probably had a more general cause. It came from the fact that, since Homer, concrete representation of abstract realities by means of personifications or any other means had always been linked in a special way to the most abstract and elusive domain of all, which demanded it all the more for that very reason: the soul, its obscure dispositions, its nature, its links with the universe and the sacred. If, at least until the *Roman de la Rose*, allegorical literature was therefore inclined to deal with religious subjects, that was not because it was inspired by scriptural exegesis. It was because its characteristic procedures, derived from linguistics, rhetoric, and poetics, essentially caused it—and always had—to be applied to the psychological domain, and from that angle it readily mingled with religious preoccupations since in the Christian world the psychological could be separated from neither the moral nor the eschatological.

For allegory to depict the amorous and not the religious soul did not therefore constitute a real break from the standpoint of literary composition. But, as has been emphasized earlier, depicting the psychological world did not in itself imply a subjective viewpoint. On the contrary, allegory seems to have been a generalizing exploration and description of the consciousness. By personifying the conflicting forces in it, allegory made them independent of the subject that was the theater of their struggle and saw in them an application of permanent, intemporal laws far more than it pointed up the particular incidents, circumstances, and immersion in the present of a subjectivity experiencing them as unique each time. It is thus not surprising first to find in French literature not a grasping by allegory of the present state of a subjectivity but a confrontation between subjectivity and allegory.

If we turn to its generalizing function, it is striking to observe that allegory was almost totally absent from troubadour and *trouvère* lyric poetry, even though the latter was based precisely on generalizing abstraction. There is, of course, Guilhem de Saint-Didier's well-known *tenson*, in which his speaker describes a wonderful orchard he has seen in a dream, all of whose elements the poet interprets allegorically. That chanson, whose author died before 1200, constitutes the earliest trace of the current that bore the rustic, springtime setting of courtly lyrics toward the allegorical dream of the *Roman de la Rose*. Shortly thereafter—in any case before 1202—Guiraut de Calanson's chanson "A leis cui am de cor e de saber" (To her that I love with body and mind) describes the (feminine) person of Love, her palace, and her empire. But this sort of allegory was so foreign to the troubadours' art that when Guiraud Riquier, at the request of Count Henri II of Rodez, ventured to gloss the chanson in 1280, he had difficulty carrying out his task. This amounts to saying that courtly poetry did not cultivate allegory. Marc-René Jung has demonstrated that it is excessive to see real personifications in the *abstracta agentia* it often had recourse to since they were never described or represented for themselves and had no function other than a grammatical one.[13] As Jung also observed, comparisons in this poetry were always presented as such, the introductory element only rarely elided, the term of comparison almost always explicit. Chansons as well known as "Atresi com l'olifanz" (Just as the elephant) by Richard de Barbezieux, "Ausi conme unicorne sui" (I am like the unicorn), "Deus est ensi comme li pellicanz" (God is like the pelican), or "Tout autresi con l'ente fet venir" (Just as a graft brings about) by Thibaud de Champagne demonstrate this quite well. Such generalizing poetry did not go so far as to represent the forces troubling the soul as permanent and autonomous entities, existing independently of the subject they inhabited. This poetry, so clever at the games and dodges of language, did not go all the way toward transposed meaning. We have demonstrated earlier that its formalism, its refusal of anecdote, and its abstraction were not, as has so often been said, the consequence of turning back upon language but of its requirement of sincerity and its inability to distinguish between love and writing on love, the poet and his persona. It is not surprising to see it rule out the duplicity of allegory. The latter, on the contrary, adapted quite well to the dramatic representation characterizing the new thirteenth-century poetry. The play of double meaning served to dramatize the self.

It could do that in two ways corresponding to the distinction, made earlier, as to whether the drama was internal or external to the subject. The latter appeared first. As we have seen, instead of constructing an ideal image of the self, the poetry of the *dit* showed the self wrestling with the contingencies of reality that determined and shaped it. When it sought to account for these contingencies and show the forces governing the world of which they were the result, it represented these forces in the form of allegory. The problem, therefore, was knowing how to treat direct confrontation between the subject and these allegorical representations—so important in this poetry—when they were separated by a long, complex chain whose links were reality and whose moral cause was their concrete representation in the allegorical system. The solution, in some cases, boiled down to a kind of juxtaposition: the poet presented himself so that the meaning of the allegory applied explicitly to him. At the start of the *Vers de la mort* (Poem of Death)—which, it must be admitted, is hardly an allegorical poem since Death simply plays the role of an *abstractum agens*—Hélinand, addressing Death, states that it has shut him up to molt in a steambath where the body sweats away the excesses it has committed in life. We must understand that the thought of death made him abandon the world and enter a monastery to do penance. At the opening of the *Besant de Dieu*, Guillaume the Clerk of Normandy explained that he was going to compose a poem about the parable of the talents because that was the only way he could make use of his talent. But the *Besant de Dieu* is not a true allegorical poem either since it was intended to develop and amplify the lesson drawn from the parable of the talents. In other words, he considered the problem of the allegory's meaning to be resolved from the start, and thus does not provide refutation of the remark that French allegorical poetry was not a product of exegesis. The additional allegories that Guillaume inserted here and there and immediately interpreted—his personification of the virtues and vices, introduced quite briefly—do not constitute the framework of his poem. Aside from these earlier or marginal cases, since the beginning of the thirteenth century the means almost always used to put the subject in contact with the allegorical world was the dream. Indeed, not only did the dream permit an affirmation of subjective experience—in other words, real-life actuality—without claiming that of its content, but it was also by nature the bearer of truth of meaning, analogous in itself to allegory.

Macrobius, whom Guillaume de Lorris does not refer to merely by chance at the start of the *Roman de la Rose*, defined the nature of this truth and the conditions of its revelation in terms that explain the association of allegory not only with dream but also with the dreamer's subjectivity. He distinguished five kinds of dreams at the start of his commentary on Scipio's dream. He rejected two of them from the outset: *insomnium* (Greek *enupnion*), designating agitated dreams—either nightmares or erotic dreams—produced by concerns of the mind or disorders of the body; and *visum* (Greek *phantasma*), designating the disjointed or indistinct images that press in during the intermediate state between wakefulness and slumber at the time of falling asleep. These two categories of dreams did not allow for interpretation or conceal any truth. Conversely, two categories were defined by the clarity of their relationship with reality. The *oraculum* (Greek *chrematismos*) was a direct prediction or warning given to the sleeper in a dream by one of his relatives, a venerable and important personage, a priest, or God himself. The *visio* (Greek *horama*) was a dream that came true exactly as dreamed. But the fifth category, *somnium* (Greek *oneir*), in which Macrobius classified Scipio's dream, was the most interesting:

> Somnium proprie vocatur, quod tegit figuris et velat ambagibus non nisi interpretatione intelligendam significationem rei quae demonstratur.

> Strictly speaking, we call *somnium* a dream that conceals with figures and veils with enigmas the meaning of what is shown, a meaning that cannot be understood without interpretation.

Somnium was thus in itself the imaged or indirect representation of a meaning that could be revealed only by decipherment. It was, by nature, the framework of allegory. At the same time, Macrobius distinguished subcategories within it, defined by the dreamer's degree of participation in the action of his dream.

> Huius [i.e., *somnii*] quinque sunt species: autenim proprium, aut alienum, aut commune, aut publicum, aut generale. Proprium est, cum se quis facientem patientemve aliquid somniat. Alienum, cum alium. Commune, cum se una cum alio.[14]

> There are five kinds of *somnium*: *proprium* (concerning only oneself), *alienum* (concerning someone else), *commune* (having aspects of both of these), *publicum* (public), *generale* (universal). In *somnium proprium* one dreams that one does or undergoes something; in *somnium alienum*

something that someone else does or undergoes; in *somnium commune* something that one does or undergoes at the same time as someone else.

Somnium publicum was a dream having a public place as its setting, *somnium generale* a dream in which parts of the universe (the sun, the moon, the stars, and so on) intervened. The criterion for classifying the differing kinds of *somnium* was thus the presence or absence of the dreamer as actor in his own dream, from the most intimate, which he filled completely, to the most general, offering a panorama of the universe from which he was totally absent. In this way Macrobius brought both allegory and representation of the subject into his definitions of dreams. The literature of the Middle Ages remained faithful to him, seeing in the first of these terms a first-class instrument for handling the encounter of the other two.

This encounter first took the form of contemplation by the subject—that is, the dreamer—of an allegorical world offered up to his interpretation. This is the situation described earlier, in which the theater of allegory was external to the subject, or allegory was not a representation of the subject, but where the latter was confronted by it while remaining foreign to it. This was the case in the poems or Latin *prosimetra* previously cited. In that regard, the very title of Boethius's *Consolatio Philosophiae* (Consolation of Philosophy) is exemplary: Philosophy personified was the subject's interlocutor and consoled him. But when this appeared in French poetry, the impersonal and timeless character of allegory was compensated for not only by the fact that it was the subject's dream but also by the presence in the dream of references to the real, contemporary world mingled with the allegorical world, in accordance with the new thirteenth-century poetics.

Thus, in the *Songe d'enfer* (Dream of Hell), Raoul de Houdenc presented both personifications and real characters.[15] A bit later Huon de Méry proceeded the same way in the *Tournoiement Antechrist* (Tourney of Antichrist), which, it is true, did not claim to be the account of a dream but rather of events the poet really experienced.[16] But the fountain of Barenton, near which he encountered

Antichrist's chamberlain, was as favorable a place for meaningful adventure as was the time of the dream. In and of itself, of course, mixing personifications with characters completely foreign to allegory was nothing new. In his descent to the infernal regions in both the *Aeneid* (VI, 273–81) and the French romance of *Eneas* (ll. 2401–12), Aeneas encountered Old Age, Fear, Hunger, Poverty, Suffering, and so on, before finding his father, his companions, his enemies, and his lover. But these personifications, mere images presenting themselves to the hero's gaze at the start of his expedition, had nothing in common with the characters he was faced with later in the abode of the dead. On the contrary, Raoul de Houdenc and Huon de Méry in particular treated all their characters—allegorical, biblical, mythological, literary (that is, borrowed from contemporary French literature, with which Huon's work was imbued)—alike and had them all participate in the allegorical story on the same basis. In addition, Raoul de Houdenc mixed real people, his contemporaries, with this disparate troop, while Huon de Méry has a host of allusions to contemporary events or flashes of ethnic satire aimed, for example, at people from Poitou, Normandy, or England. Thus, they did not set allegorical accounts farther from reality than did fictional accounts based on mimesis but rather nearer—not only because allegory revealed the meaning of the real but because the real was present in allegory. Its presence was that of its author, as spectator of the allegory and of the real people known to him mixed in with it. Huon de Méry played both roles at once, participating episodically and being wounded in the allegorical combat. It has been observed that in the *Tournoiement Antechrist* "for the first time the poet chose the framework of allegorical poetry to recount a personal adventure" (Jung, p. 290). That is true, but for Huon de Méry the "personal adventure" lay in being present at the confrontation between the Antichrist's legions and the blessed army and even playing a minor role in it. That was no small thing, and it was not granted to just anyone. But between that and being the allegorical theater's center, like the narrator of the *Roman de la Rose*—in terms of the signifier, and its setting, in terms of the signified—there was a considerable distance. The combat between the forces of Good and Evil would take place in any case, whether or not the poet, there by chance, took part in it, whereas in the *Roman de la Rose* it was the poet's love that set in motion the forces confronting one another around him. The wound received by Huon during the fighting only made the *Tournoiement Antechrist* a particular case of the kind of poem in which the narrator was spectator to an allegorical representation. But by blending the contemporary world —their world and their contemporaries—with the allegorical world, Raoul de Houdenc and Huon de Méry both demonstrated that allegory touched on reality through their own mediation.

As a dream, this mediation was by definition essential, the entire allegorical representation being played out in the dreamer's consciousness. But the reader was not to forget this: his attention had to be drawn to the relationship between the dreaming self and the waking self that is to be the dream's narrator. Indeed, it was, when the poem described the process of falling asleep and the start of the dream, or questioned the latter's nature. Description and questioning, moreover, went hand in hand. On the one hand, medieval commentators indulged in in-depth reflection on the definition of vision and dream, their differences, their relationships, the nature of their truth; numerous episodes of the Bible, the lives of the Saints, and ancient literature encouraged this. On the other, poets transformed into a literary motif the description of a state that had its origins in a technique first used by horsemen, not only in the West but among numerous peoples like the Mongols, which was intended to allow them, as Corneille wrote, "To spend entire days and nights on horseback."

This state, sometimes called *dorveille*[17] (sleep-waking or semiconsciousness), is a kind of drowsiness during which the mind maintains only a distant relationship with reality or even loses contact with it without yielding to sleep, however.[18] This was probably what Guilhem IX, the first troubadour, meant in saying that he composed a poem "en durmen / Sobre chevau" (while sleeping on horseback), and another ". . . pos mi sonelh / e'm vauc e m'estanc al solelh" (. . . since I sleep and ride along as I stay in the sun).[19]

This is what fostered the amorous ecstasies in which romance heroes like Lancelot, Perceval, and Dumart le Gallois lose all contact with external reality. This, finally, was what allowed passage into another world whose border was crossed in the half-slumber of horseback riding. If we are right, as seems likely, in interpreting Guilhem IX's poetry in that sense, it was used as motivation for the romance story, as a way into the internal adventure, and as a medium of poetic creation. The first meaning of *rêver* was "to roam, *to wander aimlessly*": this is what the knight and, at the same time, his mind did. The relationship between literal and figurative meanings is here one of both simultaneity and causality. As for the daydream's outcome, it can equally well be designated as that of the ride (arrival in another world), the affective and imaginary state of dreaming (amorous ecstasy), and the poem, which might possibly cover both, defining itself literally as the product of a wide-awake dream.

Questioning the nature of such a dream, whose incorporation in sleep was denied, placed in doubt, or left unspoken; speculating on its reality; describing the conditions of its appearance before it was recounted as personal experience: this literary exercise became increasingly fashionable, whereas the horseback ride, *dorveille*'s initial cause and justification, was forgotten. It became so, along with the development of poetry of personal narration, for reasons we have given earlier. To insist on grasping the mode of the vision's appearance is to point up the relationship between its general meaning and the particular conditions pertaining to the subjectivity that was its source and its beneficiary, through which the poem's reader became aware of it.

We would need to supply a host of examples to show how consistent a habit—almost a rule of the genre—this procedure was from the second half of the thirteenth century until the end of the Middle Ages. At the start of this period, certain of Rutebeuf's poems like the "Dit d'hypocrisie" (*Dit* of Hypocrisy) or "Voie de paradis" (Way to Paradise), whose first lines we have cited earlier, would lend themselves to such an analysis. We shall mention here only a single poet, Watriquet de Couvin, active in the first third of the fourteenth century, quoting several of his *dits*, however, to point up the enduring nature and variants of the procedure. Each time an impression or a preoccupation haunting the wide-awake poet at the start of the poem found correspondence, continuation, fulfillment, or explanation in a vision that came to him. But the passage from one state to the other was suggested in differing ways. It was quite simple in the "Dit de l'arbre royal" (*Dit* of the Royal Tree), composed in 1322: the poet's sole concern was finding a poetic subject. He prayed to God and the Virgin to help him, and since he was in bed he fell asleep while saying this prayer. God answered it by sending him a dream:

> . . . je estoie
> En mon lit .I. joudi matin,
> Si fis ma priere en latin
> A Dieu et a sa douce mere,
> Que il me moustrassent matere,
> Par aucuns signes ou par letre,
> Que je peüsse en rime metre,
> Et conter devant les haus hommes.
> En ce priant me prist .I. sommes
> Qui andeus les iex me cloï,
> Et Diex, qui ma priere oï
> Que je fis, ne m'oublia point
> Ainz m'envoia, droit en ce point,
> Endormi tout a cuer joiant,
> En .I. bel vergier verdoiant,
> Loi de la ville, en .I. destour.[20]

> . . . I was in bed one Thursday morning; I said my prayer
> in Latin to God and his sweet mother, for them to show
> me, by signs or spelled out, a subject that I could set in
> rhyme and recount before the nobles. While saying this
> prayer, I was overcome by sleep, which closed my eyes.
> And God, who had heard my prayer, did not forget me but
> at that very moment, while I was deep in joyful sleep, sent
> me to a beautiful, verdant orchard, in a remote place far
> from town.

The story of this dream allowed him both to exercise his poetic talent and to pay court to King Charles IV the Fair, since he found a tree in that orchard whose four "scions" were Philip the Fair's three sons and young John (John II the Posthumous), a tree guarded by Nature, Youth, Beauty, and Strength. The initial situation is thus analogous to that of the *Besant de Dieu*, but it is developed in the form of an allegorical dream and not as an exemplary parable. Moreover, the poet's literary concern turns completely back onto him and no other object, since it is not to write *about* something but to write something. Finally, aside from this concern itself there is no connection between the circumstances of falling asleep and the nature of the allegorical dream. The mention of Thursday morning does not seem to have any particular meaning with respect to what follows, its sole function being to create an effect of reality and anchor the vision in the unfolding of the poet's life. The end of this vision does, however, betray the dream of a man of letters: to find an audience—and a prestigious one at that:

> . . . et me fu avis
> Que je Charlon ileuc veïsse,
> le roy des Frans, et li deïsse
> Par devant lui tout ce bel conte;
> Si avoit maint duc et maint conte,
> Qui si volentiers qu'a merveille
> M'escoutoient. Et je m'esveille,
> Touz estourdis et travailliez.
> (ll. 530–37)

> . . . and I felt that I saw Charles, the King of France, and I recounted this fine story from one end to the other before him; and many dukes and many counts were there who listened to me with extraordinary good will. Thereupon I awoke, all dazed and weary.

The preoccupation preceding the dream is thus found blatantly, in extremis, in its unfolding, which includes its own literary working out.

In the "Dit des quatre sièges" (*Dit* of the Four Seats), the connection between the poet's situation and the nature of his vision would also seem to be quite loose, if not incongruous, save for an interesting hesitancy concerning the boundary between dream and reality. After a graceful, banal springtime introduction, the poet continues:

133

En celui temps que toute humaine
Creature joie demaine,
Gisoie une nuit en mon lit
En la grant joie et ou delit
D'amours, entre les bras m'amie,
Qui o moi estoit endormie,
L'un l'autre acolé vis à vis.
Tout aussi con fusse ravis
Entrai en une avision
Droit le jour de l'Asencion
L'an .XIX.: oiés comment.
Il m'avint la fui longuement
Endormis, mais parmi mon somme
Oï si com la vois d'un homme;
N'iert pas hons, mais angles des ciés,
Qui tost vers moi s'est adreciés
et doucement m'araisonna.
(ll. 11–27)

In the season when every human creature rejoices, I was lying in my bed one night, savoring the great pleasures of
love in the arms of my mistress, who was sleeping with me,
our two faces pressed one against the other. Just as if I had
been carried off from this world, a vision came to me: It
was Ascension Day in the year nineteen. Listen to how
things went. I remained asleep thus for a long time, but in
my sleep I heard something like the voice of a man; it was
not a man but an angel from heaven, who turned quickly
toward me and addressed me softly.

The angel bore Watriquet up to paradise, where there awaited him
a vision and revelations flattering to four high personages of his time,
to whom he thus paid court. There is little connection between this
edifying voyage and the way the poet spent the night. The date of Ascension, with all due reverence for the holy mysteries, was fitting for
a voyage that took him "to the highest level of paradise." Dare one
suggest that this dream of ascension on Ascension Day (that is to say,
a Thursday, let it be noted in passing, as in the "Dit de l'arbre royal")

was not entirely out of place in the midst of lovemaking? Watriquet certainly would not dream of it. Yet here is the end of his poem:

> . . . Adont m'esveille
> Esmerveillant de la merveille
> Qui en dormant m'iert avenue,
> Et cuidai entre mes bras nue
> Avoir celle que tant amoie,
> Touchant sa bouchette a la moie,
> Dont moult de joie ere garnis;
> Si me ting moult a escharnis
> Quant seuls me trouvai esveilliés
> Et ainsi en vain travailliez.
> Dont pensai que travailleroi
> Tant que ce songe esveilleroie.
> (ll. 729–40)

> . . . Then I wake up, marveling at the marvel that had be-
> fallen me in my sleep, and I thought I was holding the
> woman I so loved naked in my arms, her little mouth
> touching mine, which filled me with joy; but I felt I had
> been mocked when, upon awakening, I found myself
> alone, vainly tormented by love. So I thought I would try
> and awaken this dream to reality.

This, in conclusion, was how he wrote the story of his dream. The pleasures of love and the company of his beloved, which the begin- ning of the poem led us to believe were real, belonged, like the vision of the four seats, to the realm of dreams and vanished with them. The vision itself was a kind of dream within a dream. As the emotion of nature in springtime gave rise to the erotic dream, the joyous exalta- tion that the latter inspired in the poet made him receptive to the vi- sion he was granted. But the vision had greater reality than the amorous dream, which, once it vanished, left him with only a feeling of having been mocked (*escharnis*). Its truth, that of the senses, al- lowed him to achieve the reality of the poem at the moment when the dream disappeared forever. That is the significance of the alternating repetition of *éveiller* (awaken) and *travailler* (work, or torment) in the rhymes of lines 738–40. Upon awakening, the poet once again found himself alone and vainly tormented by love. He then decided to try and "awaken the dream" he had just had, that is, to summon it to reality by making it known through the voice of the poem, making known, as he said, "les grans biens . . . / Et prouesces aux .IIII. Contes" (the great boons . . . / and feats of prowess of the four Counts)(ll. 744–45). These were Charles de Valois, the brother of Philip the Fair and father of Philip VI; the Count of Hainaut; Constable Gaucher de Chillon; and Robert de Béthune, Count of Flanders. In paradise he learned that Arthur of Brittany, Alexander, Duke Naimes, and Girard du Fraite, respectively, lived on again in them. Their qualities and feats of prowess were real and guaranteed the truth of the poet's vision just as they were certified by it. In the face of this truth, the amorous phantoms, whose reality the beginning of the poem led us to believe in, dispersed and evaporated in the poem's haze; they were not in themselves judged worthy of being a subject for writing. Their evocation, hesitancy as to the state of consciousness on which they were imposed, uncertainty concerning the moment of falling asleep and the start of the dream—all served to show through what capricious twists, what bizarre associations of a mind set loose unchecked, the vision and the revelation it bore had become enmeshed in the erotic dream.

Nevertheless, there was no connection between the latter and the former; if the poet wished to convince us of the arbitrariness of the association of ideas, he succeeded all too well. On the contrary, elsewhere he strove to bring out the enduring nature and continuity of impressions between wakefulness and reverie or dream. Thus, in the "Dit de l'araignée et du crapaud" (*Dit* of the Spider and the Toad):

> Par .I. mardi au point du jour
> Me levai sanz faire sejour
> L'an .XXIX. ou mois de juing,
> Si m'en aloie tout en juing
> Parmi .I. Vergier vert jouant,
> Et le chant d'un oisel sivant,

Qui moult me faisoit esjoïr,
Car gracieus iert a oïr.
De branche en branche voletoit,
Et de chanter s'entremetoit
Si forment qu'a son joli son
M'endormi desouz .I. buisson,
C'onques l'oiselet n'eslongai;
Mais en cest dormant je songai
Que j'estoie a Bec Oisel
Ou Charles et maint damoisel
Iert alez pour esbanoier.
La trouvai desouz .I. noier,
Seant assez pres de la porte,
Raison . . .
(ll. 1–20)

One Tuesday, at break of day, I rose up without delay, in
the year twenty-nine, in the month of June, and I set off
before breakfast to gambol in a green orchard and follow
the singing of a bird that gave me great pleasure, for it was
most harmonious to hear. It flew from branch to branch
and sang so loudly that I fell asleep under a bush to that
joyous music, without wandering far away from the little
bird. But in my sleep I dreamt I was in Bec-Oiseau, where
Charles had gone to disport himself in the company of
many youths. There I found Reason seated right near the
gate, under a walnut tree . . .

After following the singing bird, the poet fell asleep while listening to him, but once again he immediately found all he had just left
transposed into his dream, including the bird itself, of course, which
the poet did not wander away from (l. 13); indeed, his dream trans-
ported him not only to a castle named Bec-d'Oiseau (Bird's Beak)
but also in the midst of the games of a group of children whose image may have been suggested to him by the carefree joy of the bird,
the irregular liveliness of its flight, and its chirping. These were indeed children, for the Charles in question, the second son of Guy de
Blois and future Duke of Brittany, was ten years old in 1329. Similarly, the trees in the orchard in whose branches he saw the bird were

represented in his dream by the walnut tree under which he found Reason. Driven from the pontifical court, the latter had, in fact, taken refuge in the court of the Count of Blois and burst forth in complaints and tears. When she left, the poet turned his head, and the movement awakened him:

> A itant de l'aler s'atourne
> Dame Raisons, et je retourne
> Mon chief aussi comme estourdis
> Si m'esveillai.
> (ll. 209–12)

> At that moment, Lady Reason makes ready to leave; I turn my head as if bewildered, and thus I awoke.

The transition from dream to awakening was thus noted, like falling asleep and immersion in the dream, by a movement begun in the dream and interrupting it, awakening the dreamer, and by the latter's bewilderment and difficulty in coming to, his unsteady consciousness still hesitating between the two states. Once again the poet, portrayed as Reason's confidant, was faced in a completely external manner with an allegorical world not his own. But he compensated for the passivity of his role by emphasizing the fortuity of this encounter and the subjectivity of his point of view. The very precise dating—a Tuesday in June, 1329, at break of day—as well as the attention to the conditions of falling asleep and reawakening and to the projection of the circumstances of the waking world into the imaginary dreamworld were all aimed at producing this effect. Unlike the preceding poem, these circumstances and fortuities justified by association of ideas the allegorical argument of the dream, or at least its point of departure. Falling asleep to the song of a bird, the poet dreamt of the castle of Bec-d'Oiseau and young Charles of Blois; his mind passed from this to the political activity of the Count of Blois, whose court was the refuge of reason.

The same precedure was utilized in much greater detail and more explicitly in the "Tournoi des Dames" (Ladies' Tourney), whose introduction Scheler summarizes as follows:

The poet found himself one winter's day in the pavilion of a tower of the castle of Montferrant, and was busy reflecting on the significance of a stained-glass window representing a battle fought by ladies against their knights, when he fell asleep. In his sleep, Lady Truth, driven off by all, came and urged him to follow her. After explaining to him the hidden meaning behind the curious tourney depicted on the window [the struggle between the flesh and the soul], she set out with him. . . . But the introduction itself was preceded by a quite lengthy description of the setting in which the author had his vision: Montferrant, a castle in the earldom of Blois, where he was staying with the count in October 1327, as he himself stated. The charms of the site, the castle's riches, the forests full of game surrounding it were the subject of the first hundred twenty lines, which thus took on the nature of a dedication to the lord in whose service Watriquet was engaged.[21]

This long prologue is not merely a dedication: the window in the tower's pavilion, described after all the marvels of the castle of Montferrant, is its unexpected and enigmatic crown. Its secret, as it were, is the secret of the castle, to which the poet has access only after being touched by its other charms. There is a continuity between the descriptions of the castle and of the window, and between that and the vision revealing its meaning, arising directly from his puzzled contemplation of the strange tourney represented in the window:

> Ceste œvre moult m'esbahissoit
> Comment ce pooit avenir.
> Tant i pensai que soustenir
> Ne me poi plus, ançois me couche
> Seur mon bras (n'i oi autre couche),
> Si fui si qu'entre dor et voille
> Touz raviz. Or orrés merveille
> Qu'ilec en ce penser m'avint.
> A moi une dame là vint
> Où j'estoie, en celle tornelle . . .
> (ll. 166–75)

> This work astonished me greatly and I wondered how such
> a situation might come about. I reflected on it so long
> that, no longer able to stand up, I lay down on my arm
> (there was no other bed) and was thus carried off, between
> sleep and wakefulness. Now you are going to hear about
> remarkable things that happened to me in that reverie. A
> lady came to me where I was, in that turret . . .

The poet's state, plunged, *carried off* in contemplation, is explicitly defined as *dorveille*. When Truth appears to him, she addresses him thus:

> —A quel matere
> Penses tu, compains, biaus amis;
> Di moi qui en ce point t'a mis
> Que tu ne dors ne tu ne veilles.
> (ll. 186–89)

> —What is the object of your thoughts, dear companion?
> Tell me who has put you in this state, in which you are
> neither asleep nor awake.

He is not asleep, nor has he found in a dream the deformed echo or transposed image of waking impressions. He keeps pursuing the same thoughts. But their churning and the fatigue resulting from it bring about a slackening of his attention, a relaxation of his body (ll. 168–70), withdrawn into itself, and of his mind, sinking out of consciousness of external reality, from which arises elucidation, so urgently desired, in the form of an allegorical vision. The scene continues in the same setting, the same turret, before the same window, yet in another world. The lesson that Truth gives the poet in five paragraphs is general in nature, as truth by definition is general. But the long description of the occupations and preoccupations of the poet in the castle of Montferrant during that month of October 1327, the care with which he represents the vision as their consequence and continuation, the attention given to his state of consciousness at the moment when she appears—all make a show of basing the allegory's universal lesson on random circumstances and subjective impressions.

Finally, in the "Miroir des Dames" (Ladies' Mirror) Watriquet again returned to the original association of *dorveille* and riding, but here he reversed cause and effect:

> De maintes biautez me souvint,
> De dames et de damoiselles,
> Gracieuses, plaisans et beles,
> De gens cors, de douces veües,
> Et des biens que j'en ai eüs,
> Et fui si de joie esmeüs
> C'onques si liez n'avoie esté.
> Ce fu le premier jour d'esté
> Que cis pensers me vint devant,
> Aussi qu'entour soleil levant,
> Qu'iere levez au point du jour;
> Si pensai tant et sans sejour
> Qu'en cest penser fui si pensis,
> Que mors sembloie estre ou transis
> Et ensement que touz muïz.
> Et ou penser me fu avis
> Que fusse en une grant forest,
> Si chevauchoie sanz arrest
> Parmi les bois moi déduisant.
> Li rai du cler soleil luisant
> S'espandoient parmi les buissons,
> Et cil oiselet a douz sons
> S'esforçoient de haut chanter:
> C'iert melodie a escouter.
> (ll. 24–48)

I bethought myself of many a beauty, ladies and damsels, graceful, pleasing, and beautiful, with pretty bodies offering sweet display, and of the favors I had received from them; I was so enraptured by joy, never had I been so happy. It was on the first day of summer that this thought came to me, toward sunrise, for I had arisen at daybreak; and I thought of it so long and ceaselessly, I was so deeply preoccupied by the thought, that I seemed to be dead and departed and struck dumb. And in that thought I had the feeling I was in a great forest; I was riding at my leisure,

without stopping, amid the woods. The rays of the sun
shone bright upon the bushes, and the birds sang their
sweet tunes, melodious to the ear, as loudly as they could.

According to the literary conventions of the time, the poet should
have been riding through the forest, where the sun on the foliage and
singing of the birds would plunge him into amorous reverie. Here it
is the opposite: the thought of feminine beauty arouses such ecstasy
in him that, although he is as if dead to the real world, he feels he is
riding through a forest illumined by the sun's rays and the singing of
birds. It was not rare for a narrator to find himself in his dream—
usually lost—in the depths of a forest. That is the case in Froissant's
Temple d'honneur (Temple of Honor), and in *L'Amant rendu cordelier
à l'observance d'amour* (The Lover Turned Monk in the Service of
Love). Even before them, that was also the case with the *Divine Com-
edy*, though its framework was not literally an allegorical dream.
Here, however, the forest offers the characteristics of a *locus amoenus*,
which should induce reverie on feminine beauty and not be its result.
But, at the same time, it really is the place of beauty's revelation—
only within the reverie. In this forest, where the singing nightingale
does not fly away at his approach, the poet encounters Adventure,
who offers to initiate and present him and take him to contemplate
feminine perfection:

> Je vous menrai o moi veoir
> De biauté le vrai mireoir,
> Le droit compas, le parfait monstre;
> Se je fais tant con le vous monstre,
> Faire en devriez aucun biau dit.
> (ll. 117–21)

> I shall take you with me to see the true mirror, the correct
> proportions, the perfect model of beauty; if I take the
> trouble to show it to you, you ought to make a fine poem
> of it.

The poet is led to the castle where this marvel is revealed to him,
thanks to Courtesy, Generosity, Loyalty, Nature (who created it), and

Knowledge, which "knew its explanation" (l. 1164). Like Adventure, they all urge him to write a poem about the revelation, of which they have deemed him worthy:

> Mais au partir moult me pria
> Qu'aus dames savoir le feïsse
> Et .I. dit en rime meïsse . . .
> Chascune le me semonnoit.
> (ll. 1158–66)

> But upon my departure [Loyalty] earnestly bade me to
> make it known to the ladies, and to write it in the form of
> a poem. . . . Each of them urged me on to it.

All these ladies call him by name and seem to know him quite well, following the example of Courtesy, who greets him in these terms:

> Qui t'envoia ça,
> Watriquet? Je te cognois bien.

> Who sent thee here,
> Watriquet? I know thee well.
> (ll. 402–3)

We can see that the connection between the poetic self's subjectivity and the allegory is based on a reciprocal relationship and, even more, on the interpenetration of the internal and external worlds. Instead of an external, real adventure—that is to say, one assumed to be real by literary convention—leading to meditation or ecstasy, as with Lancelot or Perceval, it is meditation that leads to ecstasy, the framework of internal adventure. But the latter is personified, which amounts to saying that, although not externalized, at least it is objectified within interiority itself. This play of interiority and exteriority corresponds in its effects to the hesitancy we have observed in the "Dit des quatre sièges" between what belongs to the vision and to the waking state; in both cases reality, elusive or indifferent, is devalued as a referent and touchstone for truth in favor of the narrator's perceptions and states of consciousness. Similarly, the literary project becomes clear not only at the start of the poem

> Por ce est mes cuers assentiz
> A ce c'un dit vous conte et die,
> A oïr plaisant melodie,
> De la plus tres bele aventure
> C'onques meïsse en escripture.
> (ll. 10–14)

> That is why my heart feels I should recount and tell you a poem—it is a pleasant tune to hear—about the finest adventure I have ever written down.

but also in the context of the vision, as we have seen earlier. It is within the vision that the text begins to be composed. Indeed, the poet immediately carries out the advice he has received:

> Chascune le me semonnoit,
> Et je du rimer m'entremis,
> Que terme ne respit n'i mis.
> (ll. 1166–68)

> Each one of them urged me on to it and I set to rhyming unremittingly and without respite.

His reawakening is noted in a similar way to what we previously found in the "Dit de l'araignée et du crapaud": upon awakening, he goes on with what he was doing in the dream and has a sense of dazedness. This time, though, it is not just a feeling but the effort of literary creation, conveyed in the expression itself by the play of *annominatio*:

> Et je en l'ombre d'une tour
> Me tournai ainssi atourné,
> S'ai tant tourné et retourné,
> Comme un hons qui est endormis,
> Qu'a moi reving touz estourdis
> En l'estudie et ou penser,
> Si ne voil tant ne quant cesser
> Que celle belle avision,
> Dont dite ai la division,
> En rime n'aie devisee.
> (ll. 1274–83)

And I, in the shadow of a tower, turned round in such a
way, I turned and turned, over and over, like a man asleep,
so that I came to, completely dazed by my reflections and
thoughts; and I could not rest until I recounted in verse
this beautiful vision I have told you of.

He turns over in his sleep: this movement, which, within the vision, is the way in which he leaves, as Nature has also just done,
awakens him and is then interpreted quite differently as the agitation
of a concerned man, whose concern is writing. This concern, so familiar to him, which arises from his dream and awakens him, is not
over writing a poetic confession. It has a general and instructive end:
to make known the canons of feminine beauty and perfection. Thus,
the vision does not have its source in the feeling of love or even admiration for a particular woman but rather in the memory of all the
beauties the poet has known. The revelation he has received thanks to
it concerns nature and the laws of beauty (see ll. 118–20)—in a word,
the idea of beauty reflected in each woman. The poem's progression
does not go from the particular to its generalization, from multiplicity to a unifying idea. A poem of this kind makes no claim to reveal
anything about the poet's feelings or life. And yet with the utmost insistence it sets forth the poet's persona and point of view. Emblematically (through the allegorical vision) and explicitly (by designating its
own composition in the text) it defines itself as the product of perception and writing. The recourse to vision, reverie, or dream is a way
to draw attention to the first of these two terms.

It is in this way that poems devoted to the account of an allegorical dream are based entirely on the narrator's subjectivity. The nature
of the allegorical argument could attenuate or accentuate this characteristic but was not decisive. Whether the poet was allowed to contemplate an allegorical system referring to a reality external to it and
whose meaning was revealed to him or whether the allegory reflected
its own interiority was certainly an important distinction. H. R. Jauss
was correct to emphasize that the latter course was initiated by Guillaume de Lorris, and that for the first time the allegory in his *Roman
de la Rose* expressed not the activities of the soul in general but the

subjectivity of the narrator. In it the dreamer's consciousness was not only the dream's theater but the subject that its action described. For a medieval reader of Macrobius it was the most extreme form of *somnium proprium*; for a modern reader it was the recognition of what all dreams are in reality. The play of time and subjectivity in the work's prologue, as we have tried to show, pointed up the introversion of the poetic self and the self-referential nature of the story. Thus the *Roman de la Rose* indeed marked the end point of an increasingly closer relationship between allegory and subjectivity. It was a logical and not a chronological end, since Watriquet de Couvin's *dits*, which we have used as examples, and from that point of view all poems like them in the fourteenth and fifteenth centuries represented a step back.

But there are two reasons why we must not exaggerate the *Roman de la Rose*'s originality in this particular respect. The first is that its action is not completely internalized, in the sense that although it is only the narrator's point of view reconnoitering its terrain, the allegory features personifications that do not represent elements of his psyche and are supposed to be external to him. In the *Roman de la Rose*, as in all similar poems of that time, the allegory deals indistinguishably with representations of consciousness and of the external world, both of them identically materialized and objectified. The second, more important, reason brings us back to the preceding analyses. The manifestation of subjectivity in the poem is marked less by the content of the allegorical story than by the expression of the perceptions of the consciousness introducing it, upon which it is based. To describe and define the states of consciousness leading to reverie or dream; to examine the border between the two states; to show that their content and form are neither arbitrary nor foreign to the dreamer but, on the contrary, are determined by the continuity of waking impressions even when consciousness of the real world is eliminated—is to demonstrate that, whatever may be the general truth of the allegorical revelation, it exists only through the incidents of subjectivity and the fortuities of real-life experience. This procedure and concern characterized all allegorical literature from the end of the twelfth century to the end of the fifteenth. Dates, times, places, and circumstances— determining the perception of the world belonging to a poet at a given time—informed the allegorical vision. The prologue to the *Roman de la Rose*, as we suggested at the beginning of this chapter, applied this principle in a particularly complex and profound way by adding to the interplay between reality and dream that between past memories and the present. Therein lay the originality of Guillaume de Lorris's poem, rendered less evident, no doubt, by its lack of completion, rather than in the plot of the dream itself, whatever its relative novelty may have been in the first third of the thirteenth century.

It is in this way, therefore, that the relationship between allegory and subjectivity is resolved. Allegory, considered to be the bearer of a general truth, in its particular expression claimed at the same time to be a product of the narrator's state of consciousness. Recourse to dreams or reveries made it most strikingly and frequently tangible. But there were other means, like that used by Huon de Méry. We may recall that the *Tournoiement Antechrist* was presented as the account not of a dream but of a real adventure. Should this difference be a decisive typological criterion? Of course not. Huon de Méry's argument makes that obvious. He related (in the prologue, as it happens) that, taking advantage of his being in Brittany with the king's army during an expedition against Pierre Mauclerc, the Count of Brittany, he penetrated deep into the forest of Brocéliande in order to *learn the truth* about the perilous fountain. He found it after four days, poured water on the *steps* as Calogrenant and Yvain had done in Chrétien de Troyes's romance *Le Chevalier au lion* (The Knight of the Lion); as expected, this unleashed a frightful storm. When morning came and it died down, a Moor from Mauritania came to disarm and oblige the hero to accompany him to the court of Antichrist, whose chamberlain, Bras-de-Fer (Iron Arm), he was. That is how the poet came to witness the combat between the forces of evil and the holy legions. It should be noted that on several occasions Huon referred explicitly and admiringly to Chrétien de Troyes, as he would later do, insistently, with respect to Raoul de Houdenc's *Songe d'Enfer* (Dream of Hell) and *Roman des ailes* (Romance of the Wings). Thus, he considered himself a modest but faithful imitator both of Chrétien's romances

> Pour ce que mors est Cretïens
> De Troies, cil qui tant ot pris
> De trover, ai hardement pris
> De mot a mot meitre en escrit
> Le tournoiement Antecrist.
> (ll. 22–26)

> Since Chrétien de Troyes, whose supremacy in the field of
> poetic creation was recognized, is dead, I have found the
> courage to write down word for word the tourney of the
> Antichrist.

and of Raoul's, and the allegorical *dream* of the poet who, as he repeatedly emphasized, had already related in much better fashion what he was only repeating. But Huon did not take up the framework of the dream again, and it is no exaggeration to say that his poem bore little resemblance to Arthurian romance.

Why did he have such strong feelings concerning his obligation toward his two predecessors? Why does he conclude his poem with the remark that they have said it all and left him only gleanings?

> Molt mis grant peine a eschiver
> Les diz Raol et Crestïen,
> C'onques bouche de crestïen
> Ne dist si bien com il disoient.
> Mes quant qu'il dirent il prenoient
> Le bel françois trestot a plain
> Si com il lor venoit a mein,
> Si c'aprés eus n'ont rien guerpi.
> Se j'ai trové aucun espi
> Apres la main as mestiviers,
> Je l'ai glané molt volentiers.
> (ll. 3534–44)

> I have been at great pains not to take up again what Raoul
> and Chrétien already said, for never did a Christian's
> mouth speak as well as they did. For all that they said they

picked up fine French language by the handful, as if it
came to them at will, and they left nothing after them.
If I have found a few good ears after the harvesters passed,
I have been only too happy to glean them.

The answer to these questions requires two preliminary observations. It is not enough to say that Huon was imitating Chrétien and
Raoul. It must be added both that he remained in the position of a
reader toward them even while writing his own poem, and that he
was imitating them jointly. He remained in the position of a reader
since he quoted them, he admitted explicitly that he was reproducing
situations he borrowed from them and, in the case of Chrétien, he
substituted himself for the romance hero and took his place in those
situations: it was he and not Calogrenant or Yvain who unleashed a
tempest by pouring water on the fountain's steps. In other words, he
was less interested in reproducing a literary model than in extending,
through identification, the feeling it had produced in him. His repeated tribute to the two poets, his sense that he could not equal
them and had nothing more to say, his difficulty in finding other
subjects than the ones they had treated—all had the same cause. He
was unable to detach himself, in order to begin writing, from the fascination he had as a reader; to write while inspired by Chrétien and
Raoul was, for him, to preserve and express the feelings he had in
reading them. Wace had returned empty-handed from his real trip to
the fountain of Barenton. The one that Huon imagined, connecting
it as closely as possible to real life, granted him complete fulfillment
since it allowed him to penetrate the world of his favorite authors.

"Penetrate the world of his favorite authors" is a metaphor. We
never penetrate it, save in an imagination excited by reading. But
Huon's reading of Chrétien and Raoul was continued in the writing
of a poem whose argument was precisely that the narrator penetrated
the world of his two models. That explains the sense of dependency
he felt toward them; his poem, which did not really resemble theirs,
was an expression of their reverberation in his mind. But it is also
understandable why he felt this sense of dependency toward the two
poets jointly and was unable to dissociate them. He could penetrate

the world of Chrétien's novels only through plunging his consciousness in the world of allegory whose model Raoul offered him. Conversely, he could escape the admitted unreality of the dream, the
usual framework for this procedure, only by replacing it with romance adventure, on which he conferred the same initiatory role.

Concerning the first point, whatever his desire for identification
might have been, the poet could not claim to have lived a Breton adventure himself: the Arthurian world's meaning lay in the radical distance of the past.[22] But at the site of the Breton adventure he could
undergo one of his own with some claim to truth. That adventure
was a subjective experience of allegorical revelation, claiming the signified as its truth. The second point illustrates our point of departure,
which we return to after a long detour: the narrator's state of consciousness, which supposedly gave rise to the allegorical adventure
and revelation, could abandon the dream form without the relationship between allegory and subjectivity being significantly modified.
The *Tournoiement Antechrist* replaced internalized experience of
reverie or dream with one triggered by the fascination of literature,
externalized and materialized in the form of a literary pilgrimage off
the beaten track. In contrast to poems utilizing dreams or visions,
nothing in the text here suggested that the story might not be literally true. Only the chronological indicators, which root the allegorical adventure in the poet's life, went from pure and simple dating to
the symbolic unfolding of liturgical time. The date of the adventure
was Louis IX's expedition against Pierre Mauclerc. Its time was the
week before the Ascension: the army of the King of the Empyrean
celebrated its victory and returned to heaven on the seventh day,
Wednesday, Ascension eve; on Thursday, Ascension Day, Huon entered the monastery of Saint-Germain-des-Prés, in a final fusion of
the symbolic time of liturgy and the chronological unfolding of
events in his own life, to which he returned in extremis. Nothing in
the text itself would invite us to doubt the factual reality of the Antichrist's battle against the King of the Empyrean or designate it as a
vision and product of the narrator's state of consciousness if literary
references did not so define the entire poem: a reader's fantasy, the re-

sult of his self's beguiling mimicry, which identified with both author and character. In this sense, the initial Breton adventure was a substitute for the dream and, like it, had as its function subordination of the allegorical account to the psychological state of the narrator.

This procedure was thus not limited to the admittedly frequent cases in which reverie or dream served as the allegory's action and setting; on the contrary, it was constant and almost the rule in allegorical poetry of the time. Allegory appeared only through one set of eyes and one point of view—the narrator's. It was a perception, that is, a coherent and significant organization of the impressions and sensations felt by a consciousness interpreting and associating them according to its psychological tendencies, intellectual frameworks, and memories. Thus, it did not show the excessive simplicity that repels a modern mind, or even the objective, stable truth that scriptural exegesis revealed behind literal meaning. It was a reflection of truth in a consciousness: a reflection blurred by the peculiar conditions of that consciousness. It was this blurring that produced allegorical discourse, along with the signifier. Allegory thus revealed just as much about the consciousness perceiving it and expressing the truth of the signified as it did about that truth itself. The particular twist given the latter, its obscurities, its haplologies,[23] its indulgences, each of its choices—all made of it a discourse of the self about the self as much as a discourse of general truth veiled beneath material clothing. Thus, allegorical poetry, in the general evolution of poetry from the thirteenth century onward, was conceived as personal poetry. That is why it was so careful to reveal the overlapping and interaction of perception of the external world—inside the consciousness—with that of the signifying revelation, and tended to show the uncertainty of reality through that of the boundaries between one and the other. That is why it was applied to describing fluctuating states of consciousness and capturing the present of subjectivity.

In this poetry writing never claimed to be simultaneous with experience and the supposed state of consciousness that it described. It preserved their memory. All the examples cited thus far have been explicit concerning this point. Only the "Miroir des dames" showed a preoccupation with writing integrated with vision and preceding reawakening, which it provoked; but it was only then that the project formed in the dream was carried out. The poem drew its value from being thought to have been written in the heat of inspiration— for instance, right upon awakening. It still went back over a past state of consciousness: a recent past, but a past nonetheless. It was precisely upon this distance that the entire reflective and, by the same token, retrospective effort of the poem was based: to define the narrator's state of consciousness as reverie or dream; to return to the circumstances of falling asleep and reawakening; to grasp the relation between external circumstances and the nature of the vision. Once again the *Roman de la Rose*—which, as we have shown, attributed great importance to the play of memory—reveals special acuity in this area by showing that the relationship with the past, of necessity present in all poems of that same genre, was not self-evident, and by integrating it into the debate on dream and reality, truth and meaning. This poetry thus pointed up mediation by memory at the same time as it claimed to follow the flow of consciousness as closely as possible in perceiving and ordering the allegorical universe.

This observation calls forth two others, one concerning the link between allegory and memory and the other that between memories and self-consciousness. With respect to the first point, we know that the method of artificial memory by visualization, expounded in the *Rhetorica ad Herennium* and later glossed by medieval thought, was based on allegorization of memories. For instance, orators, to whom this method was principally addressed, were urged to imagine a vast edifice and distribute each of the ideas they proposed to develop among its various rooms in the form of a scene, preferably a violent and bloody one, or figures of exceeding beauty or ugliness that might recall it by analogy. Thereafter, when delivering their speech it was enough for them to stroll through this edifice in their imagination and find in each room the striking scenes that represented each of their ideas. In her masterful book *The Art of Memory* Frances Yates presented the forms assumed by this method during the Middle Ages and the theory she hypothesized in the works of Boncompagno, Albertus Magnus, and Thomas Aquinas:

> The images chosen for their memorable quality in the Roman orator's art have been changed by mediaeval piety into "corporeal similitudes" of "subtle and spiritual intentions."
> . . . What becomes of the strikingly beautiful and strikingly hideous *imagines agentes* in such a memory? The immediately prescholastic memory of Boncompagno suggests an answer to this question, with its virtues and vices as "memorial notes" through which we are to direct ourselves in the paths of remembrance, reminding us of the ways to Heaven and to Hell. The *imagines agentes* would have been moralized into beautiful or hideous human figures as "corporeal similitudes" of spiritual intentions of gaining Heaven or avoiding Hell, and memorized as ranged in order in some "solemn" building.[24]

This moralizing and Christianization of the art of memory, the conviction that it essentially consisted of a striking, imaged representation of heaven and hell, the virtues and vices, so as always to remember what must be sought and what must be shunned, led Frances Yates to suggest that the didactic and edifying literature of the Middle Ages owed more to the *Artes memoriae* than one might perhaps suppose. She also compared medieval art's predilection for grotesque or terrifying figures to the strikingly hideous or bloody images that those arts required men to imagine. These were bold intuitions, and the author did not elaborate on them. But there can be no doubt that allegory was both the basic procedure for artificial memory, which replaced ideas with concrete representations designating them, and the favored mode of expression for didactic literature in the Middle Ages. It is not too much to claim that, in this latter case, allegory had the function of fixing more easily in the memory the truths that a work sought to inculcate, the function as mnemonic device played by allegory having as its counterpart the function of edification that the Middle Ages attributed to the art of memory. Perhaps the various "houses" constituting the successive stages of the "Voie de paradis" taken by Rutebeuf or the various places through which Watriquet de Couvin dreamt he was passing, in the poems commented on earlier, should be considered from this angle.

Comparisons between allegory and the exercise of memory allow us to extend and complete the analyses proposed earlier. They suggest that not only did the appropriation of states of consciousness by memory make the latter the setting for allegorical poems, but that allegory itself was elaborated according to memory. Thus, it was not only linked to the narrator's consciousness in cases where characters emanated from it, as in the *Roman de la Rose*. More generally, it was not only because it presented itself as a perception of the consciousness whose conditions and incidents it reflected. More fundamentally still, truth was revealed to the consciousness in the form of allegory because allegory fixed truth in the memory. It was this link between the two, at the very time when prescholasticism and scholasticism were revealing it or rediscovering it, which obliged allegorical poetry to be a poetry of subjectivity despite its claims to generality.

Thus, we necessarily shift from the relationship between allegory and memory to that between memories and consciousness. Allegorical poetry presumed a narrator's withdrawal into himself, retrospective attention to the circumstances of his life and their echo in his consciousness, to the nature and *alea* of his perception of himself and the world. It was written as *internal memoranda*. Rooted in the dates and incidents of life whose internalized extension it represented, it was the mirror image of the personal *dit*, which also went back over these dates and incidents, however, defining the subject in terms of exteriority alone. But, paradoxically, turning inward on the play of consciousness and memories, it was more sensitive to the function of time in deciphering the subject. Claiming to grasp the subjectivity's present through consciousness of memories and memories of consciousness, despite its avowed component of fiction, it echoed the interest in autobiography emerging in literature of that period, as well as what was newest in it: the attention given to the subject in itself, not merely as witness; to the way it was marked and shaped by events, not merely their succession; to their meaning in view of its own life—the view to the present and the view backward. The narrator of the *Roman de la Rose* proceeded in just this way, recalling an old dream because his present life suddenly revealed its meaning to him and because his life drew its own meaning from the dream.

PART III

Monodic Writings

Was there really interest in autobiography during the Middle Ages, as the preceding analysis might suggest?[1] The attention to the past of consciousness that characterized allegory, and to real-life matters that pervaded the *dit*, is not sufficient in itself to determine it. The fictional exhibition of the self—indeed, the fragmented confessions of poetry—are based on an attention to the subject quite different from what is presumed by autobiography, the subject's search for its own elucidation by going back over its past and a continuous account of its life.

Considering the place that Georg Misch's *Geschichte der Autobiographie* assigned to the Middle Ages, we would be tempted to conclude that they held autobiography in great favor. Reading gives a different impression. Most of the authors included by Misch spoke of themselves more or less in passing, by accident, in works whose central purpose was not that, or else in connection with a dedication or prologue.[2] What Misch understood as autobiography was not a mode of expression but the sum of information that an author revealed about himself. Even when he put himself at the center of his work, a medieval author was rarely writing autobiography in the modern sense, that is, not only a systematic account of his own life but an account conducted from his own life's perspective, in which the world appeared through the dual gaze that he brought to bear on himself during his existence and on this gaze itself at the moment of writing. Autobiography as a specular account was little used in the Middle Ages. The exceptional fame of the few works belonging to the form is confirmation of this. Each appears, moreover, to be a special case. It is difficult to define the rules of a genre based on them alone, or to detect an evolution. Nevertheless, these texts, which belong to Latin literature, reveal by comparison an autobiographical tendency that was gradually emerging in vernacular literature, an almost unconfessed, reticent tendency that might pass unnoticed if we were not invited to look for it, but one that had a necessary place in the new cohesiveness of this literature.

The mark of autobiography, in both the erratic fragments that were its first milestones and the more ambiguous but ongoing examples that followed, was not only a relating or outpouring of the "I" but also a taking into account of the time of life—of one's life—as a measure and setting for the relationship to the world and God. This proposition holds true in every case, whether the author substituted his own life for the model of an admirable or imitable one, shifted from chronicles to memoirs or diary, or went from the limited generality of confession to a personal unfolding of his confessions.

The first case is strikingly illustrated by Saint Valerius. This noble Visigoth of Asturia (c. 630–95) wrote a first-person account of his life that began not at his birth but at the point when he left the monastery in which he had been a monk in order to withdraw, far from the world, to a desert hermitage.[3] The main part of the account was devoted to his struggles with the devil, who subjected him to constant temptations and torments. We also learn that he had disciples who came seeking intellectual and spiritual teaching, and that he was an object of high consideration for ecclesiastical authorities. Apart from this, the text reveals nothing of its author's personality, education, development, the years he spent under monastic rule, the circumstances and personal reasons impelling him to leave the cloister, or even his religious feelings, represented only by his physical encounters with the demon.

On the other hand, these were among the commonplaces of hagiographic literature, especially recounting the lives of saintly hermits. The lives of the wilderness fathers had not yet been translated into Latin at the end of the seventh century, but those of the Irish ascetic saints offered the same characteristics. In addition, they may be compared with the story of Saint Valerius, on at least one count missing from the eastern lives: the presence of numerous disciples around the saint, providing a transition from anchoritism to cenobitism. Take, for example, the life of Saint Columban, written around the same time (642–43) by Ionas, an Italian, and the Irish monk's endless hesitation between the numerous monastic establishments that he left in his wake and the call to eremitism that kept driving him on toward new solitudes. The life of Saint Valerius was a saint's life like the others, save that its author was, or claimed to be, the saint himself. What guarantee of its authenticity do we have? That—in the final analysis, as good as any other—constituted by the unusual attribute of a first-person narration; forgers seek verisimilitude and therefore the norm. Instead of presuming that someone else was passing himself off as Valerius, it is simpler to observe that Valerius treated himself like anybody else and took inspiration from hagiography, the only model he knew, for writing his life. The use of the first person did not really modify the usual relationship in this kind of literature between the author and his character. The former submitted without reservation to the story forms and the conventions of the genre, whose object was to render the latter exemplary and admirable. In the same way, he scrupulously respected the objective representation of spiritual life in the form of a combat, in the literal sense, against the forces of evil, without privileged status as narrator of his own life leading him to give it more internalized expression. The character as he narrated himself thus was not different from an image given by an overtly hagiographic text written by a third party.

Nonetheless, at times the sharpness of his rancors gave a personal tone to his account. To torment him, the demon seemed systematically to inspire thoughts and behavior harmful to him among his acquaintances and fellow monks: one would steal the books he had just written and almost drive him mad; another burned down his hermitage; a third decapitated his disciple as he was praying before the altar. Reading of these repeated misfortunes makes us suspect the author of paranoid tendencies. On the other hand, at least in the opening lines his dual presence in the text as narrator and character was made palpable by the retrospective view he took of his past through the portrayal of his conversion. But it must be admitted that he paid no attention to the relationship between the time of his life and the point at which he was writing, which is the mark of soul-searching, the sign by which the author recognizes—with indulgence, regret, or at times astonishment—that he is indeed the same person whose story he is recounting, since he once was him. This was Saint Augustine's attitude, at every moment commenting on the episodes of his past life that he was relating, the thoughts and feelings that disturbed him then, from the point view which was his at the time he was writing the *Confessions*, illuminated by faith and distance in time, making him discover what, without his then knowing it, were the ways of God, whom his account constantly called to witness.

All in all, the distance from Saint Valerius's autobiography to hagiography is scarcely farther than that between "I" and "he" and does not involve many differences other than the grammatical ones. Should that surprise us? Not if we remember how much medieval writing patterned itself on respect for literary models. Should we be surprised if the model used by Valerius for this unusual exercise—recounting his own life—was that of hagiography? Six centuries later, Dante justified this choice at the start of the *Convivio* (I, 2). Denying the author's right to speak of himself, for reasons that were moral but justified by the authority of ancient rhetoric, he acknowledged his authorization to do so in two circumstances: to exonerate himself from unjust accusations, like Boethius, or to enlighten his reader, like Saint Augustine. Saint Valerius easily fitted within the second category, as Abelard did within the first. In addition, by choosing admirable lives as a model for writing, he showed himself to be sensitive to the hermeneutic value contained by the time of a life within itself. On a scale that the human mind could embrace not only through conceptualization but through the experience of memory, it was a revealing image of the history of salvation, in which humanity was immersed and which it therefore could not fully comprehend. It was this mirror that Saint Paul spoke of, in which we see *in aenigmate* while waiting to see *facie ad faciem* (1 Cor. 13:12): a time to follow and to live the *excellentiorem viam* (13:1) of Christ's charity. To replace "he" by "I" in relating this progress of life was thus to underscore, if only implicitly, the role of recalling the past in the revelation of the meaning of a life and what it implied.[4] It pointed up the dual nature of memory as existential experience and the faculty of synthesis. Existential experience was marked by the use of the first person, replacing memorized knowledge of another's life with personally lived memory. The faculty of synthesis was marked by the continuity of an account that pursued a life's unfolding.

The latter point contrasts Valerius's "I" with that used by Gregory the Great in his *Dialogues* half a century earlier.[5] Attention to personal memories was at the very source of that work, as is shown by its prologue. In it the saintly pope said that one day, depressed by his office's cares, he had withdrawn into solitude and yielded to a sense of nostalgia for the time when he knew the peace of the cloister:

> Quadam die nimiis quorundam saecularium tumultibus depressus, secretum locum petit amicum moeroris.

> One day, deeply depressed by the excessive agitation of certain worldly people, I went to a remote place favorable to sorrow.

Joined by his disciple, deacon Peter, who questioned him about his melancholy, he answered:

> Infelix quippe animus meus occupationis suae pulsatus vulnere, meminit qualis aliquando in monasterio fuit. . . . Et cum prioris vitae recolo, quasi post tergum ductis oculis viso litore suspiro.[6]

> It is because my unhappy mind, shocked and wounded by its occupations, remembers how it once was in the monastery. . . . And recalling my past life as if my eyes

> were turned toward my back [and] I once again saw the
> shore [of monastic life, abandoned for the turbulent waters
> of the papacy], I sigh.

In response to Peter he then decided, basing his words on trust-worthy witnesses, to speak to him of those servants of God, whom he envied, who succeeded in spending their lives far from the world. Af-terward, to develop and confirm the teachings of the anecdotes he re-lated, he frequently appealed to his own memories and to episodes that he had witnessed or even taken part in. Thus, the work opened with a retrospective view—"quasi post tergum ductis oculis" (as if my eyes were turned toward my back) as Saint Gregory spelled it out—absent from Saint Valerius's autobiography, and with emotions that memories of his past life aroused in the author. Yet it did not go on with the story of that life, as one might expect, but with a series of generally indirect recollections in which subjective memory never-theless played an essential role, not only because a certain number of them referred to events experienced by the author but because they all dealt with people who had lived a life, once his, which he missed. These recollections were thus not intended to reconstitute its course but, divided up into exempla, to illustrate and justify spiritual teach-ings. Their meaning, subordinated to those teachings, was more or less external to them, and the only value attributed to personal testi-mony was guaranteeing the authenticity of the reported facts. From an autobiographical perspective, conversely, the meaning of recollec-tions is inherent in their very nature as subjective recollections and arises from a coherent, sustained reconstitution of a life unfolding in memory.

Few texts can be situated so strikingly within the perspective of autobiography as the first lines of Gregory the Great's *Dialogues*. But the work immediately drifted toward an exemplary compilation whose memories and nostalgia for the cloister provided only its main thread. Conversely, Valerius, writing a *vita* in the first person, sug-gested that he was sensitive to the conjunction of life-time and the experience of memory in producing a meaning that remained exem-plary as well. However, by neglecting to inscribe in the text the view he was taking of the past, he passed over what defines the autobiographical enterprise itself. If we limited ourselves to works like this, we would have to agree with Philippe Lejeune, for whom autobiography was born in 1770.[7] Indeed, they do not deserve that name any more than those vernacular works, starting in the thirteenth century, in which we can detect the rough outline of an autobiographical project. But between the seventh and thirteenth centuries there was at least one work which in itself modified the image of this literature. Its importance and renown deserve mention here, so we will postpone a bit longer our reaching the chronological and linguistic limits of this study.

This was the *De vita sua*[8] of Guibert de Nogent (c. 1055–1125) Probably written around 1114–15, this is among the best known works left to us by the Middle Ages, but it enjoys a fame that is bipartite and a bit schizophrenic. Some have viewed it above all as a first-rate historical source, particularly concerning the revolt of the Laon commune in 1112. It is not too much to say that Guibert's story, summarized in the history textbooks, has struck the imaginations of generations of schoolchildren from the time they are taught French history, including Bishop Gaudry hiding in a barrel from which the rebels dragged him and put him to death, and the tax exactions of Thomas de Marle, the Lord of Coucy. But historians interested in the reported facts examined the work's autobiographical quality only insofar as it permitted them to measure the reliability of its testimony. Others, like Misch, have been concerned solely with this quality itself, being led thereby to take into account only the first book, in which it was most pronounced. The reluctance to consider the work in its entirety as a coherent whole shows how disconcerting it is to the modern mind in terms of its organization and aims. It is in three parts, which Guibert called *libelli* (booklets). In the first, after a prologue closely patterned on Saint Augustine's *Confessions*,[9] the author gives an account of his life, from birth to his election as abbot of Nogent-sous-Coucy. This part ends in a rather disjointed series of exempla testifying to the devil's interventions and the manifestations of God's justice. The second part, much briefer than the other two, is devoted to the origins of the abbey of Nogent, the author's installation as abbot, and his mother's death; like the first, it ends with some exempla. The third part is entirely taken up with the Laon affair. The author is present only insofar as he played a personal role in it, which is to say rather little. Like the preceding books, it closes with a series of exempla. The work comes to an abrupt end after the last of these, with a concluding two-line prayer.

This summary undoubtedly leaves the impression of a hodge-podge that gradually shifts from autobiography to chronicle. Are we to believe that Guibert did not remain faithful to his initial project, or that it lacked firmness? Above all, is it possible to define this project? We have two main elements at our disposal: the work's title and its prologue. The title, admittedly, does not really exist. The only manuscript we have (a late copy at that) does not have one. The first editors inserted *De vita sua*, and Edmond-René Labande kept that, translating it as "autobiography." John F. Benton used the term "memoirs"—which was more in keeping with modern usage—in speaking of a text that for the most part did not focus on the author's personality per se, even if it did derive its material from his recollections. But Guibert himself, referring to his own work, designated it elsewhere by the title *monodiae: in libris monodiarum mearum*[10] (monodies: among my books of monodies). This word, whose use reveals his taste for rare, learned terms and—to be blunt—his tendency to pedantry, should be understood, as Labande observes,[11] starting from the definition given by Isidore of Seville in his *Etymologies*:

> Cum unus canit, graece monodia, latine sicinium dicitur;
> cum vero duo canunt, bicinium apellatur; cum multi, chorus.
> (*Etym.* VI, XIX, 6)

> When a single person sings, it is called *monodia* in Greek,
> *sicinium* [solo] in Latin; when two people sing, on the
> other hand, it is called *bicinium* [duo]; when they are more
> numerous, chorus.

The title *Monodiae* thus defined not the content of the work but its mode of expression: Guibert intended to make himself alone heard.

No other voice would be mingled with his and the point of view would be deliberately subjective.

From whatever angle we examine it and however we are to understand its metaphoric sense, this unfamiliar term "monody" was well chosen. First, Guibert was expressing himself alone in his work: it had no sources, an exceptional occurrence in the Middle Ages, especially for an author who was such a bookworm. He did, of course, have a model in Saint Augustine. But for the events he was reporting as well as his accounts of miracles he "depended on no prior written source."[12] For a man who had read so much and was so proud of it, limiting himself to his own recollections or to oral information that he had gathered personally was obviously the sign of a deliberate plan, which his unexpected title further emphasized. The plural *monodiae* is certainly explained by the fact that the work was made up of three books, as the expression "in libris monodiarum mearum" confirms. From it one may deduce that in their author's view the three books had in common the fact of being *monodic*, but they constituted three separate *monodies* and the narrative made no claim to any continuity from one to the other or from an absolutely identical perspective, which would have encouraged us to seek the work's unity beyond their apparent dissonances. Finally, by drawing attention, above all, to the resonance of his own voice, the author was directing the intended reading of the prologue and, through it, of the entire work.

As we have said, this prologue was inspired by that of Saint Augustine. It was quite different in spirit, however, as we may see from its first lines:

> Confiteor amplitudini tuae, Deus, infinitorum errorum meorum decursus, et creberrimos ad te miserationis internae, quos tamen inspirasti, recursus. Confiteor pueritiae ac juventutis meae mala, adhuc etiam in matura hac aestate aestuentia, et inveterata pravitatum studia, necdum sub defatigati corporis torpore cessantia.
> (pp. 3–4)

> I confess to Thy grandeur, Oh God, the errors caused by my innumerable faults, as well as the repeated returns of

> my inner distress toward Thee, returns that Thou, in truth,
> hast inspired in me. I confess the iniquity of my childhood
> and youth, which still boils up in my maturity, as well as
> my deep-rooted penchant for guilty acts: the numbness of
> a weary body still has not put an end to it.

Like his eminent model, Guibert turned to God, whom he addressed in an elevated tone and prolix style not immune from pretentiousness (*corporis torpore*). Like him, he insisted on the bad habits of youth and inclinations of the flesh. We can take his word concerning the latter. Later on he admits to having composed a few Ovidian poems while a young monk and having been aroused by them. As for the former, what follows shows that they amounted to very little in a child destined for the clergy from birth and raised in extreme austerity and severity, who, around the age of twelve or thirteen, had been left on his own for a few months before entering the convent and at most went on a rather boisterous vacation. Finally, the opening word, *confiteor*, is obviously a tribute to the title of the *Confessions*.

But it is precisely concerning this point that divergences appear. Although their first word was not *confiteor*, Saint Augustine's *Confessions* did begin with a confession—a confession of praise. Saint Augustine first confessed not his sins but God's greatness and mercy:

> Magnus es, domine, et laudabilis valde: magna virtus tua et
> sapientiae tuae non est numerus. Et laudare te vult homo,
> aliqua portio creaturae tuae.

> Thou art great, oh Lord, and most worthy of praise. Great is Thy
> strength, and Thy wisdom is beyond calculation. And a man, a
> mere particle of Thy creation, wishes to praise Thee.[13]

There followed a long meditation on the audacity of man—who, despite his lowly and wretched state, dared to praise God, in whose eyes he should be as nothing—and on the goodness of God, who let man know, praise, and love him and deigned to appreciate this praise and love. This meditation allowed Augustine, by a dialectical process, to continue with a description of his early life.[14] In contrast to God's knowledge and endurance he placed his own ignorance, which was double and doubly linked to creation's immersion in time: he did not know whence he came into this world and had no recollection of the first years of his life. This admission of ignorance allowed him to re-orient the initial confession in three ways. It served, first of all, as a transition for him to embark on the story of his life. In addition, it was the first opportunity for him explicitly to articulate the *confiteor*, which was both that of the glory of God and that of his own insuffi-ciency:

> Confiteor tibi, domine caeli et terrae, laudem dicens tibi de primordiis et infantia mea, quae non memini.
>
> I confess to Thy glory, Lord of heaven and earth, and I praise Thee for the beginnings of my childhood, which I do not recall.[15]

Finally, in continuing the story of his childhood, it allowed him to pass from admission of his insufficiency to that of his failings, those of the child he had been, for a child was not innocent but merely weak. Thus, he went from confession of praise to confession of his sins. The former came to his lips first, since he was addressing God in the first lines of his work. But once he returned to his own self, the latter inevitably accompanied his return to past life.

Only this second confession is present in Guibert de Nogent's pro-logue; his is a *confiteor* of sins. The initial meditation he engages in, in imitation of Saint Augustine—which naturally suffers by compar-ison with its model—starts with the misery of sinning man, the ac-cumulation of his endlessly renewed sins, his obdurateness, his con-version, and God's patience and mercy. The transition between these reflections and the account of his own life is based on the idea that one must know oneself in order to know God and be illuminated by His light:

> Quomodo enim ad tui notitiam scintillarem, si ad me vi-dentum caecutirem? . . . Quia igitur utrumque constat, ut per mei notitiam tuam petam et, fruens tua, ilico mea non

caream, dignum ac singulariter salutare est, ut obscuritas ra-
tionis meae, per hujusmodi confessiones, crebra tui luminis
inquisitione tergatur, quo stabiliter illustrata numquam de-
hinceps a se nesciatur.
(pp. 6–9)

How, indeed, should I get any light from knowledge of
Thee, if I have blurred vision in respect to myself? . . . Two
things are thus evident: insofar as I know myself, I seek to
know Thee; but when I enjoy knowledge of Thee, I do not
lose thereby the knowledge I have of myself. Thus, it is
truly just and salutary for an assiduous search for Thy light
to scatter the darkness of my understanding, through such
a confession: thus lastingly enlightened, it [my under-
standing] will henceforth never lose knowledge of itself.

It is only then, as he embarks on his life story, that Guibert, re-
versing Saint Augustine's process, goes from confession of his sins to
a confession of praise, thanking God for the blessings heaped on him.
In the lines just quoted we may note that the formula "dignum ac . . .
salutare est" is not used, as in the prelude to the mass from which it
was drawn, to introduce the giving of thanks ("vere dignum et jus-
tum est, aequum et salutare, nos tibi semper et ubique gratias agere"
(it is truly worthy and just, right and salutary, for us to give thanks to
Thee always and everywhere) but rather to justify the project constituted by these confessions. Thus, it is itself deflected from praise toward confession.

So it is not enough to say that this prologue, whose first word is
confiteor and one of its last *confessiones*, was inspired by Saint Augustine. It must be added that Guibert transformed the spirit of his
model because he likened "confessions" to "confession." In so doing,
he truly appeared as a man of his time, marked by the increasing importance attributed to confession and the persistent reflection devoted to it. The evolution of penance from the Early Middle Ages to
the twelfth century, which has often been described, shows a gradual
allowance for the penitent's inner predispositions and the reality of
his repentance that, from the eleventh century on, replaced the strict,

automatic, fixed-rate penitence spread throughout the entire West during the Carolingian period by Irish monasticism. At the end of the eleventh century, the Gregorian reformation, in regulating the practice of confession, conferred new importance on it and made its practice more habitual and frequent. At the start of the following century, during which theological thought in general underwent unprecedented expansion and enrichment, attention to the penitent's repentance and the signs of the return of divine grace within him became more and more exacting. This reached its culmination in the doctrine of contritionism, according to which the remission of sins was brought about by consent to grace, manifested by tears of repentance. From this perspective, the priest's role was limited to administering the sacrament; in contrast, the penitent's actions were given greater importance, and the humiliation caused by admission of sin during confession was itself considered an important aspect of penitence. Yves de Chartres, who was born in 1035 and was thus twenty years older than Guibert, had already written in his epistle #228:

> Per internum enim gemitum satisfit [peccator] interno judici, et idcirco indilata datur ab eo remissio peccati, cui manifesta est interna conversio.[16]

> For by his inner groaning [the sinner] fulfills inner judgment, and for that reason remission of sin is granted to him without delay by Him to whom the inner conversion is visible.

It is clear that to a man nurtured on this doctrine, writing his confession and giving it the public notice of a literary work was in itself penance and atonement for his sins.

But there is more. At the abbey of Bec, Yves de Chartres had been a disciple of Lanfranc, whose most celebrated pupil was Saint Anselm of Canterbury. As he himself tells us, during his youth Guibert had an opportunity to study Anselm's teachings in the abbey of Saint-Germer de Fly. The garbled, almost unintelligible summary he gives does not let us conclude that he derived great profit from it. But this passage—the only one he devoted to problems of this kind—at least shows that the master's lessons bore particularly upon desire and will:

> Is itaque tripartito aut quadripartito mentem modo distinguere docens, sub affectu, sub voluntate, sub ratione, sub intellectu commercia totius interni mysterii tractare. . . .

> He taught me to exercise my mind according to the tripartite or quadripartite method, to develop the operations of the inner man in his entirety from the points of view of desire, will, reason, and understanding. . . .

A few lines further down we read:

> . . . cum primum quidem inter velle et affici distaret luculentissime aperuisset . . .
> (Labande, pp. 140–41)

> . . . as he had first most luminously revealed to me how will is distinguished from desire . . .

That distinction was essential to Anselm's doctrine of will, which created a considerable stir in its day. According to Saint Anselm, for the will to conform to justice it had to conform not only in its object but in its motive, which had to be nothing save the will to have a just will:

> The will is just when it maintains its righteousness because it is righteousness; and justice, that is to say moral goodness, will be defined as follows: the will to maintain the righteousness of the will out of love of righteousness [voluntas servandi rectitudinem voluntatis propter ispsam rectitudinem] (De veritate, chap. 12).[17]

The will impelled by desire—positive desire for happiness or fear of punishment—was thus evil. This Kantian conception *avant la lettre* had the consequence that the sole function of man's freedom was to allow him to keep his will good :

> Now, as we know, this moral value of man, what Saint Anselm calls justice, is righteousness of will willed for oneself, and therefore freedom shall be the power to maintain righteousness of the will for itself [potestas servandi recti-

tudinem voluntatis propter ipsam rectitudinem] (*De liber-tate arbitrii*, chap. 2).[18]

This moral doctrine had one inevitable psychological implication: the need for man to know himself in order to measure the righteousness of his will and thus be able to exercise his freedom, which was nothing but to know God and obey Him.

The end of Guibert's prologue (quoted earlier), to which we now return after a lengthy digression, said just that. The transition between the initial meditation on his obdurateness in sinning and the story of his life was based precisely on the affirmation that one must know oneself in order to know God. Neither the argument nor the sequence of ideas was arbitrary. They were a direct application of teachings he had received from his master, which, as he demonstrated elsewhere, had marked him so deeply; similarly, in conceiving his "Confessions" as a confession, he echoed the new doctrine of repentance then developing. The process of introspection and the discourse of confession combined to form the framework within which his "monodic writing" was inscribed: introspection or, rather, retrospection. From this time forward, the combination of introspection and confession characterized all spiritual literature. But Guibert—on this point the first editors, Dachery and Bourguin, were correct in their choice of title—engaged in monodies not "de conscientia sua" (on his consciousness) but "de vita sua" (on his life).

This difference presumed a broader point of view, taking into account not a given state of consciousness but a totality. It is a tautology to say that this broadening was of time, an entire life. But Guibert was not Saint Augustine. He was not meditating on time itself. Nevertheless, even in retracing the progression of his entire life, he strove to illuminate it by broadening his field of vision in another way. With respect to each stage of his life, he was careful to situate his person, his circumstances at any given time, and his experiences in their social, historical, and spiritual contexts. This concern provoked the shift in his text away from a confessional model toward that of a collection of exempla or a chronicle. This tendency appears right at the opening of the work. If he described his mother's beauty, he immediately engaged in reflections on the value of beauty—which was useless and even harmful without virtue yet worthy of praise insofar as it was in the image of God's beauty—and announced what we should all enjoy when we were with Him, after shedding the imperfections of this world. If he spoke of his tutor's ignorance, his excessive severity as well as his devotion, Guibert developed his ideas on the education of children in that connection. He did not proceed otherwise when it came to historical circumstances and political events that had influenced his life.

Thus, his mother's conversion and retirement to the convent of Fly are the occasion for a fifteen-page account of the evolution of monasticism during his time. This is introduced in terms that leave no doubt as to the function that the author attributed to it:

> Sed libet paulo altius, quantum nostri temporis mentione requiritur, statum religionum conversionumque, quas vidimus, attingere; unde et hanc ipsam . . . necnon et plerosque alios bonae mutationis contigit exempla sumsisse.
> (Labande, pp. 48–49)

> To the degree to which this brings up again what I say about our times, and in order for people to understand whence my mother and many others drew the example of a happy change in life, I intend to go a little way back into the past, to define the religious lives and conversions that we witnessed.

He speaks next of monastic crisis and renewal, the taking of orders by a number of important people, Saint Bruno's vocation and the Carthusian order, of which he gives a precise and justly celebrated description. Finally he returns to his subject:

> Ad te tandem post has ratiocinationes redeo, Deus meus, super illius bonae mulieris, matris meae, conversione.
> (pp. 74–75)

> After these digressions, now I finally return to Thee, my God, to speak of the conversion of my mother, that holy woman.

We note here that to return to his subject is to return to God and speak of his mother. The latter is hardly surprising when we think of the role his mother played in his life, the influence she had on his vocation, the close ties uniting the young widow with her last born; John Benton's analyses have shed much light on these issues.[19] As for mention of returning to God, it reaffirms the coherence of the project expressed at the end of the prologue: to confess one's life in order to attain God through knowledge of oneself. The same sort of justification is alleged for almost all his digressions; for example, to introduce the series of exempla closing the first book inserted into the account as he is about to leave Fly for Nogent:

> Sed, quoniam in hac Flaviacensi ecclesia, sub Deo parente et beati Geremari, loci ejusdem conditoris, patrocinio coaluisse nos diximus, quaedam, quae ibidem audivimus fierique vidimus, dignum ut memoriae tradamus.
> (pp. 168–69)

> However, since we have stated that we were educated at the monastery of Fly, with God as our father and the blessed Germer as our protector, founder of the above-named house, it is just for us to recount here the recollection of certain things we learned in that place or were witness to.

A similar remark serves as a preamble to the story of the founding of the abbey of Nogent that opens the second book. The same thing occurs at the end of the book, where he takes advantage of the fact that the account of his mother's death has led him from Nogent back to Fly, permitting him to continue the account of the wonders and miracles that had the monastery of his youth as their setting. But it serves no purpose to give more examples, since the confirmation they give cannot be applied to the essential point, which is that in any sense the third book no longer used the autobiographical account as its main theme. The account of events in Laon did not claim to shed light on the author's person or life and find its justification in that. Where do we find the project of confession and self-knowledge in the pages having as their sole object the condemnation of Bishop

Gaudry, Thomas de Marle, the rebellious burghers of Laon, and Jean de Soissons, or underhanded denigration of Bishop Godefroy d'Amiens, Guibert's predecessor on the abbey throne of Nogent?

However, let us recall the plural *monodiae* and suppose, as a hypothesis, that these monodies could be sung in several keys. At least three observations, then, lead us to take another look at this book. The first is that, in the mind of a son so closely tied to his mother as Guibert, the story of his life merges with that of his education and career. Once the latter has reached its apex with his election as abbot—that is, once he has given his mother satisfaction, fulfilled her hopes, fitted his image to the one she conceived of him and imposed upon him—the unfolding of his life no longer seems worth recounting in a systematic, orderly way. In the second book, scarcely has he transcribed for the reader's edification the inaugural sermon he delivered to his monks upon arriving in Nogent than he returns to Fly to relate his mother's death. The actual autobiography dies with her. Thereafter he seems unable to continue the story of a life that unfolded under her eyes, and one may wonder whether this additional parallel with Saint Augustine's *Confessions* was deliberate.[20] Henceforth he had to find another type of monody than the autobiographical account.

The second observation is that the events in Laon closely affected Guibert even though his active role in them seems to have been relatively limited. If he had wanted, he could have connected them to the story of his life much more naturally and justifiably than by the exempla in the preceding books, or even his picture of monasticism in the twelfth century. He was involved in these events simply through being one of the high church dignitaries of the diocese of Laon. He suffered personally from these events because several of his friends— even one of his relations by marriage—lost their lives in them. Finally, he himself played a role of some importance on at least two occasions. First, when he was questioned by Pope Pascal II at the time of the investigations that the latter conducted into the controversial election of Gaudry to the episcopal throne at Laon, as spokesman for the dignitaries of the diocese (because he was the one who spoke

Latin most fluently), he expressed himself with a caution akin to cowardice, as he himself indicated with admirable honesty, and refused to associate himself publicly with the accusations originally made against the newly elected bishop by the renowned Anselm of Laon (who, moreover, did not see fit to repeat them when he himself was present at the scene). He thus admitted to his share of responsibility for the pope's confirmation of Gaudry's election.[21] Second, he was the one who preached during the ceremony of reconciliation at the cathedral of Laon, stained by the murder of Gérard de Quierzy that had taken place there. In his work he provides a long excerpt of this sermon, which, he said, earned him the enmity of Bishop Gaudry and his partisans, the instigators of the murder.[22] Finally, throughout the account he neglects no opportunity to take sides, almost always violently and insidiously at times.

Thus, a new form of monodic discourse was taking shape with respect to the opening of the work: no longer an account of his own life, illuminated by contemporary events, but an engaged testimony concerning those events he witnessed, took part in, or was marked by. This reversal makes these *memoirs*—the term chosen by Benton is perfectly suited to the third book—a kind of obverse face of autobiography: not its opposite but the same reality seen from a different perspective, another view of the same *subject*, defined not through the events of his own life but through the passion of his writing and through his *commentaries*—to use the title that Caesar gave to his memoirs—upon what, though outside himself, touched and revealed him. Thus, the objectivization of the account did not signify abandonment of the project of confession announced at the start of the work, since Guibert—without conspicuously beating his breast or constantly calling God as witness, as he did in the first book—in no way sought to hide the fact that throughout Gaudry's episcopacy he felt he was in an awkward position that constantly required him to make small compromises and take great precautions. He despised the bishop, about whom he muttered as much ill as he could, but he treated him with respect and kept up an appearance of good relations with him; even the aforementioned sermon was aimed at him only indirectly, when he was far away. Basically they were on the same side; he despised the rabble that put the bishop to death, and the very principle of the commune, as much as Gaudry. It was at the bishop's side that Guibert's relatives and friends fell.

These pages depict Guibert better than the purely autobiographical part of his work: a bitter intellectual, very conscious of his intelligence but seemingly suffering more harm than good because it was not political intelligence; quick to censure his fellows but too lacking in courage to be a model of virtue himself. Of course, he gives himself away without admitting to this. But neither does he try to show himself in the best light or strike poses. Most of all, in his view the connection between the story of his life and the events in Laon was seemingly constituted by the passions aroused in him by those events, passions that made them both a part and a revelation of himself. That is why he was still writing his confession as he recounted them. That is why memoirs, in his case, constituted a pursuit of autobiography by other paths.

The validity of this proposition is confirmed—this is the third observation—by certain particularities of the marks of statement in Guibert's account. These appear in the very first words of the third book:

> De Laudunensibus, ut spopondimus, jam modo tractaturi, imo Laudunensium tragoedias acturi, primum est dicere totius mali originem ex pontificum, ut nobis videtur, perversitatibus emersisse.
> (pp. 268–69)

> When it comes to dealing now with the people of Laon as we have promised, or more precisely discussing their tragedies, it must be said that the origin of all the evil (as it seems to us) lay in their bishops' depravity.

Where does the promise to discuss the tragedies of Laon appear? Nowhere. Why this false repetition, then, this insistent fidelity to an initial project that does not exist in reality or that the author, contrary to his claims, has at least never mentioned up to this point? In proposing to examine the history of the situation and shed light on it, Guibert was faithful to the method he had practiced since the beginning of his work, examples of which we have already provided. Informing the reader that this picture reflects his personal interpretation—"ut nobis videtur" (as it seems to us)—he defines what has been called his "involved testimony." Nevertheless, in this case the historical reminder claimed to shed light not on his own life and personality but on events outside of him. Outside? The reversed, abortive act by which, instead of forgetting his promise he kept a promise that had never been made, reveals in the writing that the author, as organizer of the discourse of which he was the subject, considered himself to be closely linked to these outside events. Somewhere there was an origin to the discourse that had kept silent but whose latent existence was so strong that when it was mentioned for the first time—at the same time the discourse was being executed—it was in the form of a reminder. The autobiography itself, as has been noted, ended with his mother's death. But for this son—faithful to the image of ideal judge that he had made of her and submissive to the severe law she had set for him—for this child of the cloister, the religious scandals, political turmoils, and discovery of his own weakness in the face of ambiguous choices were like a renewed death of his mother. The tragedies of Laon, as he called them, were in that sense his own tragedy, and since he obviously could not realize this in the full light of consciousness, we should not be surprised if his intention to speak of it, in the continuation of the story of his life and the death of his mother, was both unmentioned at the origins of the discourse and recalled as long present when the time came.

Is this too much extrapolating from just two words, "ut spopondimus" (as we have promised)? Not if we note a phenomenon of the same sort that had appeared earlier in the account. In the second book, immediately after summarizing the inaugural sermon that he gave at Nogent, Guibert recounted the last days and death of his mother, who had remained at Fly. The transitional paragraph ends as follows:

> Ego autem et frater meus, tunc temporis, agebamus Novigenti, biennio, ni fallor, ante illud ad Flaviacenses postli-

minium, quod supra quidem meminimus, inconsiderantis-
sime quidem factum, sed, eo autore qui malis nostris bene
utitur, conversum in multo prosperiorem quam credi posset
enventum. Pepercit enim ejus teneritudini Deus, ne jecur
tantopere Deum amans immeritum hujus innobilis reditus
gladio carperetur.
(pp. 242–43)

At that time my brother and I were living in Nogent. If I
am not mistaken it was two years before our return to Fly,
which we have mentioned earlier, a return that was made
so thoughtlessly but that nevertheless, thanks to Him who
uses our ills for our welfare, turned out far better than
might have been expected. In any case, God spared my
mother's delicacy and did not allow her heart, which loved
Him so deeply, to be undeservedly pierced by the sword of
so disgraceful a return.

Despite what he has asserted, here again Guibert has nowhere previously mentioned this inglorious episode. Similarly, he was speaking
here for the first and last time of his brother—evidently a monk at
Nogent—who suddenly appears in the middle of a sentence and will
never be mentioned again. When we read these lines, two questions
arise. Why, at this particular moment, did he describe his brief return
to Fly, which was probably the result of difficulties with the Nogent
monks and problems in the administration of his monastery? And
why did he think or claim that he had previously mentioned it?
Guibert himself provided an answer to the first question by thanking
God for sparing his mother the sight of her son's "disgaceful" return.
At the time he was about to recount her death, he thought of a later
event in his own life that he congratulated himself for her not having
witnessed. This association of ideas confirms the impression that
Guibert viewed his life through the eyes of his mother, established as
judgmental authority. Another reason, found in the writing itself,
may be deduced in addition to this one. For him to go from the inaugural sermon in Nogent to his mother's death in Fly was to *return*
to Fly. The metaphor is so banal that it scarcely registers. Guibert
himself used it a little later on in a passage, alluded to earlier, when

he said he wished to take advantage of the return (of his account) to Fly to recount some extraordinary events that took place there: "Sed quia ad Flaviacensem ecclesiam postliminium fecimus . . ." (But since we have returned to the church at Fly . . .). This return of the account to Fly thus evoked the account of the other return to Fly, the actual return, designated by the same word, *postliminium*, two years later than the events whose report was the cause of the first one. The latter detail is not unimportant from an author as sparing of chronological indications as Guibert.

The second question remains: Why did he wrongly believe, at the point when his account returned to Fly, that he had already mentioned his actual return? He had no reason to do so since, once again, the event took place two years after those that his account had reached at this point in his story. Actually, he would not have another opportunity to do it later on since, after the death of his mother, he abandoned the continuation of a systematic account of his life; in fact, he did not speak of it again. So why should he have spoken of it earlier? Let us recall the terms used by Guibert in the passage just quoted: "illud ad Flaviacenses postliminium, quod supra quidem meminimus," which Labande translates as "that return to Fly, which we have mentioned earlier." But *meminimus*, which, associated with *supra* in the present context, undoubtedly meant "we have mentioned," first of all means "we have remembered." Guibert claimed to have recalled these events to mind earlier. That he recalled them to his own mind is beyond doubt. They certainly could not fail to be present in his mind once his account led him to speak of Nogent and his election as abbot—and even much earlier. When he spoke of his youthful intellectual success, his ambition, the plans his mother and the rest of his family made for him, the many steps they took to obtain a living for him, could he forget the stain that was, at least momentarily, to tarnish the success of all those efforts? In his inner discourse, dominated by the maternal superego, the episode was constantly present. It surfaced in his writing when a metalinguistic metaphor put it there ("returning to Fly"), at the very moment when his mother's death, averting the threat of having to face her judgment, was inscribed in the text. Even then it was recalled *for the record*[23] and discharged, not later on in the text, where it would still be threatening, but earlier on, whence it was absent in reality but had never stopped weighing down on discourse as it weighed down on memory.

This misleading reference to the text's past, like the promise never expressed and yet recalled and kept at the beginning of the third book, namely, to speak of the tragedies at Laon, is a sign in Guibert's work of a project that does not coincide with the apparent logic of the text. We wonder how much his work qualifies as autobiography and why he began by recounting his life and then totally altered his point of view and basically stopped speaking about himself. But those two categories are ours, not his. It is we who distinguish between speaking *for* oneself and speaking *of* oneself. The term *monodiae*, chosen by Guibert, did not allow for such a distinction: it meant "to sing oneself alone," without defining "oneself" as either subject or object. Preoccupations, indignations, and personal anxieties appeared in the work, perhaps directly connected to the author's life through the account of the circumstances that gave rise to them, but at least as much through other events, certain of whose signs, like the trompe-l'oeil references we have spoken of, reveal that they concerned the author as intimately and affected him as deeply as those directly constituting the fabric of his daily life. Thus—for a man who placed his account under the invocation and view of God, his judge—from the perspective of confession and hope for pardon and salvation, the exempla in which the devil's craft, man's weakness, and God's severity and mercy were shown not only did not differ from the project of the *monodiae* but were of intense interest and affected his being in the profoundest way.

The proof is that at the very end of the work, when his childhood is far away and he has long since given up recounting the story of his life, he reappears as the hero of an exemplum in which, as a little boy and gravely ill, he benefited from a miraculous cure thanks to the intervention of Saint Léger, in whose church he had been left to spend the night. A quite noisy intervention, but it did not really frighten the little invalid, who was reassured by a lighted lamp, and the two clerics to whom his mother had entrusted him, who, awakened by the supernatural din, whispered nearby.[24] This manifestation of the deity would have been terrifying had it not had a familiar setting in the glow of the lamp, amid the muffled conversations of the clerics; a child's bed set up in a church belonging to his mother, surrounded by her solicitude, that of the clerics, and that of the saint; a sickly childhood given over to austere motherly affection and the protection of God and his servants: this is the final image Guibert leaves us of himself, and it is a revealing one. It would be hard not to see that this exemplum in the form of a childhood recollection justifies the presence of all the other exempla in the work, after which it finds a place and which, as we discover, had the same meaning in its author's eyes: recalling and domesticating the presence of the sovereign judge to whom he confessed and for whom he remembered and wrote.

Thus, Guibert makes no distinction between the discourse of confession and that of an involved witness to his times, for he felt that the latter, as much as autobiographical confession, revealed his consciousness, the obscure links between external events and his own passions, the attention that God paid him through the signs of the world—in a word, made the fibers of his inner self *sing* in *monodies* of himself alone. In the eyes of the divine interlocutor to his confession, as in his own, recounting what had affected his life was as revealing as recounting his life. That is why memoirs and autobiography were two paths to the same confession.

Guibert's work is the only one of its kind. It was not a success, since it is not preserved for us in even a single manuscript, only a seventeenth-century copy. However, its conception of the literary discourse of confession as incorporating both what we call autobiography and memoir sheds light on many a later work. If, at the beginning of the twelfth century, it seems to us to have been marked by the preoccupation with confession that followed Gregorian reform, we may assume that attention to confession was still greater a century later, following Innocent III's papacy, and even more following the Fourth Lateran Council. That period also saw an affirmation of be-

lief in individual judgment immediately following death, not await-
ing Christ's return and final judgment of all living and dead, as
Jacques Le Goff revealed in connection with the "birth of purgatory."
This belief gave new urgency to the retrospective, evaluative look
back over one's own life. Within this perspective we may resituate the
vogue for "vers de la mort" (poems of death), *congés* (farewells) and,
later, *testaments*—in general, the rise of poetry of a personal nature.

However, a tendency toward emotionalism had already appeared
in spiritual literature before the mid-twelfth century, particularly in
the works of Saint Bernard. Many of his writings were translated into
French and circulated from the end of the twelfth century, among
them his admirable sermons on the Song of Solomon, where this tendency is most notable and wherein occurs, in particular, the celebrated lament on the death of his brother Gerard. Bernard interrupts
himself in the midst of his exegetical statement to give vent to the
sorrow of this recent loss, the effort that he has made until then to
hide it having become intolerable. He says: "La dolors et la grevance
ke ge soffre commandet fin a faire" (The sorrow and torment that I
suffer demand to be heard). The funeral eulogy for Gerard that follows is interspersed with a confession of the sorrow that Bernard felt
and the tears he could not hold back, although his steadfast faith
should shield him from such weakness:

> Mais la dolor rapresseie s'aracinat devenz plus parfont et si
> devint, si com seu, en tant plus aigres en com bien ne li fu
> mie sofert ke il s'en eissist. Gel gehis, vencuz sui. Mestiers
> est ke fors eisset ce ke ge soffre devenz. . . . Eissez fors, eissez
> fors, les larmes qui lo deiserent ja de piece! . . . Soient
> aovertes les fenestres del chaitif chief! Si eissent fors les
> fontaines des aigues. . . . Et se moi dist l'om: "Nel sentir
> mie!" gel sen, gel sen, seveas non, dolens; car ma force n'est
> mie force de pieres, ne ma chars n'est mie d'arain. . . . Ge ai
> gehi mi amur enver lui, ne l'ai mi noïe. Alcuns l'apelerat
> carnal? Ge ne l'ai denoïe mie estre humaine, nient plus ke
> moi estre home. Et se ce n'est assez, nel denoie mie estre
> charnel, car ge suis charnez, mis desoz pechiet, aloiez a la

mort, sugez az poines et as dolurs. Ge ne suis mie telz ke ge ne sente paines: et de la moie mort et des miens ai ge paür.[25]

But repressed sorrow took root deeper within and, as I perceived, became all the more bitter for not being allowed to come out. I confess that I am overcome. What I am suffering inside must come forth. . . . Let the fountains of my poor head be opened! Let the water of the fountains come forth. . . . And though they say to me: "Do not weep!" my innards are wrenched forth from me. And though they say to me: "Do not be moved by that!" I am moved by it, in spite of myself I am moved, I suffer; for my strength is not that of stone and my flesh is not of bronze. . . . I have confessed my love for him, I have not denied it. Some will say it is of the flesh? I have not denied it was human any more than I have denied being a man. And if that is not enough, I do not deny it is of the flesh, for I am of the flesh, prone to sin, delivered up to death, subject to pain and sorrow. I am not such that I do not feel pain: of death, both mine and that of my kin, I am afraid.

As they have come down to us, the *Sermons on the Songs of Solomon* were never given and in no way reflected Saint Bernard's real preaching.[26] Writing in the silence of his study, therefore, he judged it better to interrupt the flow of one of his sermons to insert this secret, this confession, this indication of his own tears, this avowal of weakness, all the more striking for concealing his indulgence under a mask of self-restraint. Thus, it bears witness to the value granted to emotional display in spiritual edification and elevation.

This tendency toward subjective effusiveness was accentuated in the thirteenth century under the influence of a religious feeling peculiar to the mendicant orders. In addition to Saint Francis himself or Jacopone da Todi, in the vernacular languages we may cite the mystical writings of the Flemish Beguines, particularly the poetry of Hadewijch of Antwerp, and those of the Rhenish Dominicans, Eckhart, Tauler and, still more, Heinrich Suso. Later we shall return to the case of Ramon Llull, at once exemplary and marginal. In France we could cite Gautier de Coincy, whose subjective presence is very insistent in his *Miracles de Notre Dame*, and not just in the lyric pieces.[27] Moreover, signs of sustained interest in introspection can be seen everywhere, not only in such technical works as confessors' or penitents' handbooks but in devotional works and "spiritual methods"—even in romances, whenever they took on a religious tinge; the endless meditations and confessions of the characters in the *Quête du Graal* are proof of that. Finally, the consequences of this tendency in allegorical poetry have already been analyzed at length. We do not intend to return to that here, instead choosing to recall the favorable ground that what we may term "monodic narration"—following Guibert de Nogent's example and the observations his works have suggested—found in the thirteenth century. The expression "monodic narration," we may recall, embraces the modern concepts of autobiography and memoirs. Its use is necessitated by the fact that within the framework of the first-person account Guibert did not distinguish between the kind whose subject was also its object and the kind whose object was different from its subject but chosen and expressed as a function of the latter's experience, personality, and passions. For him it was enough that first-person narration, whatever its modes might be, refer to a latent image of the "I" whose revelation, explicit or implicit, was felt to be a confession.

One may therefore realize that the absence of autobiography in the modern sense from French literature of the thirteenth century—to which we finally return—does not signify an absence of this monodic narration but rather suggests we look for it within the memoir range of confession. The thirteenth century was the age of memoirs—if, as we have noted, the chronicles in French prose whose earliest examples marked the beginning of the century were really memoirs. The three terms designating historical works in the Middle Ages are annals, chronicles, and history. The distinction between history and chronicle comes from a model furnished by the *Ecclesiastical History* and *Chronicle* of Eusebius of Caesarea, works that all medieval historians knew in Latin translation:

> *History* favored narrative; the *Chronicle* favored chronology.
> *History* was "a fully complete narrative"; the *Chronicle* was a
> "précis" that summarized world history in chronological
> tableaus.[28]

Thus, history lent itself to literary and rhetorical amplification and
even reflection upon events, which was absent from chronicles. As for
annals, they were simple chronological catalogues in which the out-
standing events of each year were noted:

> Events were recorded in them as they became known; they
> were inscribed under the number of the year during which
> they became known. In sum annals, yearly notations, were
> the raw material of history, but could not be used by just
> anyone: they were not the work of a historian.[29]

The two other genres, however, were the work of historians capable of gathering documents and making use of them. Miniatures of
those times representing a historian at work always showed him
within easy reach of the numerous books he used in writing his own
work. This task of compilation obviously left no avowed place for the
author's subjectivity or personal point of view, and it was not related
by either form or object to the writing of memoirs. That was how
medieval Latin historiography represented itself.

But in its beginnings French historical literature did not transpose
this situation into the vernacular. In the twelfth century, in the
French and especially in the Anglo-Norman area, it was the new romance that claimed to write history in broad tableaux, from the *Roman de Troie* to Benoît de Sainte-Maure's *Chronique des ducs de Normandie*, from the *Brut* to Wace's *Rou*, from the *Histoire des Bretons* to
Gaimar's *Histoire des Anglais*. When we first made this statement, we
were attempting to grasp the point at which romance ceased to lay
claim to referential truth and recognized itself as fiction, claiming a
truth of meaning based on the romance writer's authority; that point
seemed to us to coincide with its penetration by the Breton matter.
But apart from the branch that established its headquarters in King

Arthur's court and so separated itself from history, if we follow romance to where it became history of the present, we see that it also granted a new place to the author and transformed him from compiler into witness.

The first landmark works reflecting this evolution were also Anglo-Norman, and they fitted the mold that vernacular literature offered them: Jordan Fantosme adopted epic alexandrine *laisses* for his chronicle of the Anglo-Scottish war of 1173–74, and Ambrose of Normandy used romance's octosyllabic couplets for his *Histoire de la guerre sainte*, which dealt with the Third Crusade.[30] The first, a learned clerk and pupil of Gilbert de La Porrée, applied a degree of moral reflection and judgment—as it happened, rather ill-adapted to the rigidity of the form he chose—to the current events that he was relating in order to justify his side's cause, thereby showing his partisanship. The second, probably a jongleur in the service of Richard the Lion-Hearted, recounted only what he had seen, without ever introducing, designating, or explicitly representing himself except in a long, literary-style introduction devoted to reflections on the work's determinants and definition. He saw a good deal, being present at several royal meetings, but he did not breathe a word about Richard's doings and actions when he was not by his side, thus omitting important episodes. This account to the English king's glory therefore did not really focus on his person. Its sole principle of composition was restriction to the narrator's viewpoint. Nevertheless, Jordan and Ambrose were professional literary men who were writing, if not directly to order, at least because it was their trade. They were not immediately involved in their account, save as witnesses and partisans. Their project was not the fruit of any personal urgency but rather formed part of a series of dynastic romance-histories. Was it merely by chance that this genre, which later evolved into the *Histoire de Guillaume de Maréchal* and family romances with historical underpinnings like *Gui de Warewic* or *Fouke Fitz Warin*, seems to have been a specialty of Anglo-Norman literature? Would it be absurd to seek the trace of Nordic sagas here and detect the signs of the dual Scandinavian influence that so deeply influenced the literary beginnings of Saxon England and must have survived among Rollo's descendants? Family romance was to remain a specialty of English literature into the Victorian era.

But to return to French historical literature at the turn of the thirteenth century, the great new departure of that period in this area was the appearance of prose works whose authors would never have gotten involved in writing had they not felt a need to recount events they had participated in. Neither the Picardy knight Robert de Clari nor the marshal of Champagne Geoffroy de Villehardouin, nor, at the end of the century, seneschal Jean de Joinville could be defined as men of letters. It was a different case with Philip of Novara, who, apart from his *Memoirs*, wrote several works, including poems, of which he gave a list at the end of his moral treatise *Des quatre âges de l'homme* (On the Four Ages of Man); but he remained, above all, a jurist—"le meilleur pledeour deça mer" (the best lawyer on this side of the sea), according to his contemporary Hugh of Brienne—and a chancery, not a literary, man.[31]

These authors' use of prose certainly seems not to have been an easy way out, since the rules of prose are no easier than those of poetry, but rather a deliberate mark of their testimony's nonprofessionalism and starkness. The humble Robert de Clari insists on these two points in the closing lines of his work:

> Ore avés oï le verité, confaitement Coustantinoble fu conquise . . . que chis qui i fu et qui le vit et qui l'oï le tesmongne, Robers de Clari, li chevaliers, et a fait metre en escrit le verité, si come ele fu conquise; et ja soit chou que il ne l'ait si belement contee le conqueste, comme maint boin diteeur l'eussent contee, si en a il toutes eures le droite verité contee et assés de verités en a teutes qu'il ne peut mie toutes ramembrer.[32]

> You have heard the truth about the conquest of Constantinople . . . for the knight Robert de Clari, who was there, who saw and heard what went on, bears witness to it; he had the conditions of its conquest set down in writing in a truthful fashion. And although he has not related this

conquest as elegantly as many a clever storyteller might, in
any case he has told nothing but the truth, and there are
many things he has left unsaid because he could not relate
everything.

Robert emphasizes both his clumsiness as a *diteeur* (storyteller)
and the fact that he has experienced everything he has recounted and
it is true. But there is more. His last phrase—"et assés de verités en a
teutes qu'il ne peut mie toutes ramembrer" (and there are many
things he left unsaid because he could not relate everything)—was
imitating a model, only modestly attenuating its scale: the last sentence of the Gospel of Saint John:

> Sunt autem et alia multa, quae fecit Iesus: quae si scribantur
> per singula, nec ipsum arbitror mundum capere posse eos,
> qui scribendi sunt, libros.[33]

> And there are also many other things which Jesus did, the
> which, if they should be written every one, I suppose that
> even the world itself could not contain the books that
> should be written.

Robert de Clari was obviously not claiming comparison with
Saint John. If the Evangelist came to mind as he dictated his last sentence, it was because he associated imperfection of writing with truth
of testimony. In his view, prose was humble and true. He was convinced that its effectiveness was not based on effects of language. It
was the mode of expression of divine truth and the only true history:
biblical history. The idea that prose was opposed to literary ornamentation and it alone was suited to expression of the naked truth
was common in the Middle Ages. We also find it developed in the
manuscript containing Robert de Clari's chronicle, written down by
a certain Jean de Flixecourt as a prologue to his prose translation of
the *De excidio Trojae* (On the Destruction of Troy) by the Pseudo-
Dares.[34] For Robert de Clari, who implied it clearly, and for the other
memorialists of his time, prose was both a guarantor of referential
truth and a warning that its user made no claim to be a man of letters.

This status of prose is contrastingly confirmed in the verse pieces included in Philip of Novara's memoirs. Philip repeatedly quotes occasional poems he composed at the time of the events he was recounting and took part in. A refugee, after narrowly escaping from his enemies in the Hospitalers' monastery at Nicosia, where he was besieged along with women and children, he sent a long verse letter to Balian of Ibelin, the son of his suzerain the lord of Beirut, to ask for aid (IV). After the battle of Nicosia, which saw John of Ibelin's victory over the five bailiffs of Cyprus, he composed a satirical song, a *sirventois*, to celebrate the event (LXIII). Wounded at the siege of the castle of Dieudamour (Saint-Hilarion), he denied the rumor of his death circulating among the besieged by composing a song that very evening in which he compared his enemy Aimery Barlais to Reynard,[35] as he did in the letter to Balian, and the besieged castle to Maupertuis, which he called Maucreux (LXVII). At the siege of El-Kantara, after overhearing a conversation between some of the castle's defenders while on watch one night, he wrote a song about it based on the model of a "chanson d'aube" (LXIX). During the peace negotiations that followed, he wrote a new "branch" of *Reynard* (216 lines long) in which his enemies were represented by Reynard and his followers, while John of Ibelin, oddly enough, was designated as Isengrim and Philip himself was Chantecler the cock (LXXIII). Further on he repeated that he had composed a song against the Lombard garrison stationed in Beirut by Frederick II but gave only its first three lines (XCVIII). Each time the poem was a kind of personal commentary and rhetorical amplification of the prose, but it never replaced it in terms of recounting events. In that domain the poem was not sufficient unto itself even when it repeated the account in its own way, like the "branch" of *Reynard*, or when it was meant to exercise an informational function concerning those events, like his letter to Balian. Understanding of it required the preliminary account in prose and explanations concerning the rules governing the transposition of events into poetic language. Here, for example, is how the letter to Balian of Ibelin is introduced:

> Phelippe de Nevaire vost faire assaver cest fait tout pre-
> mierement a monseignor Balian d'Ybelin, son conpere, et
> puys qu'il ot comencié a escrire les letres, il prist talant de
> faire les en rime. Et por ce que sire Heimery Barlais estoit
> plus malvais que tous les autres, il le vorra contrefaire a Re-
> nart, et por ce que, au romans de Renart, Grimbert, le tais-
> son, est son cousin germain, il apela messire Amaury de Bet-
> san Grinbert, et por ce que sire Hue de Giblet avoit la
> bouche torte, et il faisoit semblant que il feïst tous jors la
> moe, Phelippe l'apela singe.[36]

> Philip of Novara wanted first of all to inform his comrade,
> my Lord Balian of Ibelin, of the events, and when he had
> begun to write the letter, he decided to put it in verse. And
> since Lord Aimery Barlais was nastier than all the others,
> he decided to make him Reynard, and since in the *Roman
> de Renart* Grimbert, the badger, is his first cousin, he called
> Lord Amaury de Bethsan Grimbert, and since Lord
> Hugues de Gibelet had a twisted mouth and always looked
> as if he was making faces, Philip called him a monkey.

Thus, we can see that it was the idea of writing the letter in verse that led to disguising as characters in the *Roman de Renart* those individuals whose intrigues it denounced. Its overshadowing of the signified and its transposition according to a code of interpretation analogous to that of allegory, as well as its recourse to the play of literary intertextuality through the use of the *Roman de Renart*, were felt to be specific to verse writing and necessary to that kind of writing as opposed to the direct statement of fact characterizing prose. It is thus true that the latter was confusedly perceived as avoiding literariness, exempt from the distance marking literary discourse associated with verse and, by the same token, *truer* than it, with regard to the signified.

In choosing prose, thirteenth-century memorialist chroniclers were showing that they made no real claim to be writing literary works. How, then, did they look upon their works? These deserve the title of chronicles traditionally given them because they were all chronological accounts of historically important public events. But the common point that distinguished them from other chronicles was that their author not only had been a direct witness to the events he was relating but took part and often played an important role in them. The account he gave of them could therefore be an expression of his passions or even deliberately take the form of a personal apologia.

The latter case is strikingly illustrated by Villehardouin. He was included in all the important decisions made by the leaders of the Fourth Crusade and bore a significant share of the responsibility for diverting it toward Constantinople. It was he who had negotiated with the doge of Venice for construction of the fleet to transport the crusaders to the Holy Land. But he had gone overboard, so to speak, and because the crusaders, who were too few in number, could not raise the sum demanded for all these ships, they had to agree to repay their debt in the form of favors—by taking Zara for the Venetians, thus incurring excommunication for attacking a Christian city. This was the beginning of a series of events leading them to Constantinople under the combined effects of chance, financial need, politics, and the personal interest of the princes, in which Villehardouin never ceased to be involved. As Jean Dufournet has shown,[37] his spare, limpid account, apparently neutral and devoid of emotion, made a show of objectivity and detachment only in order to render the extremely clever *pro domo* plea—its real aim—more effective. Similarly, seeming to distribute praise and blame with utter impartiality, he had a marvelous ability to denigrate some men without seeming to, indeed, pretending to praise them, and to highlight others. He never expressed his preferences openly and seemed not even to possess feelings or emotions. He did not write a single word that was not necessary to the organization of his account, did not devote one sentence to descriptions, and, unlike Robert de Clari, did not gape at the wonders of Constantinople. In a scant few lines he noted the imposing sight of the immense fleet sailing up the Bosphorus. Not only does he speak of himself in the third person, as all did up to Joinville, but he does it only when he played a specific part in the course of events; and even then he does not name "Geoffroy de Villehardouin, the Marshal of Champagne"—or, later, when he received his new title "the Marshal of Romania and Champagne"—either first, out of concern for his own person, or last, as in modern usage's affectation of modesty, but in the midst of others, at his precise place in the hierarchy. And yet his entire work is nothing but a settling of scores and a monument to his own image. This model of laconic coldness was in reality a passion fruit.

The other chronicler of the Fourth Crusade, Robert de Clari, obviously did not have the same preoccupations. A poor knight, the lord of a six-hectare fief near Amiens, he was swept up in the tide of events without shaping them, without any voice in matters, not sharing in the decisions of the great, not always even having been informed. Aside from his conclusion, quoted earlier, he names himself only once, and then not as author or with reference to his text but as the brother of cleric Aleaume de Clari, one of whose deeds he relates:

> S'avoit illuec un chevalier, un sien freres, Robers de Clari avoit a non.[38]

> There was a knight there who was his brother, his name was Robert de Clari.

However, we must seek the motivation for his account in the intensity of his personal feelings. First, in the wonderment of memory upon his return from the voyage: Robert de Clari, unlike Villehardouin, was sensitive to *mirabilia*; prone to astonishment if not credulity; rather attentive, at a time when people tended not to be, to what would later be called the picturesque; capable of concrete observations. But, above all, he keeps repeating his feelings of admiration and rancor. Admiration for his suzerain, Pierre d'Amiens, "the fine and brave," as he is forever calling him; for that extraordinary warrior Pierre de Bracieux; for his brother Aleaume. Rancor toward the leaders and great names of the expedition, the "rich men" concerned solely with their personal interest, insensitive to the sufferings of the common soldiers fighting for them, greedy and underhanded, who reserved for themselves the best lodgings in Constantinople despite the orders they received, and who, far from dividing the immense spoils equitably, stole the greater part of them even though

they had been entrusted with their safekeeping. In stating his griev-
ances, Robert never places himself in his own account, having his
brother represent him instead, as he represents himself only in relation to his brother. It was Aleaume who, through his rash bravery,
permitted the capture of the tower of Galatha, the main defense
structure of Constantinople; it was he who complained bitterly of being excluded from the division of the spoils on the pretext that he was
a cleric and not a knight, and who, by maintaining that he fought
better than many a knight, ended up obtaining justice. Aleaume was
the incarnation in the text of Robert's passions, his spokesman—almost his avenger. This account, from which he is virtually absent and
concerning events that were beyond him in every respect, has as its
raison d'être the subjective repercussions that they had on his emotional makeup, in an account analogous to that of the "tragedies of
Laon" in Guibert's *monodies.*

But the comparison with Guibert de Nogent is even more perti-
nent and illuminating in the case of Philip of Novara. What we call
Philip of Novara's "Memoirs" are in reality a fragment preserved for
us because it was included in a vast historical compilation known under the title of *Gestes des Chiprois* (Deeds of the Cypriots), probably
composed by Gérard de Montréal around 1320. This fragment is devoted to an account of the disturbances in Cyprus marking the mi-
nority of King Henry the First of Lusignan, called "Henry the Fat,"
and the war in which Philip fought beside the lords of Beirut, John
the First and Balian III of Ibelin, against Emperor Frederick II. It
covers the years 1218 to 1243. This was part of a much larger whole—
now lost—whose contents, however, are indicated by Philip of Novara at the end of the treatise *Des quatre âges de l'homme,* which he
wrote in his latter days. Here is what he tells us:

> Phelipes de Navarre, qui fist cest livre, en fist autres .II. Le
> premier fist de lui meesmes une partie, car la est dit dont il
> fu, et comment et por quoi il vint deça la mer, et commant
> il se contint et maintint longuement par la grace Nostre
> Seignor. Aprés i a rimes et chançons plusors, que il
> meïesmes fist, les unes des granz folies dou siecle que l'an

apele amors; et assez en i a qu'il fist d'une grant guerre qu'il
vit en son tens antre l'ampereor Fredri et le seignor de
Barut, mon seignor Jehan de Belin le viel. Et .I. mout biau
compe i a il de cele guerre meïsmes dés le commancement
jusques a la fin, ou que il sont devisé li dit et li fait et li grant
consoil des batailles et des sieges atiriez ordeneement; car
Phelipes fu a touz. Aprés i a chançons et rimes qu'il fist plu-
sors en sa viellesce de Nostre Seignor et de Nostre Dame et
des sains et des saintes. Celui livre fist il por ce que ces tro-
veüres, et li fait qui furent ou païs a son tens, et les granz
valors des bons seignors fussent et demorassent plus longuement en remembrance a cels qui sont descendu de lui et des
autres amis, et a touz ces qui les vorront oïr.[39]

Philip of Novara, who wrote this book, wrote two others.
He wrote the first in part about himself, for it is written
there whence he came, how and why he came to this side
of the sea, and how he lived for a long time, by the grace
of Our Lord. Afterward there are numerous poems and
songs that he himself wrote, some about that great worldly
folly called love, and many others about a great war that he
saw in his time between emperor Frederick and the lord of
Beirut, my lord John of Ibelin the Elder. And there is a
very fine account of the war itself, from beginning to end,
in which the words, deeds, battles, and sieges are recounted in order; for Philip was present at all of them.
Then there are songs and poems he wrote in great number
in his old age, about Our Lord, Our Lady, and male and
female saints. He wrote this book so that these poetic
works, the events that took place in this country in his
time, and the feats of the valiant lords might longer remain
in the memory of his descendants, his friends, and all
those who will listen to them.

Then Philip described his second book, a juridical work that has
come down to us, the *Livre en forme de plait* (Book in the Form of a
Legal Argument).

Thus, the first book written by Philip of Novara was composed of
an autobiography and "war memoirs" mingled with verse pieces.

What could the unifying principle of such a work have been, in the eyes of its author, except what Guibert de Nogent designated under the name *monodies*? It was a work characterized by the subjectivity of its point of view, displayed through the variations in form and object of its discourse. This object was Philip himself in the autobiographical part, of which he was both the subject and the object, or of which he was the subject in both meanings of the term; it was himself and others, or deeds and men in regard to himself, in the part constituted by memoirs that has come down to us; in the verse pieces it was necessarily either the abstraction of the self characteristic of the courtly lyric or the concrete fiction of the self represented by the new thirteenth-century poetry. Finally, a personal relationship to the author was supposed even among the book's addressees, since they were above all his descendants and friends. In his first book the future author of the *Quatre âges de l'homme* thus retraced not only the events but the movement and the ages of his lifetime through the diversity of perspectives and modes of writing. The formative years, whose account is focused on his own person and the circumstances that shaped his personality; the years of action and passion, when that personality confronted the surrounding world, in which it played a political and military role recalled in the memoirs, and whose allure he experienced, as expressed in the poems; the years of old age, marked by conversion and religious preoccupations, which are echoed in poems quite different from the earlier ones. With remarkable determination and persistence the author sets his own life at the heart of his enterprise. This life gives unity to a *book* that seems disparate only because its stages and turning points determine and are reflected in the varieties of writing. Its duration defines the time of the account; the passions that wracked it bestow order on its material.

Is it not evident that we find developed in this book, amplified but mostly clarified by the author himself, the same structure as in Guibert de Nogent's work, which was so disconcerting because we were looking at it in isolation? Like Philip, Guibert successively wrote autobiography and memoirs; both related their formative years and then the events in which they were involved as adults. One inserted the love poems of his youth in his book, the other mentioned them. As we have shown, far from disrupting the autobiographical part of his work, as it first appears, the account by Guibert of the "tragedies of Laon" extends it along other paths in accordance with the underlying coherence of his obsessions and passions, whose psychological fullness is at times revealed by an illusion of textual recurrence. The same demonstration cannot be made concerning Philip of Novara since the first part of his book is lost and we have only his memoirs. But he is more present in them than any of the authors we have discussed till now. He is present, first of all, because he played a key role in the events he relates, of which he was a central actor rather than a witness. He is also present because his account follows him step by step in his activities and travels, only rarely transporting the reader to a place where he is not present, and almost constantly represents him: he names himself frequently and often finds room for both his speeches and his doings. Most of all, his emotional presence is quite strong. He gives lively expression to his hatreds and preferences, not pretending to be objective, like Villehardouin or even Clari, not hiding the fact that these are his personal opinions. Look at the indulgence with which he includes his poems, partisan commentaries on events with which he observes the image that others reflect back at him and he owes to his poems. Thus, he describes the reception given by Balian and his entourage in the verse letter, written, we may recall, when he was besieged in the hospital at Nicosia, where the women and children of the supporters of the Ibelins had taken refuge:

> Ceste rime fut receüe a Acre a mout grant joie, et tous crierent: "Or tost a la rescouse des dames et dou Lombart!"[40]

> This poem was received with great joy in Acre, and they all shouted: "Quickly now, to the rescue of the ladies and the Lombard!"

The Lombard, of course, is Philip himself, who came from Novara in Lombardy. Similarly, when he is wounded at the siege of Dieudamour, his enemies shout: "Mort est vostre chanteor, tué est!" (Your singer is dead, he has been slain!). His account, though a dramatic one, is thus infused with a kind of hearty elation. He was also capable of suggesting, as Joinville so admirably did somewhat later, the affection that he felt for someone through a tiny, concrete notation, insignificant in itself but revealing, through the keenness of the memory, the depth of feeling sustaining it. Take, for example, the moment when he shows John of Ibelin, the old lord of Beirut, whom he obviously loved and deeply respected, assuming a stance habitual with him as he courageously and ably pleads his case before the young king of Cyprus and his court:

> La cour estoit si pleniere que tous i estoient, amis et enemis. Il se leva en estant, et il avoit une coustume, que il cruisoit ses jambes quant il demoroit en estant; il le fist ensi com il sot bien, et parla moult haut et a trait.[41]

> The entire court was assembled and so everyone was there, his friends and his enemies. He stood up straight, and he was in the habit of crossing his legs when he stood; he did so, as he knew well, and spoke in a strong, steady voice.

In this well-adjusted man there are none of those obscure torments, as in Guibert, that call for and shy away from confession. At the heart of his work there is a constant admission of what he loves and hates, what constitutes his life, as well as the admission of that admission: an admission that he is speaking of what has interested, marked, and stirred him and that he is discussing it for that very reason. He owns up to looking first at his own life and everything else after that.

Two final lessons can be drawn from Philip of Novara's summary of his book, quoted earlier. The first is precisely that nothing remains of the book save its summary and the part included in the *Gestes des Chiprois*. We do not know what Philip's descendants and friends thought of it, but they do not seem to have appreciated it in the spirit in which it was composed. Philip's monodies, his autobiography, and the subjectivity of his view held no interest in themselves. The only part that was recopied deals with historical events, since it was used as a historical document. The very fact that Gérard de Montréal included it unaltered in his compilation proves he was completely indifferent to its specific mode of writing, the voice heard in it, and the particular nature of its point of view, since he was not shocked by the break in tone and perspective from what came before and after in his own work. Perhaps he was aware of all this, and that was precisely why he copied the text so faithfully, following the taste for anthological collage so common in the Middle Ages. The fact remains that the original procedure characterizing Guibert's work and then Philip's, almost a century and a half later, was little appreciated in their time, since in one case there remains only a single copy and in the other only a fragment.

Nevertheless we may ponder the exact place that poetry occupied in Philip of Novara's book, beginning with its physical place. Reading the description that he gave of his book, we first understand that the verse pieces on love or politics were distributed between the autobiographical part and the account of the war between Frederick II and the Ibelins. But, as we have seen, that account was itself full of political poems. Are they only the ones Philip was alluding to, and are we to believe that his autobiography was strewn with love songs, just as his memoirs were with polemical pieces? It does seem, despite everything, that a special section was devoted to them, between the autobiography and the memoirs, and another one after the latter. Philip wrote: "Aprés i a rimes et chançons." (Afterward there are poems and songs.) The insertion of poems between the prose sections as well as within them was symptomatic of the distribution between verse and prose established at that time. On the one hand, they confirm observations made earlier: prose was perceived as having a lesser degree of literariness than verse by reason of its very "truth." It told the truth about the subject and the world, allowing us to recognize it when transposed and disguised in poetic language. On the other hand—and this is a consequence or, rather, a corollary of the latter—Philip combined verse and prose at about the same time (often in northern Italy, where he came from) and in a way analogous to the songbooks that introduced troubadour songs with *vidas* and *razos*. The explanations that he gave before quoting his poems, which allow us to understand them, played the role of *razos* and, indeed, adopted their tone and style. Thus, Philip showed the same reaction with respect to himself that the authors of the *vidas* and *razos* exhibited with respect to the troubadours upon whose songs they commented: dissatisfaction with the limited and ambiguous revelation of the self—what self?—in the poem; a need to root the self in time, in the course and circumstances of a life; the conviction that a prose account was the kind of discourse best suited to carrying out this "relay" function. From the perspective of monodic discourse, the poem, a witness to the moment, an occasional work, had a place—Guibert mentioned his, Philip quoted his own—but in its place, located in the time of life, embedded in writing that accounted for it.

In its fragmented complexity Philip of Novara's book is focused entirely on its author's life. Nonetheless, he never speaks of himself except in the third person. Joinville's book, on the contrary, had history and the praise of Saint Louis as its object. The plan he announced, even if its logic is not ours, was a logical one, conceived with the following aim:

> Chier sire, je vous foiz a savoir que madame la royne vostre mere, qui moult m'amoit . . . , me pria si a certes comme elle pot, que je li feisse faire un livre des saintes paroles et des bons faiz nostre roy saint Looys; et je li oi en couvenant, et a l'aide de Dieu le livre est assouvi en deux parties. La premiere partie si devise comment il se gouverna tout son tens selonc Dieu et selonc l'Eglise, et au profit de son regne. La seconde partie du livre si parle de ses granz chevaleries et de ses granz faiz d'armes.[42]

> My dear sire, I inform you that Madame the Queen, your mother, who greatly loved me . . . , asked me as insistently as she could to have a book written about the holy words and good deeds of our king Saint Louis; I promised her to do so and with God's help the book has been finished, in two parts. The first part recounts how he governed himself all his life according to God and the Church and to the benefit of his kingdom. The second part of the book talks of his great chivalric deeds and great feats of arms.

Joinville could not help observing, from his very first words, that the queen mother loved him greatly; he draws attention to himself throughout his book in a way never previously encountered with a French-language author, just as he was the first one writing in French to speak of himself in the first person. Thus, many pages of his book—more markedly than any other text of the Middle Ages—offer the characteristics of autobiography, although the work seems unrelated to autobiographical form. Or, rather, it oscillates constantly and increasingly between the lives of Saint Louis and Joinville. Therefore we may say that the succession of autobiography and memoirs characterizing Guibert's monodies, like Philip of Novara's, is here replaced by an interweaving of the two forms, whereas the explicit plan of the work was related to neither of them but rather to a hagiographical model. This model, used by Valerius for the account of his life, provided an opportunity for Joinville to gravitate toward an account of his own, starting from that of another man. Guibert de Nogent and Philip of Novara went from a discourse of the self on the self to a discourse of the self on something that was not the self but was chosen because of its effect on the self or the revelatory function it played in relationship to it, which therefore extended—beneath the surface, as with Guibert, or implicitly, as with Philip, but still indirectly—the confession of the self. Joinville combined autobiographical testimony, the self's retrospective view of the holy king, and the self's retrospective view of itself.

Did this symmetrical procedure, contrary to that of the two preceding authors, have the same basis? Should we seek as strict and close a link between Joinville's discourse on Saint Louis and on himself as between Guibert's discourse on himself and on the "tragedies of Laon"? Yes, of course; the link is particularly clear in his case: Joinville loved Saint Louis. If Philip of Novara wrote his account of the war in Cyprus out of attachment to the Ibelins and, in particular, fidelity to the memory of the "old lord of Beirut," that motivation was more striking still in the case of the old seneschal. The years spent in close contact with Saint Louis had so marked—indeed, so molded—Joinville that when he relived them through writing in his old age not only could he not speak of the king, nor of himself as well, but he could not portray the king without portraying himself at the same time. Michèle Perret, who calculated that Joinville appears in 73 percent of the paragraphs into which modern editors have divided his text,[43] showed that he so favored the relationship between the king and himself, and set himself at the center of his account with such vigor, that it was sometimes clouded as a result: one no longer knows whether he really was present at such and such an event or what his precise mode of inclusion was in a "we" involving the king or situated in relation to him. Most of all, Joinville showed the object of his account, which in principle was external to him, as being in reality close to him, putting his own self into play with remarkable force and insistence, exhibiting a skill beyond comparison with Guibert de Nogent's false recurrences or Philip of Novara's emotive commentary in poetic form.

He succeeded in doing so by playing on shifts of emotion in his writing so as to weave a tight network of affective signs between the king and himself for the reader.[44] On the one hand, at a time when it was natural and even proper to weep in public, to show one's grief or one's sympathy toward another's grief, Joinville puts on a show of modesty about tears, both his own and the king's, yet by the same token makes them more affecting by giving the reader the impression that he detects or suspects them. Thus, when he has left his castle at Joinville en route to the crusade:

> Et endementieres que je aloi a Blehecourt et a Saint-Urbain, je ne voz onques retourner mes yex vers Joinville, pour ce que le cuer ne me attendrisist du biau chastel que je lessoie et de mes deux enfans.[45]

> And as I was going to Blécourt and Saint-Urbain, I made sure never to turn my eyes back toward Joinville, lest my heart be moved by the beautiful castle I was leaving and my two children.

The effect of paralipsis used by Joinville here gives evidence of the discovery that words can express something other than what they say, that negation can be as good as affirmation, that silence is eloquent in communicating emotion to the reader. This procedure, however, was not much practiced before him in vernacular literature, and although referred to by Martianus Capella, it was not precisely categorized in the *Artes dicendi*. Strictly speaking, Joinville is not using paralipsis as a stylistic figure. He draws attention to his emotion not by saying that he will not speak of it but by saying how he managed not to be overwhelmed by it and thereby not to show it. Paralipsis is not in the turn of phrase but in Joinville's attitude as the sentence describes it, seemingly unnecessarily, since in fact he did nothing: he did not turn around. The negation bears not on the project of telling but on what is told; among all the possible actions that could have been accomplished by the character who did nothing, it chose—if only to negate it—the one that would have led him to show his emotion, the expression of fear, "pour ce que le cuer ne me attendrisist" (lest my heart be moved), prolonging the nonaction with its nonconsequence.

Thus, by saying he did not wish to show emotion in spite of himself upon departing for the crusade, Joinville lets his reader think that he is revealing it despite himself in writing the book: the reader, thinking he detects an intimacy that modesty has striven to hide from him, is moved by it.

Later on Joinville uses a similar procedure when he shows the king shedding tears despite himself that belie the serenity of his words. On the evening of an unfortunate though apparently victorious day— when the Christians, after crossing the Nile, unwisely pursued the Saracens too far from their bases, and the king's brother, the count of Artois, lost his life, a victim of his own rashness—Joinville rejoins the king and rides by his side after defending a little bridge against the Saracens with the aid of two knights:

> Endementires que nous venions, je li fis oster son hyaume et li baillé mon chapel de fer pour avoir le vent. Et lors vint frere Henri de Ronnay, prevost de l'Ospital, a li, qui avait passé la riviere, et li besa la main toute armee. Et il li demanda se il savoit nulles nouvelles du conte d'Artois, son

frere; et il li dit que il en savoit bien nouvelles, car estoit
certein que son frere le conte d'Artois estoit en paradis: "Hé!
sire, vous en ayés bon reconfort, car si grant honneur n'avint
onques a roy de France comme il vous est avenu; car pour
combattre a vos ennemis avez passé une riviere a nou, et les
avez desconfiz et chaciez du champ, et gaaingnés leur engins
et leur heberges, la ou vous gerrés encore ennuit." Et le roy
respondi que Dieu en feust aouré de ce que il li donnoit; et
lors li cheoient les lermes des yex moult grosses.[46]

Along the way, I had him take off his helmet and I gave
him my steel cap so he might get the breeze. And then
there came to him brother Henri de Ronnay, the provost
of the Hospital, who had crossed the river, and he kissed
his armored hand. And the king asked him if he had any
news about his brother, the count of Artois; and he told
him that he indeed had news, for he was certain that his
brother, the count of Artois, was in paradise: "Ha! sire, you
may take great consolation from the fact that no honor as
great as the one that has come to you has ever come to a
king of France: for to fight your enemies you have swum
across a river, you have defeated them and driven them
from the field of battle, you have taken their machines and
their tents: you will sleep in them tonight." And the king
replied that God should be adored for the gifts He gave
him; and very great tears then fell from his eyes.

The last sentence could possibly mean that the king was crying
out of gratitude for God's blessings, for which he thanked Him, since
there has been no question of the count of Artois's death for several
lines and the words of the provost of the Hospital concern only the
victory over the Saracens. Thus, Joinville leaves the formal possibility
of an exemplary, official version of his anecdote. But it seems clear
from his text that in reality the king, at the very moment he declared
that God should be adored for his blessings, could not help weeping
for his brother. If he were shedding pious tears, he would do it willingly. On the contrary, tears fall from his eyes, which shows that they
have already welled up in them, and the mere fact of speaking, as the
adverb *lors* (then) indicates, has made them fall in spite of himself.

Even the insistence on the size of the tears, shifting the adjective *moult grosses* (very great) to the end of the sentence with which the exposition ends, has meaning only if those tears are caused by grief. The pious Joinville thus reveals weakness in the king by showing him shedding tears caused not by spiritual meditation but earthly attachment. He was perhaps encouraged in this by the example of Saint Bernard weeping over the death of his brother and admitting his weakness in the passage quoted earlier. It was perhaps also the same rhetoric Saint Bernard had used—his lengthy, simultaneously overflowing and tightly argued lamentations—that permitted Joinville, a century and a half later, to say everything in a few words, to use compression and silence, to settle for juxtaposing without commentary indirect recollection of the brief words pronounced by the king and the sight of the uncontrollable tears that seem to belie them and give them deeper meaning: "Et le roy respondi que Dieu en fust aouré de ce que il li donnoit; et lors li cheoient les lermes des yex moult grosses." (And the king replied that God should be adored for the gifts He gave him; and very great tears then fell from his eyes.) This brief sentence implies Saint Bernard's lengthy analysis, thanks to which Joinville could avoid emotional outbursts and argumentation and use affective devices with an identical theme.

The king's tears were silent. To see him weep one had to be right next to him and observe him like Joinville. Thus, the reader did not need to be moved by a plangent avowal that a strong, God-fearing man made of his weakness since there was no avowal. He had to be moved by grasping the only brief moment of weakness of a man who did not want to let his sorrow show through. The entire passage is organized in this way, not only to give an impression of discretion and terseness but to make the reader believe his own insight has let him seize the importance of a detail that the text mentions seemingly in passing, almost at random, without realizing its importance. This detail moves him all the more because he is secretly flattered at having picked it up. For not only does Joinville not dwell on the king's tears, but immediately after mentioning them he moves on, without transition, to an unimportant, almost silly incident.

And yet Joinville, who was the only one to recall these tears of the king and perhaps the only one to see them, was careful to emphasize a few lines earlier that it was his concern for the king that prevented the latter from hiding them. Had he wept inside his helmet, no one would have known a thing. But Joinville, meeting him at sundown, had him take off his helmet and instead gave him his own steel cap so he would be protected and still get some air. The text thus seems to mention these tears with as much reluctance as the king shed them, making them moving in a way different from other literary tears of that period. At the same time, Joinville does not let us forget that he has revealed them twice: by his writing, in terms suited to the manner in which they flowed, but also, at that very moment, by this gesture of kindness toward a king he loved.

Joinville loved the king. Throughout the book this attachment is meant to elicit tears; a reader's tears, the tears of the old, disconsolate seneschal, writing long after the death of this king, who was just old enough that, with his greater age added to his higher rank, Joinville could move without difficulty into the role of a blindly, boundlessly devoted *famulus* (servant) without the age difference preventing moments of brotherly complicity from gratifying his desires, leaving him with the undying taste of the most precious of rewards. It is memory of these moments that moved him later on.

The mixture of insistence and coyness that he twice used to move the reader—by suggesting an opposition between the intensity of the restrained emotion that he himself or the king felt and the discreetness of these displays and, apparently if not actually, of his expression—shows that he grasped a commonplace yet important literary process. He understood that it is impossible to move the reader with the same emotion that is supposed to have moved the author or his characters by telling or showing its effects, and that the reader can be be moved only by awakening within him an emotion that is his own and quite obviously does not have the same source as that attributed to either the narrator or his characters, since the reader, seated by his fire, is in a situation totally different from theirs. The reader is moved, for example, by the contrast between the praise of God uttered by the king and the tears he could not restrain, which Joinville detected and pointed out so discreetly, and not by the death of the count of Artois, which moved the king but in itself could only leave the reader cold.

By showing himself capable of playing on displacements of emotion, Joinville makes one suspect that the image he gave of the king, the fruit of his own emotion, referred back to his own image, and that his entire text functioned in the same way as the numerous passages in which the king's personality was explicitly revealed at the same time as his own through familiar conversations between the two men that shed light on both of them. A good example is the one in which Joinville admitted that he would rather have committed thirty mortal sins than be a leper, or the reproaches the king directed at him upon seeing him drink his wine straight. Each time Joinville's image is shaped at the same time as the king's, because the latter is perceived through Joinville's subjective, deeply emotive outlook. This procedure, natural and explicit when the text reproduces a conversation between the two men, may be noted in many other contexts. For example, it appears in Joinville's close attention to fabrics and garments and the frequent mention he makes of them. Noting the garment worn by the king in such and such a circumstance was a way of making his image more alive and present by permitting us to visualize it. It was also a way to complete the saint's portrait by showing that he dressed as simply as possible, but always in conformity with his rank, and recalling his teachings on the subject of clothing.[47] Most of all, it was a way to bring out the keenness and precision of the narrator's memories after so many years, signs of the emotional interest they held for him. Philip of Novara, recollecting a stance habitual to John of Ibelin, similarly gave testimony of his attachment to him. Why should Joinville have noted that at the plenary court session in Saumur in 1241 the king "had on his head a cotton hat that ill-suited him, because he was a young man then"? Why should he have noted in detail the clothes the king wore to render justice informally in "the garden in Paris": "A camel's hair tunic, a sleeveless Tyre silk surcoat, a black taffeta mantle about his neck, very well combed, without a

headdress, and wearing a white peacock-feather hat on his head"?[48]
These details derive their value from their insignificance. They portray the king but, even more, they reveal the love Joinville bore him.

But the memory's vividness is not the only thing. Joinville's interest in fabrics in itself was a revealing trait of his own personality and
how he experienced his relationship with the king; from that point of
view it seems to be in the category of the symbolic and in dream imagery. Thus, clothing and fabrics are connected to the memory of one
of those moments of affectionate complicity with his sovereign that
were so precious to him. In one of the best known passages of his
work, he relates his dispute with Robert de Sorbon at disproportion-
ate length and with obvious pleasure. One Pentecost, while the entire
court is getting a breath of fresh air in a meadow after dinner, Robert
de Sorbon brings Joinville before the king, drawing him by the hem
of his mantle, and reproaches him for being dressed "de vair et de
vert" (in varicolored fur and green cloth), whereas the king is dressed
simply. Joinville retorts that he has a perfect right to wear these clothes,
which he inherited from his father and mother, but that Robert de
Sorbon, "the son of a peasant man and woman," has cast off his par-
ents' clothes and is dressed "in richer *camelin* [a fine cloth of camel or
goat hair] than the king." Taking the king's garment in one hand and
Robert de Sorbon's in the other, Joinville brings them together so
everyone can make the comparison. The king then sides with the
founder of the Sorbonne and defends him. Joinville continues:

> Après ces choses, monseigneur li roys appela Monseigneur
> Philippe son filz, le pere au roy qui ore est, et le roy Tybaut,
> et s'assist à l'uys de son oratoire et mist la main a terre, et
> dist: "Seez vous ci bien pres de moy, pour ce que en ne nous
> oie." "Ha! sire, firent il, nous ne nous oserions asseoir si pres
> de vous." Et il me dist: "Seneschal, seez vous ci." Et si fiz je,
> si pres de li que ma robe touchoit a la seue.[49]

> After that, my lord the king called my lord Philip, his son,
> father of the present king, and King Thibaut; he sat down
> in the doorway of his oratory, put his hand on the ground,
> and said: "Sit down right next to me here so people cannot

> hear us." "Ah! sire, they said, we would not dare sit
> down so close to you." And he said to me: "Seneschal,
> sit down here." And I did so, so close to him that my
> robe touched his.

The king explains that he defended Robert de Sorbon because he saw
he was in an awkward spot and took pity on him, but in reality
Joinville was right. He draws a sartorial moral from the incident:
"Vous vous devez bien vestir et nettement, pour ce que vos femmes
vous en ameront miex et vostre gent vous en priseront plus." ("You
must dress well and cleanly, so your women will love you better and
your servants will think more highly of you.")

Thus, after thinking he has been repudiated by the king, Joinville
has the delightful surprise of being approved by him. What is more,
this approval is a secret shared between them; he receives it in private,
whereas he had been reproached by the king one day for holding a
private conversation at table with this same Robert de Sorbon.[50] The
only people in on the king's secret with him are the two grandest personages present, both of whom the king called his sons, since King
Thibaut of Navarre was his son-in-law. Did he not get the feeling
that for the moment he was the king's third "son"? Better still,
whereas the son and son-in-law, a king and the king's son, were hesi-
tant to sit so close to the king, who would reproach them rather
sharply for it, a mere officer of King Thibaut, the seneschal of Champagne, who was neither king nor count, was the first invited to take
his place on the floor at the king's feet, so close that their robes were
touching. It was this detail that struck Joinville and is the point of this
entire story of garments placed side by side and compared: his robe
and the king's were touching, and that was a sign of their intimacy.

In his work Joinville describes two dreams he had, both of which
concern the king. The first had a garment belonging to the king at its
center. During Lent in 1267, the king summoned all his barons to
Paris. Joinville, who was busy on his lands, excused himself because
he was in the grip of a quartan fever. The king ordered him to come
anyway, adding that he had doctors capable of curing quartan fever.
Joinville arrived in Paris on the evening of March 24 and found

neither the king nor anyone able to tell him why the king had him come:

> Or avint, ainsi comme Dieu voult, que je me dormi a matines; et me fu avis en dormant, que je veoie le roy devant un autel a genoillons; et m'estoit avis que pluseurs prelas revestus le vestoient d'une chesuble vermeille de sarge de Reins. Je apelai après ceste vision monseigneur Guillaume, mon prestre, qui moult estoit sage; et li contai la vision. Et il me dit ainsi: "Sire, vous verrés que le roy se croisera demain." Je li demandai pourquoy il le cuidoit; et il me dit que il le cuidoit par le songe que j'avoie songé car le chasible de sarge vermeille senefioit la croiz, laquelle fu vermeille du sanc que Dieu y espandi de son costé et de ses mains et de ses piez. "Ce que le chasible estoit de sarge de Reins, senefie que la croiserie sera de petit esploit, aussi comme vous verrés, se Dieu vous donne vie."[51]

> Now it came to pass, as God willed, that I fell asleep around Matins; and in my sleep I thought I saw the king kneeling before an altar; and I thought a great number of prelates in ecclesiastical garb were dressing him in a scarlet chasuble made of Reims serge. After this vision I called Monsignor Guillaume, my priest, who was very wise, and I told him of my vision. And he said to me: "Sire, you will see that the king will take the cross tomorrow." I asked him why he believed that, and he told me he believed it because of the dream I had dreamt; for the serge chasuble signified the cross, which was scarlet from the blood God shed from his side, his hands, and his feet. "The fact that the chasuble was made of Reims serge signifies that the crusade will have little success, as you will see if God grants you long life."

Indeed, the king did take the cross the next day despite his extreme physical weakness. Joinville refused to do so. The army of crusaders went and laid siege to Tunis, where Saint Louis died of cholera on 25 August 1270.

It is evident that Joinville felt a need to justify himself for not accompanying the king on the crusade, and that is why he recounted his dream. The priest who interpreted it predicted that the king would take the cross the next day and the crusade would turn out badly. As the first point came true the next day, Joinville was authorized thereby to believe that the second would also come true, and that also did not fail. He thus implied that a dream sent by God, "ainsi comme Dieu voult" (as God willed), and explained by a holy priest, spared him from following the king on his ill-fated enterprise.

As Father Guillaume observed, the essential element of the dream was the chasuble, since two absurd details of the dream appeared in connection with it. The first was that the king was being dressed in a chasuble by prelates. But it is fairly easy to account for that circumstance: the king was quite pious; he showed great deference toward the religious orders—particularly the mendicants, for which he was often reproached—but authoritarian severity toward the bishops. Joinville had given some examples of these two attitudes a few pages earlier. These various elements might have been combined and reversed. In addition, summoned during Lent and having his dream on the eve of the Annunciation, Joinville expected to see the king participate in religious ceremonies that day.

The other absurd detail is that instead of costly fabric this chasuble was made of serge, an extremely common cloth, never used for church ornaments. Independent of the interpretation given by Father Guillaume, we may deem that this poor material referred to the king's spirit of poverty or, in the dream itself, to the humility of his attitude toward the prelates. But why was the serge from Reims? The name "Reims" was perhaps evoked by the image of the prelates dressing the king in a chasuble, as the archbishop of Reims had dressed him in the royal insignia on the day of his coronation. But it is perhaps also because Reims was both a city in Champagne, the seneschal's homeland, and one closely linked to the king's person, to the extent of symbolizing his function, since it was in fact the coronation town. Reims would be a point of juncture between the king and Joinville; Reims serge would be a point of contact between them, like their robes touching on that long-ago Pentecost day, signifying the closeness linking them.

Would it be unreasonable to continue the analysis of this dream by recalling that for Freud uniforms and clothing in dreams signified nakedness? Would it be too much to compare the king's position, "à genoillons" (kneeling), with another passage again dealing with fabric? In this passage the couple formed by Joinville and the king is replaced by another: Joinville is represented by one of his knights; the king is replaced by the queen. One day, toward the end of their stay in the Holy Land, the king asked Joinville to buy a hundred lengths of camel's hair cloth, which he wanted to offer to the Franciscans upon his return to France. After bringing him both the cloth and some relics that the prince of Tripoli offered him, Joinville had four extra lengths of cloth sent as a present to the queen:

> Le chevalier qui les luy presenta, les porta entorteillés en une touaille blanche. Quand la royne le vit entrer en la chambre ou elle estoit, si s'agenouilla contre li, et le chevalier se ragenoilla contre lui aussi; et la royne li dit: "Levez sus, sire chevalier; vous ne vous devez pas agenoiller qui portés les reliques." Mes le chevalier dit: "Dame, ce ne sont pas reliques, ains sont camelins que mon seigneur vous envoie." Quand la royne oy ce, et ses damoiselles, si commencierent a rire; et la royne dit a mon chevalier: "Dites a vostre seigneur que mal jour li soit donné, quand il m'a fet agenoiller contre ses camelins."[52]

> The knight who presented it to her brought it wrapped in a white cloth. When the queen saw him enter the room where she was, she knelt before him and the knight knelt before her, too; and the queen said to him: "Rise up, sir knight; you who are bearing relics should not kneel." But the knight said: "My lady, these are not relics, but lengths of camel's hair cloth my lord sends you." When the queen heard that, and her ladies in waiting, too, they burst out laughing; and the queen said to my knight: "Tell your lord that I send him my worst regards because he had me kneel before his lengths of camel's hair."

Through her humorous curse, which, ironically, was simultaneously a comical formula of thanks, the queen laughingly reproached

Joinville for having made her attribute too high a value to his fabric, to the extent of kneeling down before it, which led, in a symmetrical fashion, to Joinville's envoy kneeling. As we have seen, in Joinville's mind fabric was indeed charged with emotional value, linked as it was to his attachment to the king. The first part of the scene here is trivial: Joinville brought some cloth and relics to the king; nothing came from him since the cloth was bought with the king's money and the relics were the gift of a third party. But when the cloth becomes an offering from Joinville, paid for with his money, it replaces the relics and usurps their value, with the misunderstanding prolonged by the mutual—if we may so term it—kneeling of the two characters. But, in a kind of attenuation, the latter are no longer Joinville and the king but Joinville's knight and the queen. Why should there have been any need for attenuation? Was the misunderstanding concerning the relics not a quite innocent one? No, it was not. Over the relics, a word that literally signifies remains (*reliquia*), there hangs a suspicion of litotes. That was precisely the word that Jean de Meun, a contemporary of Joinville's, chose as a possible substitute for the word "balls" in the *Roman de la Rose* (ll. 7066–85): in and of itself the pronunciation of *reliquia* could lend itself to misunderstanding and provide material for jokes.[53] Need we add that Joinville, upon awakening and going to look for the king, found him "monté en eschafaut aus reliques" (climbing up on the relic stand)?

Concealed and revealed by the cloth's symbolism, Joinville's attachment for the king is expressed in the keenest and most violent way throughout his work. It is thus not enough to say, as at the start, that Joinville, meaning to write a life of Saint Louis, ended up speaking as much of his own as the king's. Furthermore, it is not enough to show how—by manipulating expression, paralipsis, and emotional displacement with insistent discretion—he gives his reader the feeling that he is letting him observe the king through the subjectivity of his own view. Joinville cannot help portraying his own image at the same time as the king's, not so much because these are his memories (which he might, like his predecessors, have presented in a neutral and detached manner) but because writing—the word is not exact, since he was dictating—made him discover that he, Jean de Joinville, at the age of almost ninety, was defined by his passionate attachment to the dead king. It is this revelation, almost a confession, that he offers the reader. What the cloth divulges is revealed by the entire text, including its most explicitly literal parts.

Joinville's final dream is, as it were, a final expression of that confession. The task he has assigned himself appears to have been achieved, and his book appears to be finished: he has reproduced the teachings that the dying king gave his son as a testament, reported his last moments according to the accounts he knew and, after a brief funeral eulogy, has described his canonization hearing and the ceremony that took place in Saint-Denis when canonization had been granted. This description ends with a traditional concluding formula in the form of a prayer to Saint Louis, similar to those found at the close of sanctorale sermons, with which the book seems about to end:

> Prions a li que il weille prier a Dieu que il nous doint ce que besoing nous yert aus ames et aus cors. *Amen.*

> Let us pray to him that he will pray God to give us what we shall need for our souls and for our bodies. *Amen.*

But, then, following this sentence, another development begins that the author himself seems to consider a sort of postscript:

> Encore weil je dire de nostre saint roy aucunes choses qui seront a l'onneur de li, que je veis de luy en mon dormant: c'est a savoir que il me sembloit en mon songe que je le veoie devant ma chapelle a Joinville; et estoit, si comme il me sembloit, merveilleusement lié et aise de cuer; et je meisme estoie moult aise, pour ce que je le veoie en mon chastel, et li disoie: "Sire, quant vous partirés de ci, je vous herbergerai a une moie maison qui siet en une moie ville qui a non Chevillon." Et il me respondi en riant: "Sire de Join-ville, foi que doi vous, je ne bée mie si tost à partir de ci."[54]

> I also wish to say a few things about our holy king, which will be to his honor, that I saw while sleeping: namely, in my dream it seemed to me I saw him in front of my chapel

at Joinville; and it seemed to me he was wonderfully happy
and serene; and I myself was very glad because I was seeing
him in my castle, and said to him: "Sire, when you leave
here, I shall lodge you in a house of mine that is located in
a village of mine called Chevillon." And he answered me,
laughing: "Sire de Joinville, upon the faith I owe you, I do
not feel like leaving here so soon."

The reason why Joinville relates this second dream is even clearer
than that for the first, since he gives it himself in the lines following
those just cited: he wanted to obtain some relics of Saint Louis from
King Louis X, "the Stubborn," for his chapel at Joinville. It is obvious, however, that despite what he says at the beginning as a pretext
for recounting his dream, the latter was less in the sainted king's
honor than in his own, since he was the one favored with such a vision, and upon reawakening, as he himself said, had the pious, gen-
erous idea of dedicating an altar in his chapel to Saint Louis and settling a perpetual annuity on it to celebrate masses in his honor.
Joinville thus presents his affair with a kind of craftiness, oddly seeming more intent on showing himself in a good light and getting his
relics than on stirring the reader with the account of a dream that
probably stirred him.

It is a well-known type of dream: the sleeper dreams of someone
dear to him who has died. Sometimes he knows that he has died and
weeps copiously. Sometimes, as here, he sees him alive and even particularly cheerful, but often he is surprised at it. In every case, although some are happy dreams while others are sad, the dreamer's
feelings upon awakening, once he again realizes that the person of
whom he has dreamt is dead, are oppressive.

Here the sorrow that Joinville felt at the king's death, the cause of
his dream, is shown in reverse by the king's cheerfulness, his noncha-
lance, and his air of good health. Joinville's knowledge of his death is,
in reality, negated by his insistence on keeping him and by the king's
on staying. More precisely, Joinville nonetheless has a vague feeling
that he will not be able to keep the king forever near him in his castle; he wants to know that at least he is lodged in a house belonging

to him and desperately insists on that possession: "Une moie maison qui siet en une moie ville" (a house of mine located in a town of mine). The king reassures him, gratifies his desire, and calms his anxiety by assuring him that he wants to remain in Joinville for a long time, perhaps forever, since the negative turn of phrase he uses remains imprecise.

Without stressing the symbolism of the chapel and the house, we may observe that in the dream the king is standing before the chapel of Joinville, just as, after the argument between Joinville and Robert de Sorbon, he is seated before his oratory. In particular, we may observe that the proper nouns in this dream express the link by which Joinville would like to be joined to the king. He would like to be *chevillé*[55] to him by lodging him in his house and village of *Chevillon*; he would like to be "joined" to him at Joinville. Should these puns be considered meaningless? Is it really by chance that the king, who throughout the book has never called Joinville anything but "seneschal," here addresses him for the first and only time as "sire de Joinville"? Can we say that wordplay has no meaning for Joinville, when, on the point of leaving for the crusade, he insisted on having his pilgrim's cloak and staff put on him by the abbot of *Cheminon*, whom he had summoned to Joinville expressly for that purpose, though he seems somewhat bewildered by his own choice?[56]

What gives this dream a happy tone, shown by the king's cheerfulness, is that it contains a promise for Joinville of the king's lasting closeness, which, as the proper nouns reveal, he perhaps would have liked to see go as far as touching. The happy surprise of this closeness, negating their distance through death, which Joinville suffers from when awake, and this touching, the desire for which does not directly penetrate his consciousness even in the dream, is analogous to what was felt by Joinville when the king sided with him against Robert de Sorbon, going against his own words. Earlier we demonstrated the importance for Joinville of sitting next to the king, so close that their robes brushed against each other. The same happy surprise is shown on another occasion: this time it is not robes touching but the king's hands placed on Joinville's head. After the council at Acre, where

Joinville alone maintains that the king should remain in the Holy Land, all violently reproach the seneschal; and during the dinner that follows, the king, who is seated next to him, does not address a word to him. Joinville thinks the king has decided to return to France and is irritated with him for advising him to stay:

> Tandis que le roy oy ses graces, je alai a une fenestre ferree qui estoit en une reculee devers le chevet du lit le roy; et tenoie mes bras parmi les fers de la fenestre. . . . En ce point que je estoie illec, le roy se vint apuier a mes espaules, et me tint ses deux mains sur la teste. Et je cuidai que ce feust monseigneur Phelippe d'Anemos qui trop d'ennui m'avait fait le jour pour le conseil que je li avoie donné; et dis ainsi: "Lessiés moy en pez, monseigneur Phelippe." Par malavanture, au tourner que je fiz ma teste, la main le roy me cheï parmi le visage; et cognu que c'estoit le roy a une esmeraude que il avoit en son doy.[57]

> While the king was listening to grace, I went to a barred window that was in a recess near the king's bed; and I passed my arms through the bars of the window. . . . While I was there the king came and leaned on my shoulders, and he put his two hands on my head. And I thought it was my lord Philippe de Nemours, who had given me a great deal of trouble that day because of the advice I had given the king; and I said to him: "Leave me alone, my lord Philippe." By ill chance, on turning my head the king's hand fell upon the middle of my face; and I recognized it was the king by an emerald he had on his finger.

The king makes him keep still, and after testing him one last time by expressing surprise that so young a man as he has dared defend his lone opinion against the greatest personages in the realm, confides that he has been won over to his opinion, for which he thanks him, asking him to keep it secret for a week.

Patterned on a gospel and hagiographic model of unexpected praise or blame, the movement, suspense, and outcome of the account are the same as in the scene with Robert de Sorbon. But the repudiation that Joinville thinks he is suffering is far more serious; besides, if confirmed it would separate him from the king, since Joinville has made up his mind to remain in the Holy Land in any case—that is what he is pondering at the window. Joinville thus expands on the portrayal of his distress. The dramatic surprise is therefore all the more violent and unexpected. He still thinks himself abandoned, the butt of a hostile entourage's bad jokes, whereas the king is already next to him and it is his hands on his head; thinking he is brushing away an opponent's hands, he finds the king's.

Nowhere—neither in this scene nor in the one with Robert de Sorbon—does Joinville speak of feeling abandoned by the king and then, against all expectations, of being reassured. But the repetition of identical narrative patterns and parallel episodes suggests what unhappiness was for him—to feel the king distant and severe—and, conversely, what happiness was: to be seated at the king's feet with their robes touching; to be standing by the king's bed, facing the window, whose bars imprison his arms and, defenseless in this way, to feel the king so close behind him, leaning on his shoulders with his hands on his head. Then this pattern returns for a third time: nowhere does Joinville depict the emotion that the king's death gave him, but just when he thinks they are separated by death, he finds him once again in a dream, close enough to touch him.

It is certainly remarkable, in a commissioned work devoted to Saint Louis, for Joinville to speak of himself abundantly and unrestrainedly enough to relate his own dreams and close the book with an account of one of them. It is remarkable that this passionate attention turned toward the king should have as its corollary such intimate attention turned toward oneself, through the recollection of so many detailed, poignant memories. But it is also remarkable for selfconfession to take on form and meaning during the course of the work's writing as the collection of his memories progressed. Joinville's monodies took the opposite direction from those of Guibert de Nogent or Philip of Novara. With the latter writers, testimony took over from confession. With Joinville, on the contrary, confession was in the service of testimony, which was the sole object of the work at the outset, and then overran it. Guibert realized that his testimony about the events which affected him was also a confession. Joinville, who did not claim to be writing a confession, went much further. He could not write a life of Saint Louis without writing his own life. He did not imagine he could bear witness to the king without confessing his attachment for him, thereby revealing himself to his reader and himself. The source and the lesson of his discourse were in his recognition that the truth he was revealing existed and expressed itself only through subjective sensibility. By reawakening his memories of the late king, the aged, disconsolate seneschal discovered that no one ever talks about anyone but himself. Conversely, the first French prose writer to talk about himself in the first person constructed his own image from elements outside himself—in this case the image of another through the distance of memory—in the same way that personal poetry, whose rise had begun during his youth, in the time of Saint Louis, presented the "I" as a product of life's circumstances and time's traces.

Two books of hours dating from the beginning of the fourteenth century, by Jeanne d'Evreux and Jeanne de Navarre, were illustrated with scenes from the life of Saint Louis, probably painted in both cases by the celebrated Jean Pucelle or his workshop and inspired by the king's various historiographers or hagiographers, Guillaume de Nangis, Guillaume de Saint-Pathus, perhaps Joinville himself. In Jeanne d'Evreux's book of hours, the order of these illustrations obeys the didactic and edifying intentions of the work. But in Jeanne de Navarre's they follow the biographical and chronological order of the sainted king's life. Thus, just as Joinville's work, based on a logical plan (the holy words and good deeds), ended up following chronological order under pressure from biographical and autobiographical concerns, so, around the same time and dealing with the same subject, the two approaches came face to face in the realm of iconography. The unfolding of the life in itself vied with the structures of argument for demonstrative effect and meaning.[58]

It may seem paradoxical to compare Guibert de Nogent with the French chronicler-memorialists of the thirteenth century, to show his project's similarity to Philip of Novara's, and never at any time to parallel it with Abélard's. Yet Guibert de Nogent's *De vita sua* (to retain its traditional title) and Abelard's *Historia calamitatum* (History of My Troubles) have traditionally been associated as the two works most representative of autobiography in the Middle Ages, if not the only ones. Both men wrote in the Latin tongue and they belonged to the same intellectual and monastic circle, though Guibert was raised in the cloister whereas Abelard entered it later and only under duress. They were contemporaries—at least within the time frame we are considering here—if somewhat inexactly, since Abélard (born 1079) was Guibert's (1055) junior by a quarter century. They even had common acquaintances upon whom they passed differing judgments: Guibert spoke of Anselm of Laon as an intellectual and moral authority; Abelard, who was for a time his disciple but soon became his rival, depicted him as superficial and envious.

However, two reasons have convinced us not to associate the two works too closely. The first is that they were quite different in nature and spirit. Abelard does not address God or confess his life and sins to Him. Supposedly he is writing a letter of consolation in which he recounts his misfortunes to a friend, inviting him to take comfort in the realization that his own are trifling by comparison. The retrospective view he takes of his life is thus not meant to know and judge himself but to recall his successes and tribulations, highlight his merits, and expose his adversaries' machinations. Whereas Guibert, in revealing his personality, is verbose about his childhood and upbringing, Abelard devotes only a few lines to them and his account really begins with his arrival in Paris and his first brilliant successes at the school of Guillaume de Champeaux. His project is in no way inspired by Saint Augustine's. The high opinion he has of himself and the bitterness of his resentments remind us rather of Valerius, although we may suspect both traits to be more justified in his case than in the Visigothic monk's. Nevertheless, these differences between Guibert's text and his own are not sufficient to prevent comparison between two works that in other respects are akin.

But the special fate of the *Historia calamitatum* obliges us to look at it in a completely different way. Its earliest manuscript dates from the end of the thirteenth century, which is to say a century and a half after the text was supposedly composed. Following the *Historia calamitatum*, this manuscript contains a series of four letters exchanged between Héloïse and Abelard, the first written by Héloïse after the *Historia calamitatum* had fallen into her hands by chance. Then come three letters of an impersonal nature concerning the administration of the convent of the Paraclete, whose abbess Héloïse had been since about 1129, and, finally, a Rule drawn up for the convent by Abelard. How authentic is the somewhat heterogeneous whole—possessing a certain coherence nonetheless—constituted by the *Historia calamitatum* and the correspondence between Héloïse and Abelard, collected so long after the event? This question has been the subject of debate since the mid-nineteenth century, and four hypotheses have been proposed. First, it is a genuine collection, retouched only at the time of its collation in a late manuscript. Second, it is a kind of epistolary romance composed by Abelard, who may possibly have been inspired by letters he really received from Héloïse. Third, it is Héloïse who composed this romance under the same conditions. Fourth, it is a complete forgery, elaborated at the Paraclete in the second half of the thirteenth century, perhaps based on genuine documents or orally transmitted recollections. Our purpose, obviously, is not to enter into the details of this argument.[59] But whichever side one takes—except for the only indefensible hypothesis, namely, complete authenticity—it is clear that the thirteenth century saw the fashioning and dissemination of the work as we know it. That was when it first achieved a success that has never diminished. The second half of that century is the period when the work was almost simultaneously disseminated in Latin and translated into French by Jean de Meun himself, who added to it a translation of the letter in which the Venerable Pierre, the abbot of Cluny, informed Héloïse of Abelard's death; Jean de Meun also paid homage to her virtues in the *Roman de la Rose*.[60] In a word, whatever its initial degree of authenticity, the work as we know it was a product of the thirteenth century, and it was that century, far more than the turn of the twelfth, whose literary sensibility it reflected. It is that century, through its literary sensibility, which bequeathed to posterity the image of the celebrated lovers.

In truth, two of its aspects do not belong to the thirteenth any more than the twelfth century. The first is the epistolary form, cultivated uninterruptedly by ancient and then Medieval Latin culture as a mode of expression for opinions, moods, confessions—even subjective candor. In this respect the composite formed by the *Historia calamitatum* and Héloïse and Abelard's correspondence was in a more traditional, less unusual form than Guibert's or Philip of Novara's works. It is only in a roundabout way that it might be connected with an autobiographical project and, above all, be seen as evidence of the two lovers' painful situation during a particularly dark period of their lives. Even considered separately, the *Historia calamitatum* is rooted in the present tense of dialogue, since it purports to be a letter of consolation.

Conversely, the respective personalities of Abelard and Héloïse, as they emerged from this series of letters, and the relations between the two characters were based on ancient literary conventions. One cannot read these texts without being struck by the difference in character and concerns between Héloïse and Abelard. In the *Historia calamitatum* the latter appears to be concerned almost exclusively with his reputation and intellectual battles: he himself states that he has suffered more from the Council of Soissons's condemnation of his treatise on the Trinity than from his castration. He claims to have seduced Héloïse not under the sway of passion but out of cold, deliberate calculation. Tormented by the flesh, he did not know how to satisfy his desires:

> Quia igitur scortorum immunditiam semper abhorrebam et ab accessu et frequentatione nobilium feminarum studii scolaris assiduitate revocabar nec laicarum conversationes multum noveram . . .

> Since I detested the gross company of prostitutes and the preparation of my courses did not leave time to frequent women of the nobility (I had few contacts with women of the laity) . . . [61]

Under these conditions, he felt the best solution was seducing Canon Fulbert's niece, the charming, learned Héloïse:

> . . . commodiorem censui in amorem mihi copulare, et me id facillime credidi posse. Tanti quippe tunc nominis eram et juventutis et forme gratia preminebam, ut quamcunque feminarum nostro dignarer amore nullam vererer repulsam. Tanto autem facilius hanc mihi puellam consensuram credidi, quanto amplius eam litterarum scientiam et habere et diligere noveram.

> . . . I felt it would be easy to have an affair with her. I had no doubt as to the outcome; I was outstanding in reputation, youth, beauty: there were no women from whom my love needed fear rejection. I was convinced the girl would put up all the less resistance for having a solid education and a desire to enhance it.

So he arranged to take lodgings with Fulbert and give private lessons to his niece. It is true that he portrays himself as a man deeply in love once the affair begins, but it is more accurate to say: as a man who is obsessed by a pleasure that he condemns at the time he is writing and that he deplores, particularly because for a time it affects the quality of his teaching.[62]

If we now turn to the four letters exchanged by Abelard and Héloïse, we can observe that Abelard's do not have a very personal tone. They are the letters of a spiritual director and teacher seeking the edification and instruction of Héloïse and, through her, of the entire Paraclete community. Abelard does mention his suffering and even the dangers he runs at the hands of his loathsome Saint Gildas monks, who have tried to assassinate him several times, but we find no trace of his intimate, personal feelings toward Héloïse. In her letters, on the contrary, passion can be sensed with gripping intensity, almost brazenness. Describing their union, which Abelard first speaks of with such cynicism and then with an almost offensive insistence on slavery to the flesh, she yields to a kind of ecstatic or vertiginous self-abandon, to the extent of claiming (in a famous passage) to prefer the name of "friend"—even "concubine" or "loose woman"—to that of "wife." She forgets neither the irreparable accident nor the vows she has pronounced, separating her from her husband forever, nor what she owes to God, her nuns, and herself. But the remorse hounding her only sharpens her regrets and desires:

> In tantum vero ille quas pariter exercuimus amantium voluptates dulces mihi fuerunt ut nec displicere mihi nec vix a memoria labi possint. Quocumque loco me vertam, semper se oculis meis cum suis ingerunt desideriis, nec etiam dormienti suis illusionibus parcunt. Inter ipsa missarium sollempnia, ubi plurior esse debet oratio, obscena earum voluptatum phantasmata ita sibi penitus miserrimam captivant animam ut turpitudinibus illis magis quam orationi vacem; que cum ingemiscere debeam de commissis, suspiro potius de amissis. Nec solum que egimus sed loca pariter et tempora in quibus hec egimus ita tecum nostro infixa sunt animo ut in ipsis omnia tecum agam nec dormiens etiam ab his quiescam. Nonumquam etiam ipso motu corporis animi mei cogitationes deprehenduntur, nec a verbis temperant improvisis.[63]

> The amorous pleasures that we have tasted together have such sweetness for me that I cannot hate them or even drive them from my memory. Wherever I turn, they appear before my eyes and awaken my desires. Their illusion does not spare my sleep. Even during the solemnities of the mass, when prayer should be the purer, obscene images assail my poor soul and preoccupy it more than the services. Far from grieving over the sins that I have committed, I think, sighing, of those I can no longer commit. Not only have our mere gestures, along with your image, remained deeply inscribed in my memory; but also the places, the hours that witnessed them, to the extent that I find myself there with you, repeating those gestures, and these memories give me no respite even in sleep. At times my body's movements betray my soul's thoughts, and I utter revealing words.

The relief into which this correspondence as a whole throws the personalities of the two characters and the contrasts opposing them has often been interpreted as an indication or even proof of its authenticity. After all, is there not some plausibility to Abelard's egocentric intellectual figure, and to Héloïse, overwhelmed by humble admiration and prey to a passion that mingles self-denial and sensuality? But we must realize that these figures were modeled upon conventional images provided long before by literature and religion. This observation in itself should in no way serve as an argument negating the work's authenticity, since nothing was more natural—in the Middle Ages even more than now—than a tendency to match the image one gave of oneself to a literary or ideological model.

In the case in question, the operative models were of two sorts. One type, appearing in the four letters exchanged by Abelard and Héloïse, was that of spiritual guidance. Abelard's letters are akin in tone and manner to edifying treatises that have come down to us in great numbers; most often, like these two letters, they were addressed to women, either nuns or pious women living in the world. Héloïse's, with their humility and long passages of introspection and self-accusation, place their author in the role of the penitent woman. They are like a practical application of treatises on repentance and a reply to the questions in confessors' manuals, both of which were numerous. The passage quoted may be read as a model of confession, tracing the guilty impulses of the soul and noting aggravating circumstances with dogged scrupulousness and a sincerity that could pass for immodesty. Finally, the four letters apply a technique used in sermons, which consisted of supporting each development with a scriptural quotation. Thus, the contrast between Abelard's letters and Héloïse's, which seemingly reflects the two personalities, is above all a contrast between two opposing, complementary roles taken by the two correspondents, those of spiritual advisor and penitent.

The other model was more strictly literary and secular. The depiction of deliberate seduction in the *Historia calamitatum*, which might easily seem to reveal a nasty character trait, was from the outset borrowed from the lyric genre of the chanson of amorous encounter, in which the search for erotic adventure was completely dissociated from feelings of love. That lyric genre was practiced in both the vernacular and goliardic Latin poetry. It could not but be familiar to Abelard, whose own chansons in honor of Héloïse, as he tells us in the *Historia calamitatum*, were on everyone's lips at the time of his writing. More strikingly still, Héloïse's sensuality, at once burning and resigned, conforms to the image of feminine love offered by the "chansons de femmes," whether they were "chansons de toile," one of Guiot de Dijon's "chansons de croisade," one *canso* or another by women troubadours themselves, the somewhat later Portuguese "cantigas d'amigo," or what we can glimpse of the much earlier Mozarabic *khardjas*. This figure of a woman tormented by grave desire, waiting with distressed passivity for a satisfaction that is long in coming or will come no more, was quite an ancient constant in Western poetry. No doubt the readers of Héloïse's letters took pleasure in discovering it reflected in them. A century and a half later, Christine de Pizan would make use of her widowhood in the same vein.

But if all these conventions predate the thirteenth century, how can we maintain that the work as such bears the mark of the period? It does so in making them serve the subjective representation of a life. The formalized stereotypes of lyric poetry, the rhetorical rules of spiritual literature, the requirements of penance, and the order of confession were all assimilated, merged, and rethought by a consciousness that transformed them into so many instruments of contemplation and expression of the self. The backward look assumed by all these forms—erotic memory of a brief encounter, examination of conscience, recollection and evaluation of sins—was, if not diverted, at least extended to embrace synthetically a life's past, to situate one's representation by oneself within the recollection of one's own past, to show that a self-portrait was not a snapshot. This demonstration is emphasized all the more by the work, as we know it, playing on a dual temporality, of memory and the epistolary exchange's duration; and, of course, in the latter case on dual points of view, each speaking to the other of itself and the other and portraying itself through this dual discourse. This process is further complicated by the fact that Héloïse takes as her starting point Abelard's image and her own in the *Historia calamitatum*, addressed not to her but to a third party.

This synthesis of diverse forms within the confessions of a subjectivity, through a retrospective glance at the self as well as an exchange of
glances, was tailor-made to captivate the reader, whatever the real
date and circumstances of its composition, in an age that was discovering emotional display in all fields, from religion to literature, and
that associated the idea of poetry with a confession of the self rooted
in time.

Emotional display, lyric flights, even tenderly expressed religious
feeling owed a great deal, of course, to a major phenomenon of
piety—especially popular piety—in the thirteenth century: Francis-
canism. Guibert de Nogent and Abelard were contemporaries, the
latter being a player in the vast movement of reflection on introspection connected with the notion of responsibility in the sacrament of
penance, one of whose practical consequences, at the start of the thirteenth century, would be the obligation of annual confession for all
the faithful. In the thirteenth century, following Saint Francis's example, subjective emotional display went beyond the framework of
penance, in the administration of which, moreover, the Franciscans
played an essential role, stirring up polemics by competing for penitents with parish priests. Saint Francis and his children were a source
of tender devotion to the infant Jesus and the crèche, at the same
time that they generally exalted the innocence and holy weakness of
childhood.[64] Saint Francis's *Laudes* and those of Franciscan poets who
succeeded him, like Jacopone da Todi, transformed the theme of
"Caeli enarrant gloriam Dei" (Ps. 18:1: The heavens declare the Glory
of God)[65] into personal religious feeling at the wonders of nature and
expressed it in the lyrical forms of the time. All these elements were
present at the end of the century in the works of a writer who occupies a totally original and essential place on the fringes of autobiographical literature—as he does on the fringes of theology, mysticism,
logic, Islamic studies, the encyclopedic spirit, and poetry: the Catalan Ramon Llull (1232?-1315), who, from the time of his conversion,
lived in the Franciscans' orbit without ever actually joining the
order.[66]

Ramon Llull is both an exemplary and a marginal character. He is obviously examplary: a troubadour who converted, as so many did. His absolute confidence in reason to account for faith was to a certain extent a natural attitude at the end of the thirteenth century, following the theological expansion and development of scholasticism during the preceding two centuries. The influence of the mendicant orders, which he experienced so powerfully, was universal in the intellectual and spiritual domain at that time; in addition, it was natural for someone not possessing a classical university education to feel more at ease among Franciscans than among Dominicans. His concern for education in the vernacular—seen in several of his works (*Doctrina pueril* [The Teaching of Children], *Libre del orde de cavalleria* [Book of the Order of Knighthood], *Evast e Blanquerna* [Evast and Blanquerna], *Libre apellat felix de les maravelles del mon* [Felix, or the Book of Wonders])—belonged to a time when the first Romance treatises on education, such as the *Miroir du monde* (Mirror of the World) and the *Somme le roi* (The King's Summa), or translations of the *Disciplina clericalis* (Clerical Instruction), appeared and when vernacular allegorical compilations and allegorical moralizing poetry flourished. His all-inclusive, systematic mind reflected a century of summas and encyclopedias. Finally, his missionary calling, oriented toward non-Christians, seemingly an original trait, may be found in the period 1230 to 1250 among the millennialist Beghards, who also drew their inspiration from Saint Francis and, as it happens, flourished in Aragon. Ramon Llull's father, a Catalan noble, is known to have been a close companion to the king of Aragon, James I, in 1229, at the time of the conquest of Majorca, where he settled in a fief granted him by the king. Llull's missionary calling—which certainly owed much to his being a Majorcan, inhabiting an island newly retaken from Islam—can also be compared with that of Saint Anthony of Padua and the voyage to the Orient of Saint Francis.

At the same time, each of these traits possesses a particular nuance that made Llull's character marginal and his work unique. A troubadour convert, he was not just a convert: he benefited from mystical experience and left mystical writings of a very special kind. As a self-taught philosopher, he failed to see the limits of reason applied to faith, something already mentioned by Saint Anselm and emphasized by Saint Thomas; that explains the ambition of his *Art*, the extreme systematization of his logic, and his belief in its fruitfulness. He did live in the shadow of the Franciscans and practically became the superior of the monastery of Miramar, which was founded at his instigation; but he never entered the order and never took holy orders; if we are to believe the inquisitor Nicolas Eymerich, he settled for becoming a member of the Franciscan Third Order. Neither a clerk nor a monk nor a simple layman, he was regarded with mistrust all his life or was considered a visionary. It was probably the first time that the vernacular held so important a place in an original, speculative work; not content with using Catalan, Ramon Llull developed a theory of the vernacular's use in education and attached considerable importance to knowledge of languages (Arabic, Turkish, etc.). Finally, his interest in Islam was remarkable. He learned Arabic and his works reflect the influence of Muslim mysticism. He wrote the *Book of the Gentile and the Three Wise Men* and *Liber contemplationis* (Book of Contemplation) directly in Arabic before translating them into Latin and Catalan.

These paradoxes may be found throughout his work, in which he is entirely present at all times. Not only does he often allude, in his poems as well as his treatises, to precise events in his life, but he also quite obviously inspired the composition of his own biography, written during his lifetime and generally designated under the title *Vita coetanea* (Contemporaneous Life), which exists in Latin and Catalan versions.[67] He also portrayed himself from multiple points of view and in multiple disguises in the *Book of Evast and Blanquerna*, which is the only work of its genre.[68] It is simultaneously an edifying allegorical tale, a review of worldly states, an educational tract, a politico-religious utopia and, in addition, a romance whose characters are not reduced to algebraic symbols of moral life and whose plot is complex and rich with the profuseness of reality. In short, it is a romance, but not an autobiographical one; rather, it is a projection of the author's biographical dream in the manner, one might say, of Frederick Rolfe's

Hadrian the Seventh, for the two works' arguments are not dissimilar and Baron Corvo's personality was not unlike Ramon Llull's.

The plan of the romance makes it a review of worldly states, since it is divided into five books dealing, respectively, with marriage, religion, the priesthood, apostledom, and hermitism.[69] Without belying this plan, the contents are far more complex than it might suggest. The unfolding of the story itself is presented in the following manner. A rich merchant, Evast, and his wife, Alome, after raising their son, Blanquerna, give up the enjoyment of their wealth, found a hospice, and devote themselves to serving the poor and ill in chastity and poverty, converting sinners by their example. Blanquerna refuses to take up his father's business and marry. His fiancée, Natane, converted by him, takes the veil and, becoming an abbess, reforms her convent. Blanquerna goes into the forest and becomes a hermit; there he encounters various exemplary or allegorical characters: an emperor, a jongleur, a knight in love, Merit in the form of a lady, the Ten Commandments, and so forth. Then he becomes a monk and, as abbot, reforms his monastery; he becomes a bishop and reforms his diocese; he becomes pope and reforms the Church and the world. Finally, he gives up the papacy and returns to life as a hermit, which the emperor, having given up his throne, will share with him.

One of the disconcerting yet appealing aspects of this book is that its numerous characters are based on differing models and their nature—imaginary, half-real, allegorical, or exemplary—is not coherent from one to the other. Some are exemplary characters defined by a moral quality, like the seven characters, each addicted to one of the deadly sins, who are converted by Evast and Alome. Others are an allegorical personification of abstract concepts, like some of those encountered by Blanquerna in his wanderings through the forest: Ten Commandments, Faith, Truth, Understanding, Piety, and Merit.

Still others are characters representing worldly states: a king's majordomo, a squire, a merchant, a litigant, a superstitious knight, a shepherd, the emperor, the hypocritical monk Narpan. These characters, with the exception of the emperor, whose role is more substantial, and Narpan, who eludes purely social definition by receiving a name, are the heroes of brief exempla and in this way attain the same value as the characters of the first category; but they are more complex, since they are defined by their place in society and the sometimes complex character traits—as with the shepherd—that they illustrate. Conversely, another squire wronged by Narpan recounts two animal fables to Blanquerna, who answers them with a third fable, the moral of which is the opposite of the first two. The allegory, therefore, is not in the characters; rather, the characters tell the allegory in a form familiar to Ramon Llull, since it is the one he used in the *Llibre de les besties* (Book of the Animals), inspired by an Arabic collection entitled *Calila and Dimna*.

Even stranger are the characters who incarnate a function of the Church: beatitude/canons and Gloria/cardinals. Blanquerna, as bishop, gives each of his canons the name of a beatitude from the Sermon on the Mount, entrusting each with a mission in keeping with that beatitude. Similarly, once he is pope he gives each cardinal the name of a verse of the Gloria in excelsis Deo and assigns him a role illustrating it. Thus, the canon of Persecution, whose beatitude is "Blessed are they which are persecuted for righteousness' sake" (Matt. 5:10), is a sort of holy fool—God's jongleur, as Saint Bernard would say—and almost a rebel. He accepts humiliation and outrage; he dances and drinks in taverns with thieves in order to convert them; he interrupts a Christmas mass to denounce its pomp and lavishness, since it is out of keeping with the poverty of the manger; and he reproaches the king with his injustices. Several of his Gloria/cardinals carry on missionary activity both within Christianity and outside it. Cardinal "Domine fili unigenite Jhesu Christe" (Lord Jesus Christ, Only-begotten Son), for example, gets from the "king of the Tartarins" four Turkish-speaking clerics to preach in Turkey. Each of these canons and cardinals has a complex function, just as the connection between his name and function is complex. Each one also has his own personality, existential solidity, a life fertile in concrete events whose meaning is direct and not allegorical.

With the literary characters from courtly romances encountered by Blanquerna we leave the realm of allegory completely: the knight errant, in love and a poet; the young girl, victim of an evil knight. Though Blanquerna draws a lesson from their presence, they are nothing but themselves, literary types who have strayed into a fiction that is not theirs, like the nursery-rhyme characters encountered by Alice in Wonderland or through the looking-glass.

Close to these main characters in their very transparency, we find verbal characters who are defined as a pure function of literary communication or mystical effusion: the jongleur of Merit, as his role is defined by the emperor, or Raymond the Fool, a repentant jongleur.

Finally, the central characters are true romance characters, but as a group they all show ways to salvation: differing ways, though all marked by detachment from the world and hierarchically ordered on the royal road to contemplation, toward which they are headed and which Blanquerna will finally choose after serving in the world and the Church. These characters express and put into practice principles of instruction, education, and government on the level of the family, the city, the monastery, the diocese, the Church, and the world, including the still pagan world. They illustrate the five worldly states that give their titles to the five books of the romance. They are Evast and Alome; Natane and her mother, Nastasia; and Blanquerna.

The latter, the hero of the romance, which originally seems to have had only his name as its title, goes well beyond the limits of his character. He is an exemplary image of perfect progress toward God in all its stages. But he is also—and this is the essential point for us—Ramon Llull himself. Yet he does not resemble him either by birth or in the circumstances of his vocation or fate. By birth he is bourgeois, not a nobleman. His vocation is the fruit of slow ripening, not the result of a sudden conversion. Llull's own conversion, tradition has it, took place in far more fantastic circumstances than his hero's. Ramon was smitten with a lady who finally granted him a rendezvous. But just as he thought to win her favors, she revealed her breast, eaten away by a horrible ulcer, thus showing him that the flesh he coveted was already given up to corruption. Deeply shaken by this scene, some time later, as he was preparing to compose a love song in the vernacular, he had a vision of Christ on the Cross. The vision was repeated several times, and on the fifth he was converted, vowing to devote himself to converting infidels, to write a book of apologetics that could be used in support of that mission, and, finally, to learn Arabic and arrange for the establishment of monasteries where different languages would be taught. If the character's conversion is less spectacular than the writer's, it is because he never lived in sin. Similarly, Blanquerna's fate goes beyond Llull's. He is what Llull would have liked to be: a great reformer of the Church, intellectually and spiritually and in a missionary sense. That is why his story is the dream biography of Llull, whose *Vita coetanea* was a real one. Llull identified with Blanquerna so completely that he makes him his figurehead and presents him as the author of edifying or mystical pamphlets that he inserts in his romance, some of which he had written years earlier: the *Libre d'Ave Maria* (Book of Ave Maria), the *Libre de amich e amat* (Book of the Lover and the Beloved), and the *Liber contemplationis*. He also makes him the author of several others of his works too long to be reproduced in the romance: the *Libre del gentil e dels tres savis* (Book of the Gentile and the Three Wise Men), the *Art demostrativa* (Art of Demonstration), the *Art breu* (Abridged Art [of Seeking the Truth]), which Blanquerna supposedly writes in his hermitage and—as is predicted at the end of the romance—will be universally studied. Neither Ramon Llull's missionary undertakings nor his writings approached in reality the success achieved under the name of Pope Blanquerna. Rarely has a literary work so explicitly reproduced its author's self-gratifying fantasies.

But Blanquerna is not the only character in the romance who represents Ramon Llull. He is also embodied in the verbal characters, who are either his self-portrait or else a mouthpiece for other characters at the precise moment when Llull speaks through them or attributes his own work to them. Thus, Raymond the Fool, a converted buffoon who has become a holy fool, follows the same path, bears the same name, and displays the same feverish and disconcerting piety as Llull. Merit's jongleur performs and distributes the emperor's book concerning her; but neither one has seen lady Merit, only Blanquerna having had that privilege. The same jongleur concludes the romance by performing the emperor's last poem, which assigns to Llull what he says of Blanquerna, since it names the actual monastery of Miramar, which is never mentioned in the romance. Merit's jongleur is thus only a voice behind which stand the emperor and Blanquerna. But this voice is speaking of Llull and it is Llull speaking through it. Similarly, at the end of the romance the repentant jongleur undertakes to travel everywhere reciting the *Book of Evast and Blanquerna*. Finally, the emperor not only tends to merge with Blanquerna in the last chapter—where he seeks to have him lead the "vie hermitainne" (hermit's life) with him, one having given up the papacy and the other the empire—and not only is he the author of the final poem, but he proves to be a perfect Llullian by leaving a *Book of the Education of Princes* to his son when he abdicates, just as Llull wrote the *Book of the Order of Knighthood* for his own son, whom he had not seen since he separated from his wife and gave his possessions away upon conversion.

The emperor and Merit's jongleur, as author and performer of works included or mentioned in the romance; the canon of Persecution, as author of a poem to the Virgin in which he calls on men to go and convert the infidels in Syria; Blanquerna himself, as reputed author of Llull's treatises, included or mentioned in the romance—all make Llull's voice heard directly. In addition, Raymond the Fool and Blanquerna are two images of Llull, the first exemplary and almost a caricature, the second utopian and idealized.

Finally, Llull's presence permeates the concluding poem—whose supposed author is the emperor and whose performer is Merit's jongleur—to the point of shifting its meaning. The last chapter, in which the poem appears, is itself surprising and significant. The romance ought to end with the death of Blanquerna, but such is not the case. It ends formally with a mystical poem in which the quest for God is represented thematically by Blanquerna's search, expressed both in the poem, as a corollary to the quest for God, and in the story, when the emperor seeks out Blanquerna in order to lead a hermit's life under his guidance. Other quests or progressions are simultaneously revealed in this last chapter; they collectively contribute to the expression of the quest for God according to the principle of the radiation of meanings from a single nucleus into various orders, which is in Ramon Llull's manner. The center is constituted by Blanquerna himself, both as the medium through which God's glory and truth are shown to the world and as Llull's double, since the works that Llull wrote are attributed to him.

Thus, in this last chapter a jongleur does penance under the guidance of Blanquerna; returning his art, which has strayed in the pursuit of secular aims, to its true calling, he devotes it to the praise of God and the explanation of worldly states, reciting in "squares, courts, and abbeys" the *Romance of Evast and Blanquerna*, that is to say, both the exemplary story of Blanquerna and Llull's romance itself, which we are reading. As for the emperor, seeking the hermitage of Blanquerna as a place to retire after leaving the empire to his son, he encounters a bishop who is on his way to bring to the court in Rome the *Art breu* or *Ars brevis*, condensed from Llull's *Ars magna*. The emperor beseeches the bishop to be Merit's attorney at the Roman court and asks Merit's jongleur to sing the poem he has composed. After hearing it, the bishop leaves the emperor, the two having been mutually edified: the former will make the poem known in Rome and, thanks to his directions, the latter will no doubt find Blanquerna's hermitage.

The poem itself points with peculiar intensity to Blanquerna as Llull's double and model, to a certain extent his ideal of the self. The first lines are at once mystical and courtly: mystical because they are an invocation to the glorious, redeeming Lord; courtly since by their very rhythm and technique and the terms with which they designate God they are strongly reminiscent of prayers formulated by troubadours in more frivolous circumstances, in particular a celebrated *aube* (dawn song) by Guiraut de Borneilh:

> Sènyer ver Déus, rey gloriós,
> qui ab vos volgués hom unir!
> Membre-us dels vostres servidors
> qui per vos volen mort sufrir,

e fayts-los ardits lausadors
en vos honrar e obeir
de lur poder;
car vos ets plaent, dous desir
de lur esper.[70]

Our Lord true God, glorious king,
who were willing to unite man with yourself!
Remember your servants
who are willing to suffer death for you,
and make them bold singers of praise
to honor and obey you
with all their power;
for you are the pleasing, sweet desire
of their hope.

It is striking that the definition of the servants of God, in whose name the poet supplicates Him, applies to Llull himself more strictly than the characters in his romance. Although a number of them are always concerned with speaking the praise of God, none of them— not even Blanquerna—either desires or undergoes martyrdom. On the contrary, the search for martyrdom was part of Llull's vow on his conversion, and we know he fulfilled that vow, once unsuccessfully in Tunis and a second time successfully, it would seem, since tradition has it that he was stoned to death in 1315 in Bougie.[71] Nevertheless, expressing praise of God was the raison d'être of his calling, both in learning Arabic for missionary aims and in the composition of the *Ars magna* and his literary activity in general. Is it not curious that Blanquerna, Llull's ideal double, does not precede him in martyrdom, and that this difference is emphasized, perhaps implicitly but clearly, in the poem that concludes the romance? Did Llull consider his hero sufficiently perfect to be able to reach God without undergoing a baptism of blood? Did he dismiss from the fabric of his romance, without knowing it, the depiction of a death that his vow would force him to confront but that daunted him to the point of fleeing its risk the first time by letting a ship bound for Tunis leave without him, before getting a grip on himself and sailing on another one? Simply stated, would the expression "Your servants who are willing to suffer death for you" designate those who, placing themselves entirely in God's hands without necessarily being destined for martyrdom, accept in advance all trials, including the ultimate one? The rest of the poem shows both that in reality Llull was speaking of martyrdom in the literal sense, and that he had his own fate in mind when writing the poem.

He was speaking of it in the literal sense, since at the start of the second stanza he evokes the apostles' martyrdom, which God's new servants must relive:

> Nada és novella frevos
> e renovellen li desir
> dels apostols, qui lausant vos
> anaven mort plaent sentir.

> A new fervor is born,
> and the desires of the apostles
> are renewed, they who went
> praising you to experience a happy death.

He had his own fate in mind, not only because he was alluding to this renewal of missionary, apostolic zeal but, in particular, because in the third and fourth stanzas he mentions episodes of his own life, that of Ramon Llull and not the emperor or Blanquerna:

> Remembrat han fratres menors
> lo Salvador, qui volc vestir
> ab si lo sant religiós
> e han fayt Miramar bastir
> al rey de Mallorca'morós:
> iran serraïns convertir
> per far plaer
> a Déu, qui a mort volc venir
> per nos haver.

> E doncs què fan preycadors,
> pus amen tant en Déu fruir?
> ni què fant abats ni priors,
> bisbes, prelats, qui enantir
> amen tant lurs possessions?

ni què fan reys qui ab durmir
e ab haver
cuydon a parais tenir
e Déus veser?

The Minorite friars have remembered
the Savior, who was willing to clothe
every holy monk,
and they had Miramar built
by the lovesick king of Majorca:
they will go and convert the Saracens
to be pleasing
to God, who was willing to die
in order to have us for himself.

And so what are the preaching friars doing,
if they so love to have their enjoyment in God?
And what are the abbots and priors doing,
the bishops, the prelates, who so love
to increase their possessions?
And what are the kings doing, whose sleep
and possessions
make them think they own paradise
and see God?

It was Ramon Llull, not a character in his romance, who in 1276 got
the king of Majorca to found the monastery of Miramar, where he
prepared thirteen Franciscans to go and convert the Saracens. The
Vita relates the founding in the following terms:

> At the same time, Ramon obtained from the king of Ma-
> jorca that that ruler would have a monastery built in his
> kingdom, endowed with possessions sufficient for training
> thirteen Minorite friars, who would learn the Arabic lan-
> guage with a view to converting the infidels. Five hundred
> florins would be allocated annually for their maintenance,
> to them and those who would succeed them in perpetuity
> in that monastery.[72]

It was Ramon Llull and not someone else who spent his life soliciting
condescending, skeptical prelates and rulers to obtain the aid neces-

sary to realize his great missionary projects. The happy memory of the success achieved at the founding of Miramar, the bitter memory of the indifference and refusals encountered thereafter, succeed each other in these two stanzas where the parallelism between "fratres menors" (Minorite friars) and "preycadors" (preaching friars) may introduce an additional polemical element.[73]

After these two stanzas devoted to the life of Ramon Llull, the reader is inclined to refer the "I" that appears in the following stanza for the first time in the poem to Llull and not the emperor. The temptation is even greater because this "I" complains, in the manner of the psalmist, of the outrage and mockery heaped upon him, complaints that were more fitting in Llull's mouth than in the emperor's and that followed naturally after the invective of the preceding stanza:

> Menors e mijans e majors
> han placer en mi scarnir,
> e amors, lègremes e plors
> e suspirs fan mon cors languir.

> The small, the middle, and the great
> take pleasure in mocking me
> and loves, tears and weeping,
> and sighs make my heart pine.

Thus, the final envoi of the poem is filled with ambiguity:

> Blanquerna! Qui'm sabria dir
> on dey tener
> vas vostra cella, on desir
> sol Déus haver?

> Blanquerna, who might tell me
> how I must go
> toward your cell, where I desire
> to have God alone?

This time the question is indeed that of the emperor, who is looking for Blanquerna's hermitage. But how can we forget Llull's fierce presence in the preceding stanzas? And how can we not attribute to him the real question of these final verses, which concerns not the road to take to find Blanquerna but the one to take to find God, the object of the only desire? After the reminder of his missionary enthusiasm and his disappointed hopes, was it not Llull who was addressing this final appeal to Blanquerna, his creation and ideal double, who had achieved what he could never expect to accomplish in reality, that part of himself that was leading him to God? Moreover, as we have said, in the romance he also identified with the emperor, the supposed author of the poem. And the latter, having it sung and circulated by a jongleur, leaves to others than himself, the real author of the romance and the poem in particular, the possibility of recognizing in themselves the "I" expressed there.

It will perhaps be objected that despite the rhetorical balance of the portrait we have sketched of him, the "Visionary Doctor" was too marginal a personage to be exemplary, and his intrusive personality, his extravagant—in both the ordinary and etymological senses of the term—life, his bizarre intellectual system, ill suited him to represent a general evolution of sensibility and letters. He was a solitary figure who left neither disciples nor an immediate intellectual posterity. Yet it is quite true that he turned to advantage everything his times offered him; most of the characteristics that we associate with the literary turn and the turning point of the thirteenth century are to be found conjoined in his works. We have already mentioned several of them: the sense of totality and synthesis appearing in the form of a speculative summa like the *Ars magna* or an encyclopedic one like the *Book of Wonders*; the attention to pedagogical questions linked to it; and the affective cast of its spirituality. But we can now add to this his conception of poetics, which brings us back to the object of this study. On the one hand, narrative fiction, even when its ambitions were instructive or didactic, had the meaning and value of confession. The forms and motifs of the "roman d'aventures" or allegorical romance masked a personal revelation. Earlier we demonstrated, using the example of Saint Valerius, that autobiography's subjection to the hagiographic model prevented the introspective and retrospective view that gave it its value from appearing in the text. Ramon Llull assigned each point of view its place, but he separated them. The *Vita coetanea* is a biography that followed the rules of hagiographic literature, with some liberties, but made no claim to be an autobiography. On the other hand, introspective and retrospective views were at the heart of *Evast e Blanquerna*, disguised since it was a work of fiction and the biography of an imaginary character and yet revealing since that character was Llull's ideal self. Elsewhere, as in the prologues to certain treatises or the poem "Desconhort" (Desolation), autobiographical elements are present and indicated as such, albeit in conformity with a fiction conceived as more revealing of the self than the progress of life itself. Just as Llull's speculative works reveal the omnipresence of a single God through the multiplicity and variety of His attributes, so he conceived literary creation only as a manifestation of the self and its history through the multiplicity of forms of fiction and writing. It was the ultimate extension of the principle of monodic writing and biographical reading.

Moreover, Llull illustrates a new relationship between verse and prose with regard to expression of the self. A poem like "Desconhort"[74] reveals aspects that have seemed characteristic of the *dit* as it developed in the thirteenth century: a fictional plot—at the heart of which, however, autobiographical elements and references maintain the illusion of reality—presents the poet so defined and indicated by name and in such a manner as to reveal the supposed truth of his self. In this poem Ramon confides—even confesses—to a hermit, retraces the stages of his spiritual itinerary, speaks about the five visions that he has had of Christ on the Cross, about the writing of his *Art*, the experience of Miramar, and so forth. But in a prose romance studded with several poems, like *Evast e Blanquerna*, it is clear that prose took over narration and verse a certain expression of emotion. This was the point at which verse, as opposed to prose, began to reflect the new idea of poetry. *Evast e Blanquerna*, Llull's imaginary autobiography, illustrates the various modes of expression and self-dissimulation in both forms of writing, whose antithetical coupling henceforth defined literature.

It is true that by delving a bit further into the fourteenth century we would have found more striking examples, from less marginal authors, of the fragmented presence of autobiography, the interplay between the fiction of history and the truth of the self, and their pressure on the evolution of the new literary forms. Froissart, viewed in isolation in his chronicles and *dits*, would deserve some attention, not to mention the cardinal importance of the works of Machaut or Christine de Pizan with respect to all these questions.[75] Completing the evolution glimpsed at the end of our first chapter, King René of Anjou was explicitly inspired by both the *Roman de la Rose* and Arthurian romance, in the *Livre du coeur d'amour épris* (Book of the Heart Smitten by Love), to write in the form of an allegorical dream the fiction of a sentimental autobiography. At the end of the Middle Ages, memoirs and intimate diaries—which were actually not all that intimate—increased in number. By trying to cross the boundaries of the thirteenth century as little as possible, we have sought to point up the fact that the change in the conception of the literary self was not a trait of the waning Middle Ages but contemporary with the spread of the most ancient works of French literature, or at least their spread as we know it, since practically no literary manuscripts in the vernacular exist before the thirteenth century. The period when the romances of the twelfth century, chansons de geste, and lyric poetry were copied and circulated, and when more were written based upon the same model, was also the one in which a new idea of literature—or even, perhaps, the new idea of literature—appeared in the reading of biography and the writing of autobiography: a period when the time of life, in literature, was the measure of all.

▌ *Notes*

Introduction

1. [François-René de Chateaubriand's apology of Catholicism (1802); its praise of the Middle Ages provided a model for French Romantic writers to come. Trans.]

2. [Jules Michelet (1798–1874), a renowned French nationalist historian; Ernest Lavisse (1842–1922), author of a *History of France* (1900–1912); Charles Péguy (1873–1914), a Catholic mystic and socialist who inspired pilgrimages to the cathedral of Chartres. Trans.]

3. [Christine de Pizan, or Pisan (1364–1430), a French woman poet born in Italy. Trans.]

4. [Jeanne Bourin was the author of a popular historical romance entitled *La Chambre des dames* (Paris: Table Ronde, 1979). Trans.]

5. René Girard is a well-known example of this.

6. In the field of medieval studies, see Paul Zumthor's clarification in *Parler du Moyen Age* (Paris: Editions de Minuit, 1980), esp. pp. 55–64.

7. [A type of French academic criticism concentrating on the study of the prepublication history, or "genèse" (genesis), of literary texts. Trans.]

8. *L'Enonciation de la subjectivité dans le langage* (Paris: Armand Colin, 1980).

9. Ibid., p. 10.

10. *La Parole médiévale: Discours, syntaxe, texte* (Paris: Editions de Minuit, 1981).

11. This undertaking had distinguished precedents; see, e.g., Leo Spitzer, "Note on the Poetic and the Empirical 'I' in Medieval Authors," *Romanische Literaturstudien, 1936–1956* (Tübingen: Max Niemeyer, 1959), pp. 100–112.

12. Thus, Rainer Warning notes that in the context of such criticism the theory of narrative "has not so much made the identity of the subject of the narrative text transparent as it has diluted it in a transcendentalism of deductive models devoid of a subject, which the communicative dimension of a narrative has eluded bit by bit." ("Formen narrativer Identitätskonstitution im höfischen Roman," in *Grundriss der romanischen Literaturen des Mittelalters. IV/I: Le Roman jusqu'à la fin du XIIIᵉ siècle,* ed. Hans Robert Jauss and Erich Köhler (Heidelberg: Carl Winter, 1978), pp. 26–27.

13. Joël H. Grisward, *Archéologie de l'épopée médiévale: Structures trifonctionnelles et mythes indo-européens dans le cycle des Narbonnais,* with a preface by Georges Dumézil (Paris: Payot, 1981).

14. *Sermones in Cantica,* X, 1–2, ed. J. Leclercq, in *S. Bernardi Opera,* vol. 1 (Rome: Editiones Cistercienses, 1957), p. 49.

15. See, e.g., Jean-Charles Payen, *Le Motif du repentir dans la littérature française médiévale (des origines à 1230)* (Geneva: Droz, 1967), pp. 17–93; André Vauchez, *La Spiritualité du Moyen Age occidental (VIIIᵉ-XIIᵉ siècle),* Collection Sup (Paris: Presses Universitaires de France, 1975); Jacques le Goff, *Naissance du purgatoire,* Bibliothèque des histoires (Paris: Gallimard, 1981), esp. pp. 284–304.

16. *The Stones of Venice,* vol. 1, chap. 21, sec. 13–14; vol. 2, chap. 6, sec. 9–14.

17. Hegel, *Vorlesungen über die Aesthetik,* vol. 1, ed. Rüdiger Bubner (Stuttgart: Philipp Reclam. Jun., 1971), p. 50. See also pp. 48–49, 574, and 586.

18. See *VIIᵉ centenaire de la mort de saint Louis,* Actes des Colloques de Royaumont et de Paris, 21–27 mai 1970 (Paris: Les Belles-Lettres, 1976); Gérard Sivéry, *Saint Louis et son siècle* (Paris: Tallandier, 1983); Jean Richard, *Saint Louis* (Paris: Fayard, 1983).

19. Jean Leclercq, *Monks and Love in Twelfth-Century France* (Oxford: Clarendon Press, 1979), pp. 9–12.

20. That is why Jacques Le Goff opens volume 2 of the *Histoire de la France urbaine: La Ville médiévale des Carolingiens à la Renaissance* (Paris:

Le Seuil, 1980), with these words: "In the *Perceval* that Chrétien de Troyes wrote around 1180, Sir Gawain one day perceives *a castle and a town*" (p. 9; italics ours).

21. ["La rue étourdissante autour de moi hurlait" is the first line of "A une passante," one of Charles Baudelaire's "Tableaux parisiens" in *Les Fleurs du Mal*; see his *Œuvres complètes*, ed. Claude Pichois (Paris: Gallimard, 1961), pp. 88–89. Trans.]

22. [The original text has "Contemple-les [rather than "Regardeles"], mon âme, ils sont vraiment affreux," in "Les Aveugles," another of Baudelaire's "Tableaux parisiens" in *Les Fleurs du Mal*, p. 88. Trans.]

23. ["Lundi, rue Christine" is the title of one of Guillaume Apollinaire's *Calligrammes*; see his *Œuvres poétiques*, ed. Marcel Adema and Michel Decaudin (Paris: Gallimard, 1959), pp. 180–82. Trans.]

A Change in Literary Consciousness

The first part of this chapter is a summary of an article entitled "Une mutation de la conscience littéraire: Le Langage romanesque à travers des exemples français du XIIe siècle" that appeared in the *Cahiers de civilisation médiévale* 24 (1981): 3–27, where a more fully developed and nuanced discussion is presented.

1. The so-called Carolingian forgeries may still have literary significance; cf. Pseudo-Turpin's Chronicle.

2. [Zink's "avancer masqué" is a French translation of the Latin "larvatus prodeo" in René Descartes's early writings; see *Œuvres philosophiques de Descartes*, vol. 1 (1618–37) (Paris: Garnier, 1963), p. 45. Trans.]

3. See, in an extensive bibliography, the excellent synthesis in Robert Marichal's essay "Naissance du roman" in *Entretiens sur la renaissance du XIIᵉ siècle*, Décades de Cerisy, n.s., 9, ed. Maurice de Gandillac and Edouard Jeauneau (Paris: Mouton, 1968), pp. 449–92; see also the essays making up the first part of the *Grundriss der romanischen Literaturen des Mittelalters*. IV/1: *Le Roman jusqu'à la fin du XIIIᵉ siècle*, ed. Hans Robert Jauss and Erich Köhler (Heidelberg: Carl Winter, 1978), particularly the one by Paul Zumthor entitled "Genèse et évolution du genre," pp. 60–73.

4. For the effects derived by the chanson de geste from its strophic structure, see Jean Rychner, *La Chanson de geste: Essai sur l'art épique des jongleurs* (Geneva: Droz, 1955).

5. Concerning listening or reading of chansons de geste and novels, see Zink, "Une mutation de la conscience littéraire," pp. 6–7.

6. Thus, in the *Roman de philosophie* of Simon de Freine, an adaptation of Boethius's *De Consolatione Philosophiae*, we read:

> Solaz dune e tout ire
> Icest romanz ki l'ot lire.
> (ll. 1–2)
>
> This romance consoles and calms
> Anyone who hears it read.

In the *Vie de Saint Georges* by the same author we read:

> N'i ad rens en cest romanz
> Dunt le profit ne seit granz.
> (ll. 5–6)
>
> There is nothing in this romance
> That does not give great benefit.

On the relationship between the first French romances and hagiographic literature, see Omer Jodogne, "Le Caractère des oeuvres 'antiques' dans la littérature française du XIIᵉ et XIIIᵉ siècles," in *L'Humanisme médiéval dans les littératures romanes du XIIᵉ au XIVᵉ siècle*, ed. Anthime Fourrier (Paris: Klincksieck, 1964), pp. 55–59, and H. U. Gumbrecht, "Faszinationtyp Hagiographie: Ein historisches Experiment zur Gattungstheorie," in *Gedenkschrift für Hugo Kuhn*, ed. C. Cormeau, W. Hang, and B. Wachinger (Munich: Metzler, 1979).

7. L. Constans, *Le Roman de Troie par Benoît de Sainte-Maure*, 6 vols. (Paris: Firmin-Didot, 1904–12), ll. 139–41.

8. Ivor Arnold, *Le Roman de Brut de Wace*, 2 vols. (Paris: Société des anciens textes français, 1938–40), ll. 7–8.

9. Reto R. Bezzola, *Les Origines et la formation de la littérature courtoise en Occident (500–1200)*, part 3, vol. 1 (Paris: E. Champion, 1967), pp. 148–49; Marichal, "Naissance du roman," p. 467.

10. This theory by Ph. Aug. Becker (*Epenfragen* [special issue of *Wissenschaftlichen Zeitschrift der Fr. Schiller Universität Jena*, 4, nos. 1–2 (1954–55)]), which Bezzola's grand synthesis only confirms, was rejected a bit too quickly by Jean Frappier; see the latter's essay "Remarques sur la peinture de la vie et des héros antiques dans la littérature française du XIIᵉ et du XIIIᵉ siècle," in *L'Humanisme médiéval*, p. 15.

11. Bezzola, *Les Origines et la formation de la littérature courtoise*, part 2, vol. 1, pp. 65–67, 119–22; Arnold, *Le Roman de Brut de Wace*, vol. 1, pp. lxxxiii-iv. In claiming a Celtic source, Geoffrey thereby himself reversed the genealogy of historical truth and introduced an element of doubt.

12. Chrétien's romances are cited from the editions of the Guyot copy in the collection "Classiques français du Moyen Age," published by Champion (*Erec et Enide, Le Chevalier de la charrette, Le Chevalier au lion*, ed. Mario Roques; *Cligès*, ed. Alexandre Micha; *Le Conte du Graal*, ed. Félix Lecoy). The translations are the ones published in the same collection (*Erec et Enide*, René Louis; *Cligès*, Micha; *Le Chevalier de la charrette*, Jean Frappier; *Le Conte du Graal*, Jacques Ribard).

13. Roger Dragonetti (*La Vie de la lettre au Moyen Age* [Paris: Le Seuil, 1980, pp. 108–9]) sees a sign of the authority that Chrétien claimed for himself in the fact that he ventured to decide on his own the comparative merits of Philip of Alsace and Alexander, the epic-romance hero, in lines 13–15 of the prologue.

14. *Ille et Galeron*, ed. Frederick A. G. Cowper, Société des anciens textes français [= SATF](Paris: A. & J. Picard, 1956), ll. 932–37 of the Paris ms; *Escoufle*, ed. Franklin Sweetser (Geneva: Droz, 1974), ll. 10–25.

15. *"Le Roman de la Rose" ou de "Guillaume de Dole" de Jean Renart*, ed. Félix Lecoy (Paris: Champion, 1962).

16. Michel Zink, *Roman rose et rose rouge* (Paris, Nizet, 1979).

17. Jacques Lacan, *Ecrits I*, collection "Points" (Paris: Le Seuil, 1966–71), p. 93.

18. *Lancelot*, ed. Alexandre Micha (Geneva: Droz, 1978–83), vol. 5, pp. 61–62.

19. Daniel Poirion, "Ecriture et ré-écriture au Moyen Age," *Littérature* 81 (1981): 114.

20. See Philippe Ménard, *Le Rire et le sourire dans le roman courtois en France au Moyen Age, 1150–1250* (Geneva: Droz, 1969), pp. 494–96.

21. *Joufroi de Poitiers*, ed. Percival B. Fay and John L. Grigsby (Geneva: Droz, 1972).

22. *Parthonopeus de Blois*, ed. Joseph Gildea (Villanova, Pa.: Villanova University Press, 1967).

23. Pierre-Yves Badel, *"Le Roman de la Rose" au XIVe siècle: Etude de la réception de l'oeuvre* (Geneva: Droz, 1980), p. 348.

From Lyric Poetry to Personal Poetry

Parts of this chapter are based on an article published in *Cahiers de civilisation médiévale* (25 [1982]: 225–32) and a chapter entitled "Die Dichtung der Trouvères," in *Die französische Lyrik*, Grundriss der Literaturgeschichten bei Gattungen, ed. Dieter Janik (Darmstadt: Wissenschaftliche Buchgesellschaft, 1987).

1. [The French word "trouveur" is used here with reference to the northern or langue d'oïl equivalent of the southern "troubadour." The more usual form "trouvère" is used later on in this chapter and throughout. Trans.]

2. Robert Guiette, "D'une poésie formelle en France au Moyen Age," *Romanica Gandensia* 8 (1960): 9–23; idem, *Forme et senefiance* (Geneva: Droz, 1978), pp. 1–15; Roger Dragonetti, *La Technique poétique des trouvères dans la chanson courtoise* (Bruges: De Tempel, 1960); Paul Zumthor, *Essai de poétique médiévale* (Paris: Le Seuil, 1972).

3. Paul Zumthor, "'Roman' et 'gothique': Deux aspects de la poésie médiévale," in his *Studi in onore di I. Siciliano*, vol. 2 (Florence, 1966), pp. 1223–34. This article was republished, with modifications, as "Le 'je' de la chanson et le moi du poète" in *Langue, texte, énigme* (Paris: Le Seuil, 1975), pp. 181–96.

4. [Langue d'oïl, the language of the north of France and thus of the *trouvères*. Trans.]

5. [Langue d'oc, the language of the south and thus of the troubadours. Trans.]

6. Gédéon Huet, *Chansons de Gace Brulé* (Paris: Firmin Didot, 1902), chanson 8.

7. Jean Boutière and A. H. Schutz, *Biographies des troubadours: Textes provençaux des XIIIᵉ et XIVᵉ siècles,* ed. rev. by Jean Boutière and I.-M. Cluzel (Paris: Nizet, 1964), p. 14.

8. [Zink here uses an untranslatable pun on the word "temps," which in French means both time and weather. Trans.]

9. Quoted in Dragonetti, *La Technique poétique des trouvères,* p. 169.

10. [In French this alludes to the Proustian title *Les Plaisirs et les jours.* Trans.]

11. ["Sanderaladon / It is so good / To sleep among the bushes." Trans.]

12. ["Flowers and violets / And new roses / On a chess-board." Trans.] Both quotations are from Karl Bartsch, *Altfranzösische Romanzen und Pastourellen* (Leipzig, 1870), vol. 1, 28, 27; vol. 2, 2.

13. A. Wallensköld, *Les Chansons de Thibaut de Champagne, roi de Navarre,* SATF (Paris: E. Champion, 1925), chanson 4.

14. Alberto Del Monte, *Peire d'Alvernha: Liriche* (Turin: Loescher-Chiantore, 1944), VIII, ll. 1–6.

15. W. T. Pattison, *The Life and Works of the Troubadour Raimbaut d'Orange* (Minneapolis: University of Minnesota Press, 1952), p. 41.

16. Ulrich Mölk, *Trobar clus, trobar leu: Studien zur Dichtungstheorie der Trobadors* (Munich: Wilhelm Fink, 1968), p. 106.

17. Del Monte, *Peire d'Alvernha,* vol. 1, pp. 16–22. Cf. Mölk, *Trobar clus, trobar leu,* p. 108.

18. [Hélinand de Froidmont's title no doubt reflected a traditional play on two meanings of the word "vers" in French, namely, verse and worms, as did later poets like Malherbe and Baudelaire in writing on death. Trans.]

19. Fr. Wulff and Em. Walberg, *"Les Vers de la mort" par Hélinand de Froidmont,* SATF (Paris: Firmin Didot, 1905). It has been translated into modern French by M. Boyer and M. Santucci (Paris: H. Champion, 1983).

20. Pierre Ruelle, *Les Congés d'Arras: Jean Bodel, Baude Fastoul, Adam de la Halle* (Brussels: Presses universitaires de Bruxelles, 1965).

21. [The hillock or mound on which poetic recitations were traditionally given; the term could also refer to the assembly at a poetic contest. Trans.]

22. *Adam le Bossu, trouvère artésien du XIIIe siècle: "Le Jeu de la feuillée",* 2d ed., ed. Ernest Langlois (Paris: H. Champion, 1923). On the aesthetics of Adam de La Halle, see P. Zumthor, "Entre deux esthétiques: Adam de La Halle," in *Mélanges Frappier,* vol. 2 (Geneva: Droz, 1970), pp. 1155–71.

23. [The *dit* derives its name from the French verb "dire" (to say). A late medieval poetic genre, it can be translated variously as tale or speech and is related (through the form "ditié") to the English word "ditty." Trans.]

24. *Œuvres complètes de Rutebeuf,* 2 vols., ed. Edmond Faral and Julia Bastin (Paris: A. & J. Picard, 1959–60). All quotations refer to this edition. The interpretation of Rutebeuf's poetics in this and the next chapter owes a good deal to Nancy Freeman Regalado's work *Poetic Patterns in Rutebeuf* (New Haven: Yale University Press, 1970).

25. [Jehan Rictus, born Gabriel Randon de Saint-Amand (1867–1933), the author of *Soliloques du pauvre*; the spelling of his first name reflected medieval French usage. Trans.]

26. For an interpretation of the tavern scenes in the *Jeu de saint Nicolas*, see Henri Rey-Flaud, *Pour une dramaturgie du Moyen Age* (Paris: Presses Universitaires de France, 1980), pp. 102–28.

27. See Michel Zink, "Le ladre de l'exil au Royaume: Comparaison entre les *Congés* de Jean Bodel et ceux de Baude Fastoul," in *Exclus et systèmes d'exclusion dans la littérature et la civilisation médiévales*, Senefiance 5 (Aix-en-Provence and Paris, 1978, pp. 71–87. [The expression "de l'exil au Royaume" is a reminiscence of Albert Camus's volume of short stories *L'Exil et le royaume* (The Exile and the Kingdom). Trans.]

28. *La Chanson de Roland*, l. 302; Béroul's *Tristan*, 4th ed., ed. E. Muret, (Paris: E. Champion, 1947), ll. 1343–47.

29. [A group of French court poets of the later Middle Ages known for their ostentatious formal virtuosity. See Denis Hollier, ed., *A New History of French Literature* (Cambridge, Mass.: Harvard University Press, 1989), p. 120. Trans.]

30. See the edition and commentary by Gérard Gonfroy, "La Rédaction catalane en prose des *Leys d'amors*," 3 vols., thesis, University of Poitiers, 1981.

31. *Rimas novadas* would seem to correspond to *dits* and, in any case, are not to be confused with the quite particular genre of "saluts d'amour," itself indeed marginal.

32. [In this quotation Cerquiglini plays on the double sense of the French word *dit*, which means both a specific medieval verse genre and "spoken." Trans.]

33. Jacqueline Cerquiglini, "Le Clerc et l'écriture: Le *Voir dit* de Guillaume de Machaut et la définition du *dit*," in *Literatur in der Gesellschaft des Spätmittelalters* [companion to *Grundriss der romanischen Literaturen des Mittelalters*], ed. Hans Ulrich Gumbrecht (Heidelberg: Carl Winter, 1980), pp. 159–60.

Periods and Dates in Literary Works

Elements of this chapter were taken up and expanded in the following: *Origines, codification et diffusion d'un genre médiéval: la nouvelle*, ed. M. Picone, G. Di Stefano and P. Stewart (Montreal: Plato Academy Press, 1983), pp. 27–44; "Time and Representation of the Self in Thirteenth-Century French Poetry," trans. Monique Briand-Walker, *Poetics Today* 5, no. 3 (1984): 611–27.

1. See Bernard Guenée, "Histoires, annales, chroniques: Essai sur les genres historiques au Moyen Age," in *Annales (ESC)* (Paris: Albin Michel, 1973), pp. 997–1016; idem, *Histoire et culture historique dans l'Occident médiéval* (Paris: Aubier, 1980).

2. See Bede's treatises *De temporibus, De temporum ratione,* and *De ratione computi,* in Jacques-Paul Migne, *Patrologia latina* (Paris: J.-P. Migne, 1844–64), vol. 90, pp. 277–91, 293–578, 579–600, resp.

3. *Les Merveilles de Rigomer,* ed. Wendelin Foerster, 2 vols.(Dresden-Halle: Gesellschaft für romanische Literatur, 1908–15), vol. 1, ll. 7–8.

4. *Roman de Rou,* ed. A. J. Holden, 3 vols. (Paris: A. & J. Picard, 1970), vol. 1, ll. 2–7.

5. He presents himself in a similar way at the start of another work: "Je sui Normanz, s'ai a non Guace" (I am a Norman and my name is Wace). *Vie de saint Nicolas,* ed. Einar Ronsjo (Lund: Gleerup, 1942), l. 25.

6. *Estoire du Graal,* ed. William Nitze (Paris: H. Champion, 1927), ll. 11–20.

7. *Del sot chevalier,* in *Le Jongleur Gautier le Leu: Etude sur les fabliaux,* ed. Charles H. Livingston (Cambridge, Mass.: Harvard University Press, 1951), pp. 186–87.

8. *Des deux vilains,* in *Le Jongleur Gautier le Leu,* p. 201.

9. *Des deux chevaus,* in *Jean Bodel: Fabliaux,* ed. Pierre Nardin (Paris: Nizet, 1965), p. 149. Line 8 contains an untranslatable play on words. It means both "the pricks that the lady had to handle" and "the pricks for which the lady had to shake hands [with the merchant to conclude the deal]."

10. *Du prestre et d'Alison,* in *Fabliaux français du Moyen Age,* ed. Philippe Ménard, (Geneva: Droz, 1979), p. 59.

11. Luciano Rossi has shown that the title of this fabliau is *Li sohaiz des viz* and not, as Nardin believed, *Li sohaiz desvez* (The Mad Wish). See "Jean Bodel et l'origine du fabliau," in *Origines,* p. 51.

12. See Michel Zink, "Boivin, auteur et personnage," *Littératures* 6 (1982): 7–13.

13. For example, *Du chevalier qui recovra l'amour de sa dame,* ll. 1–5, in A. de Montaiglon and G. Raymond, *Recueil général et complet des fabliaux des 13ᵉ et 14ᵉ siècles imprimés ou inédits,* (Paris: Librairie des Bibliophiles, 1872–90), vol. 6, p. 138.

14. [The French text plays on the various definitions of "green," which also means racy, and "ripe," which also means mature. Trans.]

15. Alfons Hilka, *Die Wundergeschichten des Caesarius von Heisterbach*

(Bonn: Publikationen der Gesellschaft für rheinische Geschichtskunde 43, 1937), vol. 3, pp. 45–46.

16. André Lecoy de La Marche, *Anecdotes historiques, légendes et apologues tirés du recueil inédit d'Etienne de Bourbon, dominicain du XIIIe siècle* (Paris: Librairie Renouard, H. Loones, successeur, 1877), pp. 139–40.

17. Frederic C. Tubach, *Index Exemplorum: A Handbook of Medieval Religious Tales* (Helsinki: Suomalainen Tiedeakatemia, 1969), no. 4883; Antti Aarne and Stith Thompson, *The Types of the Folktale*, 2nd rev. ed. (Helsinki: Suomalainen Tiedeakatemia, 1973), no. 980 D.

18. [Zink is playing on words: the French *canard*, literally a duck, here refers to a story about a chicken and a toad. Trans.]

19. Lecoy de La Marche, *Anecdotes*, p. 270.

20. Hilka, *Wundergeschichten*, vol. 3, pp. 16–17.

21. [Zink uses the word *lai*, which usually refers to a brief octosyllabic medieval narrative poem; but the title is often given as *Lais* (or *Legs*), meaning "Legacy" or "Will," the form adopted in the remainder of the poem. Trans.]

22. [Literally, the second line would read: "When I had swallowed all my shame." Trans]

23. [The Old French *griesche* means "bad luck" (generally at gambling); the title might be translated as "Winter Jinx." Trans.]

24. This poem's celebrity, its relative simplicity, as well as the abundance of plays on words and linguistic effects (whose importance our commentary will show) would make translation misplaced. We have therefore settled for translating difficult words or passages facing the text. We have added a comma lacking in the Faral-Bastin edition to the end of line 5, since the rhythm requires connecting "Contre l'yver" to the body of the passage and not just to the clause "Pauvreté me fait la guerre." [In this instance—as opposed to other medieval texts quoted in Old French, Provençal, or Latin—I have based my English version on Zink's own translation into modern French in his edition of Rutebeuf's works: *Œuvres complètes de Rutebeuf*, 2 vols. (Paris: Classiques Garnier, 1989), vol. 1, p. 185. Trans.]

25. [See later discussion of the literal meaning of this passage, with its play on the Old French *vers*. Trans.]

26. [Zink is here referring to the equivocal rhyme between *d'yver* (of winter) and *diver* (different) Trans.]

27. [The authors of several volumes of poetic pastiches entitled *A la manière de . . .* (Paris: Grasset, [1930]). Trans.]

28. ["Eight days" in the original; but French uses "eight days" to mean "a week," as it does *quinze jours* (fifteen days) for "two weeks." As Zink points out later, the Feast of the Circumcision occurs one week after the Nativity. Trans.]

29. [Zink is here playing on the similarity of the French words *renseignements* (information) and *enseignements* (lessons). Trans.]

30. Louis Aragon, "Le paysan de Paris chante" (l. 11), in his *En étrange pays dans mon pays lui-même* (Paris: Seghers, 1946), p. 43.

31. [Here and in the remainder of this sentence Zink plays on the fact that the French word *temps* means both "time" and "weather." Trans.]

32. See Michel Rousse, "'Le Mariage Rutebeuf' et la fête des fous," *Le Moyen Age* 88 (1982): 435–49.

33. Edmond Faral and Julia Bastin, *Œuvres complètes de Rutebeuf*, 2 vols. (Paris: A. and J. Picard, 1959–60), vol. 1, p. 546.

34. *Les Dits du Clerc de Vaudoy*, ed. Pierre Ruelle (Brussels: Presses Universitaires de Bruxelles, 1969), p. 50.

35. *Dits de Watriquet de Couvin*, ed. Aug. Scheler (Brussels: V. Devaux et Cie, 1868), p. 359.

36. For example, ballades LV, CCXXII, DXXI. Eustache Deschamps, *Œuvres complètes*, ed. A. de Queux de Saint-Hilaire and G. Raynaud, 11 volumes, SATF (Paris: Firmin Didot, 1878–1904). This procedure can be found in numerous poets of the fourteenth and fifteenth centuries.

37. [The title *Le Besant de Dieu* refers to a Byzantine coin associated with the Crusades. The original text implies no pun on "talent" in line 1163 since the word used is *besant*. Trans.]

38. *Le Besant de Dieu de Guillaume le Clerc de Normandie*, ed. Pierre Ruelle (Brussels: Editions de l'Université de Bruxelles, 1973), pp. 75–77. Lines 100–116 allude successively to the parables of the wise and foolish virgins, the wedding guest, and the talents.

39. Philippe Ménard, "Le Dit de la maille," in *Mélanges de langue et de littérature médiévales offerts à Pierre Le Gentil* (Paris: SEDES, 1973), pp. 541–52.

40. Roger Berger, *Littérature et société arrageoises au XIIIᵉ siècle: Les Chansons et dits artésiens* (Arras: Commission départementale des monuments historiques du Pas-de-Calais, 1981), VI, pp. 147–48.

41. Ibid., XII, p. 170.

The Present Interior

1. We shall quote from Félix Lecoy's three-volume edition of the *Roman de la Rose* (Paris: H. Champion, 1965–70).

2. See Rita Lejeune, "A propos de la structure du *Roman de la Rose* de Guillaume de Lorris," in *Etudes de langue et de littérature du Moyen Age: Offertes a Félix Lecoy par ses collègues, ses élèves et ses amis* (Paris: H. Champion, 1973), pp. 314–48; see also David F. Hult, *Self-fulfilling Prophecies: Readership and Authority in the First "Roman de la Rose"* (New York: Cambridge University Press, 1986), whose analyses are executed with great insight.

3. See Evelyn Birge Vitz, "Inside/Outside: First-Person Narrative in Guillaume de Lorris' *Roman de la Rose*," *Yale French Studies* 51 (1979): 148–64.

4. In the view of Hans Robert Jauss, this link constitutes the innovation of Guillaume de Lorris's romance in the evolution of allegorical literature. See his essay "La Transformation de la forme allégorique entre 1180 et 1240: D'Alain de Lille à Guillaume de Lorris," in *L'Humanisme médiéval dans les littératures romanes du XIIᵉ au XIVᵉ siècle*, ed. Anthime Fourrier (Paris: Klincksieck, 1964), pp. 107–45; idem, "Entstehung und Strukturwandel der allegorischen Dichtung," in *Grundriss der romanischen Literaturen des Mittelalters*, vol. VI/1: *Littérature didactique, allégorique et satirique*, ed. Hans Robert Jauss (Heidelberg: Carl Winter, 1968), pp. 146–244.

5. As is known, Quintilian defined allegory as a continuous metaphor. Donatus proposed a definition for it that went back to Heraclitus and appeared in almost identical terms in the works of Saint Augustine, Isidore of Seville, the Venerable Bede, and every medieval grammarian: *Allegoria est tropus, quod aliud significatur quam dicitur* (Allegory is a trope that signifies something other than it says). But he placed it among the tropes, between hyperbole and homœse, and the example he gave belongs to metaphor, in our view: *et iam tempus equum fumantia solvere colla* (*Georgics* 2, 542), *hoc est "carmen finire"*; finally, the seven categories he identified within it (*ironia, antiphrasis, aenigma, charientismos, paroemia, sarcasmos, astismos*), together with the examples he gave, made it a simple linguistic figure.

6. E. R. Dodds, *The Greeks and the Irrational* (Berkeley: University of California Press, 1951), pp. 1–27.

7. *Phaedo*, 94 c and d; *Republic*, IV, 441 b and d; cf. Dodds, *Greeks*, p.

213. [In Samuel Butler's English version the text is rendered as follows: "He beat his breast and said, 'Heart, be still. . . .'" Trans.]

8. See Jean Pépin, *Dante et la tradition de l'allégorie* (Montreal: Institut d'études médiévales/Paris: Librairie J. Vrin, 1970).

9. Alain Michel, "Rhétorique, poétique et nature chez Alain de Lille," in *Alain de Lille, Gautier de Châtillon, Jakemart Giélée et leur temps*, comp. H. Roussell et F. Suard (Lille: Presses Universitaires de Lille, 1980), pp. 117–18.

10. See Marc-René Jung, *Etudes sur le poème allégorique en France au Moyen Age* (Bern: Francke, 1971), pp. 43–44.

11. See Armand Strubel, "'Allegoria in factis' et 'allegoria in verbis,'" *Poétique* 23 (1975): 343.

12. The word "allegory" was itself never used in the Middle Ages in reference to the *Roman de la Rose* or works of similar inspiration. According to Pierre-Yves Badel, all its uses in French texts of that period "have as their counterpart those of the Latin *allegoria* . . . and it is noteworthy that they refer to the field of exegesis, not that of rhetoric." *"Le Roman de la Rose" au XIVᵉ siècle* (Geneva: Droz, 1980), p. 13. It is only for the sake of convenience that we apply the word "allegory" to secular literature in conformity with modern usage.

13. Jung, *Etudes sur le poème allégorique*, pp. 126–46.

14. We are quoting Macrobius here according to the edition *Macrobij Ambrosij Aurelij Theodosij uiri consularis . . . In Somnium Scipionis lib. II* (Lyons: Seb. Gryphius, 1550), pp. 19–23.

15. Auguste Scheler, *Trouvères belges*, n.s. (Louvain: Impr. de P. et J. Lefever, 1879).

16. Margaret O. Bender, *"Le Torneiment Anticrist" by Huon de Mery*, Romance Monographs 17 (University, Miss.: Romance Monographs, Inc., 1976). Since we were not able to use this edition, we will quote the *Tournoiement Antechrist* from Georg Wimmer, *Li tornoiemenz Antecrit von Huon de Mery* (Marburg: N. G. Elwert, 1888).

17. [There seems to be no precise English equivalent of the French term used by Zink, a neologism combining the verbs *dormir* (to sleep) and *veiller* (to be or stay awake). Trans.]

18. See Robert Morrissey, "La Préhistoire de la rêverie," *Modern Philology* 77 (1980): 261–90. See also Michel Stanesco, "Aspects ludiques de la fonction guerrière dans la littérature française à la fin du Moyen Age," thesis, University of Toulouse, 1982, pp. 280–314. [This was later published as *Jeux d'errance du chevalier médiéval: Aspects ludiques de la*

fonction guerrière dans la littérature du Moyen Age flamboyant (Leiden: Brill, 1988). Trans.]

19. Alberto Del Monte, "En durmen sobre chevau," *Filologia Romanza* 2 (1955): 140–47.

20. Auguste Scheler, *Dits de Watriquet de Couvin* (Brussels: V. Devaux et Cie, 1868), p. 83.

21. Ibid., pp. 473–74.

22. Jung, emphasizing Huon's persistent interest in "[ce] qui de novel avient" (l. 9) ([what] happens that is new) and in "une aventure novele" (l. 11) (a new [kind of] adventure), contrasts this attitude with Chrétien's in the prologue to the *Chevalier au lion* (Knight of the Lion), where he "prefers to speak of those who *once were*, given the decadence of his times." *Etudes sur le poème allégorique*, p. 288.

23. According to Pépin, in the first century A.D. "the grammarian Demetrius joined together symbol and allegory, observing that the strength of those figures, greater than that of plain language, comes from their brachylogical nature, which with one word makes us understand the rest." *Dante et la tradition de l'allégorie*, p. 16.

24. Frances Yates, *The Art of Memory* (Chicago: University of Chicago Press, 1966), pp. 76–77.

Monodic Writings

1. The opening words of Paul Zumthor's essay "Autobiographie au Moyen Age?" are as follows: "The question mark is indeed part of the title: I am asking a question rather than dealing with some indisputable material." And a few lines later he proposes the following definition: "We shall admit that *autobiography* comprises two elements: an *I*, and a narration given as nonfiction. These elements are united by a functional link: the *I*, at once the uttering voice and the subject of the utterance, in fact constitutes the 'theme' of which the successive actions engendering the account are the predicates" (*Langue, texte, énigme*, p. 165). This definition agrees, while formalizing it, with Philippe Lejeune's: "The retrospective account in prose that a real person makes of its own existence, when it places the accent on its individual life, particularly on the history of its personality." *Le Pacte autobiographique* (Paris: Le Seuil, 1975), p. 14. We shall leave aside the expression "in prose," which raises special problems for the Middle Ages, a period which Philippe Lejeune does not take into account. Nevertheless, the final distinction, missing from Paul

Zumthor's formulation, is very important. Philippe Lejeune gave it striking expression later on: "All autobiography is an expansion of the sentence: 'I have become myself'" (p. 241).

2. Georg Misch, *Geschichte der Autobiographie*, vols. 2–4 (Frankfurt am Main: G. Schulte-Bulmke, 1955–67). Misch observes (vol. 2, pp. 310–59) that the *Vies des anciens pères* (Lives of the Early Fathers) give a role to autobiography through their claim to have gathered a good deal of testimony from the lips of the venerable ancients themselves. This was particularly the case with the Byzantine compilation of Simeon Metaphrastes. But in these accounts the narration in the first person is a fiction. Nevertheless, since they were read aloud on the saint's feast day from the fourth century on, they may have familiarized their audience with autobiographical form. In the Latin world, between the sixth and tenth centuries we find scarcely any independent autobiographies, only fragments offering autobiographical information, whether the author was speaking of his intellectual works (prefaces) or his relationships with others (letters) or with God (*confessio*). In the first category we can cite Anglo-Saxon authors like Bede, Alfred the Great, Eadmer, Cynewulf (late eighth-late ninth centuries) or, in the Germanic area, Otfrid von Weissenburg or Notker Balbulus (ninth century). We could also mention the "Memoirs" constituted by Gregory of Tours's works and the personal engagement shown in them.

3. Migne, *Patrologia latina*, vol. 87, pp. 439–47; cf. Misch, *Geschichte der Autobiographie*, vol. 2, pp. 317–55.

4. See Eugene Vance's subtly reasoned essay "Saint Augustine, Language as Temporality," in *Mimesis: From Mirror to Method, Augustine to Descartes*, ed. John D. Lyons and Stephen G. Nichols Jr. (Hanover, N.H.: University Press of New England, 1982), pp. 20–35. We should not fail to note that if Saint Augustine took the dialectic of succession of sounds and synthetic comprehension of meaning (or of alternation of long and short syllables and perception of poetic rhythm) as an example of the role of temporality in knowledge, it was not—it would be anachronistic to believe so—through a reduction of the world to language but because language was for the human mind the vehicle of the senses and provided the clearest analogy for the revelation of the world's meaning. Vance's study pursues the basic reflection he undertook in an earlier article entitled "Le Moi comme langage: Saint Augustin et l'autobiographie," in *Poétique* 13 (1973): 163–77.

5. One of Gregory the Great's models may have been the *Vie de saint*

Martin, written in the fifth century, consisting of a presumed dialogue between Saint Martin and a disciple.

6. Wendelin Foerster, *Li dialoge Gregoire lo Pape* (Paris: H. Champion, 1876), p. 1.

7. Lejeune nevertheless added: "This does not mean we must deny the existence of personal literature before 1770, or outside Europe, but simply that the way we have of thinking of autobiography today becomes anachronistic or of little relevance outside that area." *Le Pacte autobiographique*, pp. 13–14. Even with this restriction, the judgment is open to debate.

8. *Guibert de Nogent: Autobiographie*, ed. and trans. with an introd. by Edmond René Labande (Paris: Les Belles-Lettres, 1981). This edition will be used for our quotations. See also John F. Benton, *Self and Society in Medieval France: The Memoirs of Abbot Guibert of Nogent* (New York: Harper Torchbooks, 1970), an English translation preceded by an incisive introduction. In addition to the *De vita sua*, probably his final work, Guibert wrote exegetical commentaries, a treatise defending Christian revelation against Judaism, a handbook on preaching, and especially the *De pignoribus sanctorum* (On Saints' Relics), a treatise on relics in which he showed a remarkably critical attitude, and the *Gesta Dei per Francos* (God's Deeds for the Franks), an account of the First Crusade in which appear the first signs of "French" patriotism.

9. See Pierre Courcelle, *Les Confessions de saint Augustin dans la tradition littéraire* (Paris: Etudes Augustiniennes, 1963).

10. Migne, *Patrologia latina*, vol. 156, p. 622b.

11. Labande, *Guibert de Nogent*, pp. 2–3.

12. Ibid., p. xviii. The only exception, pointed out by Labande, is the story of King Quillius at the beginning of book 2, which Guibert says he got from a written source, now lost.

13. Saint Augustine, *Les Confessions*, I, I, 1, ed. M. Skutella and A. Solignac, in *Œuvres de saint Augustin*, Bibliothèque Augustinienne, 74 vols. (Paris: Desclée de Brouwer, 1962), vol. 13, p. 272. The translation is by Louis de Mondadon in the series Le Livre de Poche Chrétien (Paris: Pierre Heray, 1947), p. 19. [Rather than use one of the numerous existing English translations of Augustine's works, I have translated from Zink's text in order better to reflect his ideas. Trans.]

14. On the connection between the Christian search for divine grace and forgiveness, on the one hand, and the development of autobiography and its ability to grasp individual destiny, on the other, see the fol-

lowing articles in *Identität* (special issue: "Poetik und Hermeneutik," vol. 81, ed. Odo Marquard and Karlheinz Stierle [Munich: W. Fink, 1979]): Manfred Fuhrmann, "Rechtfertigung durch Identität—über eine Wurzel des Autobiographischen," pp. 685–90; Hans Robert Jauss, "Gottesprädikate als Identitätsvorgaben in der augustinischen Tradition der Autobiographie," pp. 708–17; for a general overview of the problem, see Odo Marquard, "Identität-Autobiographie-Verantwortung (ein Annäherungsversuch)," pp. 690–99.

15. *Confessions*, I, VI, 10, p. 288; trans. p. 25.

16. Migne, *Patrologia latina*, vol. 162, p. 232, cited by Payen, *Le Motif du repentir*, p. 55.

17. S. Vanni Rovighi, "Notes sur l'influence de saint Anselme au XIIe siècle," *Cahiers de civilisation médiévale* 7 (1964): 423–37; 8 (1965): 43–58, art. 2, p. 51.

18. Ibid., p. 52.

19. Benton, *Self and Society*, pp. 13–22. In this regard, we might compare Guibert's work with the *Manuel pour mon fils* (Manual for My Son) written between 841 and 843 by Huoda, the wife of Duke Bernard of Septimania (ed. Pierre Riché, trans. [into French] Bernard de Vrégille and Claude Mondesert, collection Sources Chrétiennes [Paris: Le Cerf, 1975]). Huoda's "mother's book" merits being set alongside Guibert's "son's book." Concerning Guibert's relationship with his mother, see Jean Batany, "L'Amère maternité du français médiéval," *Langue française* (May 1982): 29–39; see also Georges Duby, *Le Guerrier, la femme et le prêtre* (Paris: Gallimard, 1980), chap. 8.

20. We know that the actual biographical account of Saint Augustine ends with Monica's death and that the end of the work consists of a long spiritual meditation.

21. Labande, *Guibert de Nogent*, pp. 286–93.

22. Ibid., pp. 306–11.

23. [Zink's text here plays on the double meaning of the French expression "pour mémoire," which can mean either "for memory" or "for the record" Trans.]

24. Labande, *Guibert de Nogent*, pp. 464–67.

25. *Sermones super Cantica Canticorum*, XXVI, ed. Jean Leclercq, Sancti Bernardi Opera, 8 vols. (Rome: Editiones Cistercienses, 1957), vol. 1, pp. 171–81. The Old French version quoted here is taken from the edition by Albert Henry, "Traduction en oïl de la déploration de saint Bernard sur la mort de son frère," in *Mélanges . . . Pierre Le Gentil*, pp.

353–65. [Part of Zink's modern French translation is based on material not cited here in the Old French text. Trans.]

26. Jean Leclerq, "Les Sermons sur les Cantiques ont-ils été prononcés?" *Revue Bénédictine* 64 (1954): 222–43.

27. See Brigitte Cazelles, *La Faiblesse chez Gautier de Coincy,* Stanford French and Italian Studies, 14 (Saratoga, Calif.: Anma Libri, 1978).

28. Guenée, *Histoire et culture historique,* p. 203.

29. Ibid., p. 204.

30. R. C. Johnston, *Jordan Fantosme's Chronicle* (Oxford: Clarendon Press, 1981); Gaston Paris, *Ambroise, l'Estoire de la Guerre sainte* (Paris: Imprimerie nationale, 1897).

31. Robert de Clari (c. 1170–after 1216), a knight of modest rank, accompanied his suzerain, Pierre d'Amiens, on the Fourth Crusade (1201). The account that he left of it reflects the point of view of the lowly fighting men, including their loyalty and rancor toward the great (ed. Philippe Lauer [Paris: Champion, 1924]). Geoffroy de Villehardouin (before 1150–after 1212), the marshal of Champagne, left a very different account of the same expedition, in which he played an important role: its aim was to justify the diversion of the crusade toward Constantinople and to support the party of Boniface of Montferrat (ed. Edmond Faral, 2 vols. [Paris: Les Belles-Lettres, 1938–39]). Jean de Joinville (1225–1317), the seneschal of Champagne and a friend of Saint Louis, made use of an earlier account dating from 1272 in writing his *Histoire des saintes paroles et des bons faits de notre saint roi Louis* (History of the Saintly Words and Good Deeds of Our Saintly King Louis) in 1309 for the future Louis X "the Stubborn" (ed. Natalis de Wailly [Paris: A. Le Clère et Cie, 1867]). Philip of Novara (c. 1195–after 1264), an Italian nobleman who went to the Holy Land as a young man, became a vassal of the Ibelins and took an active part in their struggle against Frederick II. Aside from his legal and moral works, he left some memoirs (ed. Charles Kohler [Paris: H. Champion, 1913]).

32. Lauer, CXX, p. 190; cf. XCII, ll. 24–26, pp. 89–90.

33. John 21:25; cf. John 20:30 [The English text given here is that of the King James version. Trans.]

34. Quoted by Lauer, pp. iii–iv.

35. [The wily, amoral fox hero of a series of medieval fabliaux, in particular the twelfth-century *Roman de Renart.* Usually his opponent was Isengrim, a greedy, dull-witted wolf; his home was called Maupertuis, literally "bad hole." Trans.]

36. Kohler, p. 29.

37. Jean Dufournet, *Les Ecrivains de la IVᵉ croisade: Villehardouin et Clari*, 2 vols. (Paris: SEDES, 1973).

38. Lauer, LXXVI, p. 76.

39. Marcel de Fréville, *Les Quatre âges de l'homme: Traité moral de Philippe de Novare*, SATF (Paris: Firmin Didot, 1888), pp. 122–23.

40. Kohler, pp. 32–33.

41. Kohler, p. 54. This position—standing with crossed legs—was frequent in the iconography of the time, from romanesque sculpture to miniatures of the late Middle Ages. The display of naturalness thus passes through the imitation of art in the case of John of Ibelin.

42. De Wailly, pp. 2–3.

43. Michèle Perret, "A la fin de sa vie ne fuz je mie," *Revue des Sciences humaines* 183 (1981–83): 17–37. De Wailly divided the text into 149 paragraphs, not 769, as Perret states.

44. Michel Zink, "Joinville ne pleure pas, mais il rêve," *Poétique* 33 (1978): 28–45. The following pages rework certain aspects of this article.

45. De Wailly, p. 82.

46. Ibid., pp. 162–64.

47. Ibid., pp. 16–17, 24–27.

48. Ibid., pp. 42–43.

49. Ibid., pp. 22–24.

50. Ibid.

51. Ibid., p. 486.

52. Ibid., p. 402.

53. [Zink is here referring to the last two syllables of the Latin word *reliquia*, which in French bear a similar pronunciation to the French word *couilles* (balls or testicles). Trans.]

54. De Wailly, p. 504.

55. [The French word *chevillé* may be translated as "attached with pegs." In the following clause Zink uses the word *joint*, which means "joined" as translated here. Trans.]

56. De Wailly, pp. 80–82. [The name "Cheminon" earlier in this sentence contains the word *chemin* (way or road) and would therefore be apt for someone setting forth on a crusade. Trans.]

57. Ibid., pp. 284–86.

58. See Marcel Thomas, "Les Heures de Jeanne de Navarre," in *VIIᵉ centenaire de la mort de saint Louis*, p. 211.

59. For a review of the argument, see Peter von Moos, *Mittelalter-*

forschung und Ideologiekritik: Der Gelehrtenstreit um Heloise (Munich: Wilhelm Fink, 1974).

60. It has even been asserted that Jean de Meun may himself have been the author of the *Historia calamitatum* and the correspondence. Thus, the work purportedly was a complete forgery, inspired by Roscelin's epistle to Abelard, through which the author of the *Roman de la Rose* pressed Héloïse's example into service for his own ideas on free love. See Hubert Silvestre, "Pourquoi Roscelin n'est-il pas mentionné dans l'*Historia calamitatum?*," *Recherches de théologie ancienne et médiévale* 48 (1981): 218–24.

61. Jacques Monfrin, *Abélard. "Historia Calamitatum": Texte et commentaires* (Paris: Vrin, 1967), p. 71. The translation, an excellent one, is Paul Zumthor's *Abélard et Héloïse: Correspondance* ([Paris: Editions de Minuit 10/18 1979], p. 53), which we have taken the liberty of modifying slightly. [The English translation is based on Zink's version. Trans.]

62. Concerning the *Historia calamitatum*, see Evelyne Birge Vitz, "Type et individu dans l'autobiographie' médiévale," trans. Philippe Lejeune, *Poétique* 24 (1975): 426–45.

63. Monfrin, *Abélard*, p. 122; Zumthor, *Abélard et Héloïse*, pp. 157–58.

64. This characteristic extended beyond the Franciscan world. See Cazelles, *La Faiblesse*, esp. pp. 14–21, 78–92.

65. See Etienne Delaruelle, "L'Influence de saint François d'Assise sur la piété populaire," in *La Piété populaire au Moyen Age* (Turin: Bottega d'Erasmo, 1975), pp. 229–46. [This is Psalm 19 in the King James version; the numbering of the Psalms differs in the Latin Vulgate Bible. Trans.]

66. From a very extensive bibliography, see Martin de Riquer, *Historia de la literatura catalana*, vol. 1 (Barcelona, Edicions Ariel, 1964); and L. Sala-Molins, *Raymond Lulle* (Paris: Aubier-Montaigne, 1967).

67. Excerpts from this text can be found in *Histoire littéraire de la France*, vol. 29 (Paris: Imprimerie nationale, 1733–19–), pp. 1–49.

68. Ramon Llull, *Obres essencials*, vol. 1 (Barcelona: Editorial Selecta, 1957–60; Catalan text); R. Llull, *Obras literarias* (Madrid: Biblioteca de Autores Cristianos, 1948; Spanish trans.). The French translation, probably written during Llull's lifetime, was edited by Armand Llinarès as *"Livre d'Evast et de Blaquerne" [par] Raymond Lulle* (Paris: Presses Universitaires de France, 1970).

69. This passage is based on portions of an article that first appeared in *Perspectives médiévales* 1 (1975): 52–60.

70. The Catalan text is reproduced according to *Obras literarias*, p. 578. The translation is the one made of the Catalan text by A. Llinarès (this poem does not figure in the French version) and added to his edition of the latter (p. 337). We have taken the liberty of modifying it slightly.

71. [Now Bejaïa, Algeria; some commentators, however, place the events at Tunis. Trans.]

72. *Histoire littéraire de la France*, vol. 29, p. 11.

73. The *Vita coetanea* relates a curious episode from 1291. Ill in Genoa, Llull was informed in a vision that he could be saved only by entering the order of the Preaching Friars. He was prepared to obey when, his taking of holy orders having been delayed for an incidental reason, he reflected that his *Art* had been better received by the Minorite Friars than the Preaching Friars: "So Ramon, considering eternal damnation to be certain if he did not remain with the Preaching Friars, and the loss of his *Art* and his books if he did not remain with the Minorite Friars . . . preferred damnation to the loss of his books (*Histoire littéraire de la France*, vol. 29, pp. 15–16). Such was the pride of the man of letters beneath the holy man's humility.

74. R. Llull, *Obras literarias*, pp. 1095–1147.

75. See the following: Daniel Poirion, *Le Poète et le Prince: L'Evolution du lyrisme courtois de Guillaume de Machaut à Charles d'Orléans* (Paris: Presses Universitaires de France, 1965), esp. pp. 191–270; Kevin Brownlee, "The Poetic Oeuvre of Guillaume de Machaut: The Identity of Discourse and the Discourse of Identity," in *Machaut's World: Science and Art in the Fourteenth Century*, ed. Madeleine P. Cosnan and Bruce Chandler (New York: Annals of the New York Academy of Sciences, 1978), 219–33; idem, *Poetic Identity in Guillaume de Machaut* (Madison: University of Wisconsin Press, 1984); Jacqueline Cerquiglini, *Guillaume de Machaut et l'écriture au XIVᵉ siècle: "Un engin si soutil"* (Paris: H. Champion, 1985); Friedrich Wolfzettel, "Zur Poetik der Subjektivität bei Christine de Pizan," in *Chloe. Beihefte zum Daphnis* (Amsterdam: Rodopi, 1984), vol. 1, pp. 379–97.